Scottish Family History

Scottish Family History

David Moody

B.T. Batsford · London

Typeset by Progress Fine Art London
and printed in Great Britain by
Billings, Worcester.

Published by B.T. Batsford Ltd
4 Fitzhardinge Street
London W1H 0AH

British Library Cataloguing in Publication Data

Moody, David, 1948–
   Scottish family history
   – (Batsford Local History Series)
   1. Scotland.   Family
   G. Genealogical aspects
   I. Title
   929.2'09411

   ISBN 0-7134-5724-4

   ISBN 0-7134-5725-2 Pbk

CONTENTS

1 The humble and the mighty: sources of biography 7

Getting started in family history – Photographic sources – Official records – Printed biographical sources – Primary sources of biography – Reconstructing daily life – Techniques of biography

2 Working lives *37*

Life on the land – Trades and professions – Urban employment – A soldier's life – Labour and industry

3 Living, dying, moving house: the study of demography *54*

Demographic records – Demographic technique – Studying the family – Mortality – Migration – Local migration – Immigration – Emigration – Population geography

4 Kin, clan and community *82*

Genealogy – Surnames – Genealogical records – The family in history – Clans – Anthropology and family history – Community

5 Exploring local society *113*

Self-help groups – Philanthropic institutions – Sociology and family history – Sociology of the family – Social relationships – Social geography

6 Culture and beliefs *137*

Folklore – Religion – Religious denomination – Individual theology – Church and community – Freemasonry – Secular culture

7 Family, church and state *160*

Social welfare – Local politics – Law

Notes and Further Reading *179*

References *206*

Index 214

Chapter One

THE HUMBLE AND THE MIGHTY: SOURCES OF BIOGRAPHY

Family history is today one of the most popular of amateur historical themes, yet many family historians are acting, as it were, under false pretences. Progressing hardly at all beyond the compilation of their own family tree, they are genealogists, strictly speaking, and not family historians. A genealogy is only a skeleton, and the most interesting part of family historical work is to paint in the flesh and to catch the breath of the spirit. This book sets out to show more than the techniques necessary for the investigation of pedigree; it aims to demonstrate the means by which one can get to know one's Scots ancestors (humble and mighty alike) as individuals, in their daily lives and in their local communities.

Such a task might appear daunting. One researcher, for example, has warned that in popular genealogy 'one cannot expect much biographical detail. What there is comes mainly from collisions with the law, even if it be only the Poor Law ... The ancestor who emerges from the records as an individual is sadly rare in most times, places and stations' (Wagner, 1975). A short checklist of biographical information that one should be able to establish about most ancestors of the last 200 years or so would include only basic demographic data (such as dates of birth and death, offspring, place of residence (themes which are pursued in Chapter Three), occupation (discussed in the next chapter) and possibly religious denomination, discussed in Chapter Six).

But armed with even these small clues and fragments, much can be achieved, particularly in the study of ancestors by proxy, as it were. Thus if one's forebear was a weaver living in Glasgow, one can illuminate his existence through a general study of the life of weavers or of Glasgow at that time, even though one has no direct historical references to the ancestor concerned. In this sense, the family historian is also a local historian, able to point to the buildings and institutions in his or her town and to tell a story of the lives and aspirations of those who built them, lived in them and worked in them.

To study the milieu in which our ancestors lived is one objective of the family historian. It is also valuable to take this reasoning a stage further and to argue that from one point of view an individual is merely a vessel for the transmission of inherited cultural values in the same way as he or she transmits the genes of family and race. Individuality, in this respect, is no more than the freedom to juggle a few of the elements with which one has been presented. One method of studying biography, therefore, is to identify a variety of structural roles – social, economic and political – in which an individual's life is cast. Redfield (1956) argues that 'the usefulness of these abstractions depends upon the fact that they leave out very much of what goes on in human life.' Indeed they do, and the advantage of this simplification is that they allow us to understand better the complex reality of human lives. Such models of social, economic and political behaviour are developed in the last three chapters of this book.

Direct biographical sources are discussed in this chapter and Chapter Three. Elsewhere the initial premise is that a biography of an individual or group must take into account the fact that life is experienced on a variety of planes, ranging from the most private – one's psychological and physiological heritage or the physics and chemistry of life (explored in Chapter Three) – to the most public – one's participation in political and cultural affairs (Chapters Six and Seven). At the same time the institutions which are the mediators of human experience themselves range from the private sphere of the family and clan (Chapter Four), through the wider world of local communities and social groups (Chapter Five) to the more formalized and distant influences of church and state (Chapters Six and Seven). The organization of this book in part reflects this progression from the 'micro' to the 'macro' scale of history and pays close attention to the crucial significance of family, particularly the way in which broader groupings have arisen by an extension of feelings and associations originating in the family group.

The 'micro' scale of history is particularly relevant to family historians, for whom affairs of state, and political and religious ideologies are important mostly for their impact on local communities. Ideologies are the preoccupation of very few, but have received disproportionate attention from historians, who have sometimes ignored the fact that their import is much diminished when filtered through the minds of others. Local history is national history cut down to size, imbued in the process with a more tangible yet more complex reality – an inconsistent jumble of pagan ritual and christian sacrament, of taboos and fetishes and scientific rationality, all contributing to the richness and colour which can make family and local studies so rewarding.

The themes to be emphasized therefore are those concerned with universal and unchanging endeavours: making a living, farming the land, getting married, having children, generating affection or mistrust, in a spirit of co-operation or competition. Such themes have traditionally been studied by anthropologists and Chapter Four devotes much space to techniques developed within this sister discipline. Anthropologists also see the family as a key element in social structure, setting the 'biological and psychological parameters of human social existence' which are 'sucked in with the mother's milk' (Freeman 1973). The kinship originating from these primary bonds of attachment has underpinned societies in the past to an extent unimaginable today. But to understand even today's world one must take into account such basic facts of child-rearing as: 'attention inevitably leads to contentious situations in which an infant becomes irritated, angered or enraged with his caretaker . . . [causing] the coexistence of contradictory impulses and emotions towards the same individual' (Freeman, 1973). Such ambivalent feelings and latent hostility explain tensions in society as well as in families.

'Society' is a broader concept than 'community', and the term is applied particularly to the forms of organization prevalent in urban civilizations such as our own, where ties of kin have diminished in importance. Instead, wider social groupings and relationships are maintained – topics which are studied by sociologists, and discussed in Chapter Five.

The mental world of our ancestors must also be considered in order to complete the picture. We must study their religious beliefs, moral standards, the spread of ideas and their grip on the imagination. One also needs to understand the residual para-phernalia – the constructs of previous cultures and the ways of thought which remain as the constraints, confusions and ultimately the litter of subsequent worlds.

It will be evident from the foregoing that the family biographer will never produce studies of breadth and under-standing unless he or she incorporates material from both the microcosm and the macrocosm, showing the relationship between the two. An example from our current world will illustrate this point. If we look at localities today – and of course, localities will always exist, even in the 'global village' – we must also look at the whole of the world, for through the likes of television it impinges upon us and helps to form us. So in previous eras, we must investigate the totality of influences felt in the local community – the books that were read, the sermons preached by the ministers, the system of law as well as the physical symbol of territorial power which was the baron's castle. These themes are pursued in Chapters Six and Seven.

The value of family historical research can be considerable. There is the pleasurable shock of recognition when one sees abstract social processes described in books brought vividly to life in the experiences of a relative; a similar pleasure can be found in the minor details of past lives and the realization that these things have an immense amount of *meaning*, that nothing in life is arbitrary. It is a discovery of the twentieth century that trivia are charged with import. In looking at the minuscule, one seems to stand on the edge of an awesome abyss, for family history has something of the nature of the *memento mori*: our ancestors are dead, and in bringing them all the more sharply to life we realize that their exuberance and discovery is like ours – fragile. In no other area of history does one get to know individuals so well, and appreciate their vulnerability.

History is not only a lesson in our own mortality, a twentieth-century version of the skulls kept on dressing tables in Elizabethan times. It also teaches us about the way we are behaving now. For it destroys illusions, not only of our importance but also of our control over our destiny, and even our motives. For we too are the creatures of our social class and our genes, and we too are the prey of prejudice. History is unpalatable truth; it declares the *historicity* of our mental world: ideas are born, develop and die, just like individuals. Such a perception is an antidote to bigotry and this can be contrasted with religious perception, which seeks permanence in a core of ideas. The salutary shock for the historian is to encounter behaviour and moral values very different from his or her own, and consequently to view *all* values relatively.

To reach this position is to prepare the way for the cultivation of sympathy. The charge that it is pointless to have sympathy for the dead when one could be sympathizing with the problems of the living is countered by the argument that the two are not incompatible. The feelings and ideas with which our ancestors grappled did not die with them but were transmitted to their successors. Our minds and characters consist of a myriad of elements, some ancient, some new. The historian is concerned with putting labels on a few of the bits and pieces, to enable us to understand them better and act more thoughtfully.

Getting started in family history

The researcher into Scottish family history should make his or her starting point the storehouse of information preserved by relatives and friends. By direct questioning of those close at hand and through correspondence with those further afield, it should be possible to construct at the very least a recent pedigree which includes grandparents and a fair amount of information about each individual. Where possible, dates of births, marriages and deaths should be established, however tentatively at this stage. All the collected data is best recorded on loose-leaf sheets or cards (which should be substantial in size – preferably as large as A4). Information about different individuals should not be recorded on the same sheet; indeed, the best practice is to use a different sheet to record the comments of each informant about *any* individual, whether themself or another. These are simple enough procedures to implement, yet they put the humblest amateur on a par with the most experienced scholar: scholarship is little more than being scrupulous and systematic in keeping records.

Eliciting information competently is a skill which needs to be worked upon, and some preparation is necessary. Checklists or profiles should be drawn up, listing themes to be pursued. The first section should consist of basic *demographic data* (date of birth, physical characteristics, medical history, marriage, name and dates of birth of partners and offspring, date and cause of death, siblings and different domiciles). Deeper probing will reveal something of *family life* – such things as courtship rituals, punishment and authority in the home, contact with relatives, the organization of formal occasions, funeral customs, and even intimate areas such as sexual relationships and habits. Of course topics of this kind have to be broached with care, but it must be said that they constitute the most valuable contribution that oral history can make to historical studies: intimate experiences are lacking above all in the traditional written record of the past.

A natural extension of the study of family life is the study of the *local environment*, most immediately the home, and its furniture and equipment. Kitchens, for instance, have seen profound changes in the last fifty years, from the days of water gathered at the pump and bread baked in a coal-fired stove to today's 'mod cons'. To ask intelligent questions in this area of study demands no wide knowledge of history – merely a familiarity with the problems of running a home today. A broader set of questions can follow, about the environment of the local street, shop and town.

School days often evoke vivid recall, and are frequently the best place to start an interview, with a question such as 'What is your earliest memory of school?' A question of this kind is neither too specific nor too general. A too-general question (say for instance 'what do you remember of school?') presents a problem for the interviewee, who cannot focus his or her mind on a particular experience. Very specific questions, which can be answered with 'yes' and 'no' or other one word answers (these are called 'closed' questions) make the interviewer do all the work, and can lead to an embarrassing 'drying-up' after a few minutes of struggle.

Subsequent checklists should cover *employment history*, *leisure pursuits* (cinema, home entertainment, dancing, radio, holidays), *social welfare* (poor relief, hospitals, etc.) and the remembered impact of *historical events*, such as the two world wars. A few sample groups of questions are given in the notes to this chapter.

Another section should concern the *character* of the individual, in which one is basically looking for a series of adjectives covering different aspects of behaviour. Classical writers considered that there were four basic types of people according to the dominance of one of four 'humours': the sanguine, the melancholic, the phlegmatic and the choleric. Modern psychology has to some extent endorsed their observations, though psychologists have their own terminology for these clusters of behaviour patterns. There are other typologies that can be used, for example the psychologists' own scale of introversion/extraversion, warmth/coldness, activity/passivity. One could also construct a detailed checklist of adjectives using a tool such as Roget's Thesaurus. Use of psychological techniques in biography has spawned a hybrid discipline – 'psychobiography' – which has been successfully applied to political studies, but could be adapted for ancestry research. Some might enjoy turning their hands to specific psychological devices such as graphology – the reading of character through the study of handwriting.

Two final categories of study are the measurement of *ability* (intellectual, artistic, technical or practical) and the investigation of *beliefs and attitudes* (for example, what political views did the person hold, and what were his or her religious affiliations). Incidentally, these latter categories are basically the same as those widely used by employers when conducting job interviews and they have proved their worth as a means of obtaining a rounded picture of an individual. The juxtaposition of factual material with data on personality also provides the sounding board for critical biographical study, for it gives us a key to answering the essential question '*why*' – the investigation of motive. What were the reasons for the choices made by an individual, and how do they compare with choices made by siblings or parents? Part of the answer lies in just those aspects of character which have been investigated, whilst another part is due to historical factors which impinge on the lives of all of us – factors such as those to be pursued in subsequent chapters of this book. Their interplay with individual personality is the essence of biographical study.

It is a pity that the compilation of such a biographical data-bank as is outlined above is not undertaken by more family historians, with the result that most of the information is lost with the death of the potential informants. Ironically, the information which most do collect – the genealogical – is readily available from government records, as will be shown below.

There are three different ways of recording biographical data. The first method is to ask the informant to write down for you what he or she knows. This is the least satisfactory in that one is forced to rely entirely on the skills of the informant – which may well not equal those which you have perfected in the production of your profiles and checklists. Some correspondents however have a natural flair and enthusiasm which can outweigh any disadvantages. Correspondence is sometimes inevitable, where informants are not close at hand; perhaps in these cases it is best to broach the subject category by category in a series of letters, so that the recipient is not overwhelmed by the sheer quantity of material requested.

The second method is for you yourself to record the information in the course of an oral interview. This is simple enough in the case of straightforward data such a date of birth or name of employer, where once again your questionnaire sheets will come in useful for quick matching of details. But to write down a description of an important event or illustration of character is much more problematic. Failing a good knowledge of shorthand, one must have recourse to taking rough notes which can be written up in fuller form immediately after the interview. If one waits any longer, inaccuracies and misrepresentations are likely to appear.

Alternatively, one can adopt a third approach – that of oral recording (with a tape recorder) or video recording. The tapes so produced are a complete record of the conversation and can be interrogated at leisure. The amateur however should not plunge into oral or video recording without some initial training. Technical expertise is essential: whatever skills have been brought to the crafting of an interview, all is wasted if not a word of it can be heard. Interview craft is of course a second important area – though one may be armed with checklists and questionnaires, it is best to conceal the fact. An interviewer should be prepared yet relaxed, as formality can cause freezing. Preparation should also extend to research into historical background – the intelligent introduction of points from the social history will both stimulate the flow of conversation and encourage an atmosphere of confidence. Another important point to remember is that it is the interviewee who does the talking, not the interviewer – the ratio should be around 90 per cent to 10 per cent. A final element of training concerns more general aspects. The best practitioners are at one and the same time scriptwriters, editors, producers and directors of their work. In radio and television these will all be specialized professions in themselves, so one can hardly hope to match their level of proficiency. However, knowledge of the basics is bound to improve the quality of your results.

How can the beginner get advice and assistance in oral and video recording? There are firstly a number of practical guides which can be borrowed from public libraries (see the notes to this chapter). Secondly, many courses are run by local history groups, television and radio companies, commercial media firms and groups such as Workers' Educational Associations. You can get details of most of these from your public library; commercial courses are advertised in the media supplement to Monday's *Guardian*. Your third course of action is to seek advice from the School of Scottish Studies, 27 George Square, Edinburgh, EH8 9LD. The school is part of Edinburgh University and pioneered oral recording in Scotland after the Second World War. Its library of tape and film is a major record of social history, of rural Scotland in particular, during the twentieth century.

Photographic sources

The potential contribution of relatives and their friends does not finish with their reminiscences. They may also be able to provide supporting material such as birth or marriage certificates, school reports, family bibles, property deeds, newspaper cuttings, medals and other memorabilia and, most commonly, family photographs.

The identification of photographs often involves a degree of detective work, given that the original owners knew the scenes and people being depicted and therefore did not normally feel moved to record that information on the backs. Where those concerned are still living, they can be questioned, but for older photographs, internal evidence must be used as a means of dating if for nothing else.

The origin of the family photograph can be traced back to the portrait painting. Indeed, early photographs were commissed much like paintings and executed in a studio, the style of composition adopted being a pointer to the date:

> In the 1850s the subject was frequently seated in a chair, holding a book. By the 1860s standing poses were being adopted, perhaps with one hand resting on the chair back, and a curtain, column or balustrade in the background. A cardboard swan, a font or a flight of steps were characteristic props. The 1870s introduced the rustic bridge and stile, the 1880s an artificial rock, hammock, swing or railway carriage, and the 1890s cockatoos and bicycles, and the practice of posing babies on white fur rugs or inside sea shells. (Steel and Taylor, 1984)

The props, being expensive, had a long lifespan; for the purpose of dating they can only be used to establish an earliest possible date. William Welling's *Collector's Guide to Nineteenth-Century Photographers*, published by Macmillan (New York) in 1976, includes lists of Scottish photographers operating in the 1840s and 1850s.

Other means of dating include the photographic process used and the costume of the sitter. Quite small details of dress can be significant. Mary Bone in Steel and Taylor (1984) mentions 'the 'M' notch sometimes seen on a gentleman's collar in the 1840s, but hardly ever after then; the large loose cravat of the 1850s; the square-toed shoes of the 1840s and 1850s, and the more pointed toe which appeared in the 1870s and 1880s.'

Dress is not only a pointer to date. As Mary Bone remarks: 'Clothes in the more formal days before the First World War were silent social labels usually worn with pride . . . The clothes of even the dowdiest, in the most apparently undistinguished of family albums, are a significant index to their tastes and attitudes . . .'. Thus, for example, the dress of children will reflect the prevalent conception of their role and status and social class is mirrored in the downward transmission of fashions. Even a detail such as the length of dress permitted for sisters of different ages is an interesting example of attitudes towards sexuality.

Family photographs, argue Steel and Taylor, came to be 'a universally important way of recording group solidarity as expressed in kinship rituals', acting, for the bourgeoisie who were in a financial position to enjoy the new technology, as 'vicarious tokens of a world of potential possessions'. The photographs were certainly considered as prized items, being mounted in handsome decorative albums such as those one can still find in antique shops.

The first mass-produced cameras were made by the Kodak Company in the 1880s, giving the middle-class *paterfamilias* scope to extend the range of his family photographs. He could now record his house and his summer holidays much as aristocrats of previous generations had commissioned artists to paint their country seats and to accompany them on their travels, recording their progress on the grand tour. The earliest photographs of working-class subjects are often school groups (state primary education was introduced in 1872) featuring grubby street urchins, often barefooted. Examples of these can normally be found in the local history collections of libraries. Camera ownership among all classes only became common in the 1930s.

Official records

At this stage the family history researcher is presented with a choice. He or she can either concentrate on developing the biographies of those members of the family already identified, or decide to push the frontier back into previous generations. If the first option is chosen, investigation can concentrate on areas such as work and leisure, and changing social patterns in the local environment over the last hundred years. This reconstruction of recent daily life is pursued at various points through this book.

If, on the other hand, one is interested in extending one's study to earlier ancestors, one must take a radical departure in terms of working methods. The major source of information for this area of study will be written historical records, not the evidence of friends and relatives. The starting point should always be the *civil registers of births, marriages and deaths*, for they supply the basic genealogical background from the year 1855. These and other demographic records are described in Chapter Three. Use of the General Register Office, New Register House, Princes Street, Edinburgh, where these are kept is competently outlined in several books (see notes to this chapter), so there is no point in giving more than a brief resumé here.

As indicated above, civil registration was introduced in 1855 and records the births, marriages and deaths of all Scottish residents since then. Easy-to-use annual indexes provide access to the actual certificates on which further information is recorded. Birth certificates give date and place of birth, occupation of father, mother's maiden name and date of marriage. Marriage certificates supply cross-references to births; and death certificates even give names of both parents, which at a stroke provides genealogical details about the previous generation. Bede (1982) gives as an example: 'a death entry of an ancestor expiring in 1858 . . . at the age of 60 would take you backwards to a birth around 1798 and name parents who could have been born around 1770.'

The addresses recorded on birth and death certificates are absolutely essential for pursuing references in the two other major genealogical sources – the *census enumeration books 1841–91* (the two censuses which are pre–civil registration are particularly useful) and the *parish registers of births, marriages and deaths* (*c.*1600–1854). These two sources are also held in the General Register Office, but microfilm copies have been purchased by most local library authorities. Their use in libraries will be more leisurely, and usually free of charge. Their content is discussed in Chapter Three.

For those unable to visit Edinburgh, specific postal enquiries can be handled by the staff. If more is required however, you will need to make use of the services of a professional searcher, a list of whose names appears in a fact-sheet available from the General Register Office. Given these circumstances, it is essential to exhaust all local and family sources of information before resorting to Edinburgh; besides, the pressure there is very intense indeed and progress in the crowded search room can be slow. It is pointless to waste time and money acquiring information which could have been obtained elsewhere.

This said, the General Register Office is the only place to go once a certain stage of study has been reached. One might be tempted by the presence of local registry offices (listed in the telephone directories under 'registration of births, marriages and deaths' and more often than not located in local government offices) where duplicates of certificates are sometimes held. The drawback here is that local registry offices keep certificates relating to their neighbourhood only, so unless you have clear evidence that your ancestors were not mobile (even to the extent of moving a couple of miles up the road) you are likely to find the experience frustrating, particularly if lack of records is compounded by lack of accommodation to consult them and lack of staff to assist you.

The use of historical records brings with it its own disciplines and problems, and nowhere do mistakes occur more frequently than in genealogical and family history research, for reasons discussed further in Chapter Four. Even prestigious publications are not immune to this – indeed the very emphasis on prestige is at the heart of the problem. Horace Round (1901) spoke of the 'hold on the public at large of the old fables' citing in blame 'the sanction they appeared to receive from their quasi-official and persistent repetition in the pages of Burke's Peerage and of other Burke publications.'

Misconceptions are not restricted to aristocratic genealogies; they occur among ordinary family researchers who, for instance, conceive the preposterous notion that if they share the surname of an aristocrat, they are in some degree related. In fact they most likely share the name because they worked on the noble's estate; or it could be that the similarity is a mere coincidence. The spelling of names was quite arbitrary until 250 years ago and 'the same or similar names were given to quite different places [so that] . . . individuals or families who came from different parts of the country and shared neither blood nor territorial affinity could nevertheless have the same surname' (Donaldson, 1981). The same is true of the so-called patronymic surnames: 'half-a-dozen different Robertsons, shall we say, are probably descended from half-a-dozen different Roberts who lived in different parts of the country at different times and have no ground at all for claiming kinship with each other; not only so, but it is only chance they are called Robertson and not, shall we say, Johnson or Anderson' (Donaldson, 1981). Surnames in fact only became fixed at the end of the sixteenth century (and only in the eighteenth in the highlands). Donaldson cites instances from the sixteenth century 'which show that some people still had more than one designation and it may be hard to say which if any of the designations was even yet a real surname'. These and similar problems are discussed in more detail in Chapter Four.

The combination of personal communication, birth, marriage and death registers and census enumeration books will, with any luck, supply a pedigree from the middle eighteenth century onwards. It is often difficult to proceed any further, however, at least not without making the kinds of unwarranted assumptions against which Gordon Donaldson warns. For though there are plenty of other records, none of them are primarily demographic in character – in other words, any genealogical clues they contain are incidental to their main purpose. Thus even though one may be looking for an ancestor with a known name from the early eighteenth century and may find a person with that name at the right time and in the right parish with the right occupation, one cannot guarantee that one has found the right person if the source does not explicitly establish the relationship with the identified descendant.

Few of these other records will supply any such connection, the main exception being records of the transmission of property, which under Scots law was inherited according to strict principles. Two sorts of property are involved: *heritable property* (the land and the buildings on it) and *moveable property* (personal effects). The first is of limited value to the historian in that only a minority of the population owned land before the nineteenth century. There are two sets of records – *the registers of sasines* (Scotland's complete register of land ownership since 1600) and *the records of service of heirs* (or *retours*) in which heirs established their right to their inheritance prior to being permitted to register sasine on their own behalf. Indexes of many of these records have been published, and full indexes are held in the Scottish Record Office, where the records are also kept. Abridged sasines for landward areas have been published since 1780 and may be available in local history libraries, sheriff courts or solicitors' offices. Moveable property was transmitted via testament and is further discussed later in this chapter. Of the other records, the most useful are perhaps poor law records (Chapter Seven) and court registers such as *the registers of deeds*. (Deeds are any kind of legal agreement deposited with a court for preservation and protection from the court's authority in the event of default.)

Most of the above-mentioned records are held in the Scottish Record Office, of which the General Register Office is a part. It is situated in Princes Street, Edinburgh, with a second building (West Register House) in Charlotte Square, Edinburgh, and is the major depository for Scottish archives, which can be consulted in the historical search rooms in each building. Explanation of its organization and outlines of the major sources of use to family and local historians are given in David Moody's *Scottish Local History: an Introductory Guide*, published by Batsford (1986). Local record offices also exist in many parts of the country; they have various names – including 'regional archives' and 'archive centres' – and are sometimes housed with local history library collections. Their principal records are those from local government and a file of them all is maintained in West Register House. Local government records are considered in Chapter Seven.

Printed biographical sources

The skeleton outline of a biography formed from the historical records discussed in this chapter can occasionally be supplemented by published secondary sources. Granted that few individuals will be featured in biographical dictionaries of great Scots, many more will be celebrated with a short obituary in a local newspaper. For the few, the principal traditional source has been the *Dictionary of National Biography*, a multi-volume work originally covering those deceased before 1900. Supplementary decennial volumes for this century have been cumulated, and the whole work has appeared in a micro-print two-volume edition. Bibliographical references at the end of each article provide clues to further research. A new venture of ambitious proportion is the *British Biographical Archive* (K.G. Saur, 1984) which aims to include numerous individuals not featured in the *Dictionary of National Biography*. It is published on microfiche but only the early letters of the alphabet have so far appeared. Because of its high cost, it will not be found other than in very large reference libraries, whereas the *Dictionary of National Biography* is ubiquitous, albeit often in a concise version, which can be useful for checking inclusions prior to consulting the full text. A third source is the series of volumes of *Who was Who*, published (mostly at ten-year intervals) since the late nineteenth century. It comprises the biographies of deceased entrants in *Who's Who*. Predecessors are the *Biographia Britannica* which only got as far as the letter F (1747–66) and *Men of the time* (1853, –56, –62).

These major reference works apart, most of the general biographical guides of the 'One Hundred Famous Scotsmen' type are of limited value, the information they contain being derived from these other sources and showing little originality, either in thought or research. The most valuable are the dictionaries of contemporaries, for the judgement of peers is in many ways a primary source of information about an individual's significance. The best of these other directories are listed in the notes to this chapter. One should also mention the ten illustrated county biographical dictionaries published around 1900, which cover nearly two thousand local figures. An index of all the names included in them has been compiled by Peter Bell in *Who Was Who in Edwardian Scotland* (1986).

Biographical dictionaries of specific professions are more widely useful, and can include quite humble individuals. The most laconic are trade directories which give little more than names and addresses and occupations. The oldest general Scottish directory is *Pigot's Commercial Directory* which first appeared in 1820, subsequent editions being published in 1825–6, 1826–7 and 1837. *Slater's* (later *Kelly's*) directories saw the light of day in the 1850s, but the runs of local *Kelly's* directories typical of England are not found. The largest cities – Aberdeen, Edinburgh, Glasgow and Perth – boast post office directories from the early nineteenth century; many counties also have their own locally produced examples. The most likely locations for these are local history libraries maintained by public library authorities. Most Scottish Districts have a special library of this type in their area.

Similar in a sense to trade directories are the rolls of university graduates and school pupils. In this field, much greater antiquity can be claimed, as for example in D.E.R. Watt's *Biographical Dictionary of Scottish Graduates to AD 1410*, published by the Clarendon Press (1977). Of Scotland's four traditional universities, matriculation rolls of three – Aberdeen, Glasgow and St Andrews – have been published (details in the notes to this chapter). The more prestigious public schools have produced lists of pupils, though not all of these will be from Scotland. In the case of both schools and universities, a direct application will often be the most effective way of pursuing a specific reference, as there are obviously many unpublished registers held by these institutions. The same is also true for many professions, whose trade associations are listed in the *Directory of British Associations*, a regularly-updated publication of CBD Research Ltd. The amount of published biographical data for different professions varies enormously, by far the most extensive being that of churchmen. Pre-Reformation figures are covered in D.E.R. Watts, *Fasti ecclesiae Scoticanae medii Aevi ad annum 1638*, Scottish Record Society (1969), and in C.H. Haws, *Scottish Parish Clergy at the Reformation, 1540–1574*, published by the Scottish Record Society (1972). All Church of Scotland ministers receive a biographical notice in *Fasti Ecclesiae Scoticanae*, originally published in three volumes and subsequently expanded to seven (Oliver and Boyd, 1915–28) since which time supplements have been produced by the St Andrews Press (details in the notes to this chapter). The major secessionist churches boast their own *fasti* – the years 1743–1876 being covered in William James Couper's *The Reformed Presbyterian Church in Scotland, its Congregations, Ministers and Students*, published by the Scottish Church History Society (1925); the Free Church is covered in W. Ewing's *Annals of the Free Church of Scotland 1843–1900*, published by T. & T. Clark (1914, 2 vols), and John Alexander Lamb's *The Fasti of The United Free Church of Scotland 1900–1929*, published by Oliver and Boyd (1956). A quite different kind of religious biography is the hagiographic celebration of martyrs and victims of religious contention.

No profession is as old as that of the church, though lawyers and doctors become relatively numerous from the seventeenth century. Biographical details of Scottish advocates are contained in F.S. Grant's *The Faculty of Advocates in Scotland 1532–1943*, published by the Scottish Record Society (1944). For the medical profession one is once again reduced to consulting rolls of members – the *List of Fellows of the Royal College of Surgeons of Edinburgh from . . . 1581 . . . to 1873*, published by the college in 1874, and the *Historical Sketch and Laws of the Royal College of Physicians in Edinburgh*, published by the college in 1925. The latter contains a list of fellows from 1681–1925.

The most prolific source of biographical information about professionals is the journals of their associations; obituaries feature strongly, as well as articles about their activities. A useful starting point for major nineteenth-century figures is the *Wellesley Index to Victorian Periodicals* to be found in the larger public reference libraries. Identification and location of other periodicals prior to the completion of the *Waterloo Index* (see notes to this chapter) can be established on application to your library authority, who will have the National Library of Scotland's *Current Periodicals* (now published in microfiche) and possibly the *British Union Catalogue of Periodicals*. If you know the details of the article required (i.e. volume number, date and page numbers) your library can easily obtain a photocopy for you. If, however, your interest is more speculative in that you are merely *hoping* to find references, you will need to consult the journals yourself, remembering of course to look for any cumulative indexes produced in the journal. Where the institutions concerned still exist, a direct approach may be worthwhile.

The next most likely source is the files of local newspapers; if you look at any of these today, they will feature obituaries and anniversary celebrations of local residents with no claim to eminence. Local newspapers as we know them evolved in the mid-nineteenth century, and a comprehensive location guide is given in Joan P.S. Ferguson, *Directory of Scottish Newspapers*, published by the National Library of Scotland (1984). Many of these locations are local history libraries, though sometimes the only sets are held by newspaper proprietors themselves or by the British Newspaper Library at Colindale in North London. A visit there might be out of the question, but once again you can obtain a photocopy of a specific known item through your local library. Another possibility is to use the scrapbooks of newspaper cuttings found in many local history libraries; these often include biographical pieces and there is the bonus that the scrapbooks have often been indexed by library staff (a few newspaper runs have been indexed too). Indeed you are likely to find many miscellaneous indexes held in libraries that can save a lot of fruitless searching. Parish and burgh histories are examples of library material that is often indexed; though they vary considerably in subject matter and approach, many are based on the personal reminiscences of local characters. The local history library is also invaluable in that it will most probably hold a comprehensive collection of the monographs written about local inhabitants as well as their own published autobiographical material such as diaries and letters. Published family histories form another category of material to be found on library shelves, though the majority of these relate to aristocratic families. This latter area is dealt with in Chapter Four. Libraries will of course also hold any local biographical dictionaries.

Primary sources of biography

The published sources of biography discussed in the last section are primarily secondary sources, i.e. they are summaries or interpretations of lives made by a third person. Primary sources by contrast are the raw data of biographical study. It has already been suggested that such data is scanty, but surviving historical archives do throw up a surprising amount of material in respect of a few favoured individuals at least, even though they may have no special claim to be remembered.

As a random example, one can cite a series of letters from John Rattray, factor for the Craighall estate in Perthshire, to Baron Clerk Rattray, owner of the estate, written in 1815 and 1816. The letters concern a Mr Dow, stampmaster of Blairgowrie, then a small town with a population in 1811 of 1025, a good proportion of whom were engaged in the hand-loom weaving industry. Two of the heritors (landowners) had written unfavourably of Mr Dow, and John Rattray is at pains to explain the reason:

> Several years ago, for Mr Dow waiting upon that gentleman when he was seated at dinner, Mr Whitson sent a message that he could not then receive his Feu [the payment due to one's superior if one possessed land] for the reason above assigned. Mr Dow sent him word that he could not wait as people were waiting for him in the office and he knew not when he could return. Mr W. came down, did the business, but threatened to kick him. Mr Dow told him if he did so, that two could play at that Game. Mr Whitson is very Hot and does not always consider the propriety of his language before he makes use of it.

Apart from illustrating the character of two very minor historical figures, the letter raises the interesting questions of whether Mr Dow was infected by the spirit of radical egalitarianism prevalent in hand-loom weaving communities at this time – or was merely a drunken boor (for which see below). Also we would want to ask why John Rattray is trying to take his part against a powerful local landowner.

A slightly earlier letter provides more background, with John Rattray's assertion that the stampmaster general, Mr Blair, was attempting to 'break the present stampmaster for the alledged crime of Drunkenness and Incapacity'. He adduces in evidence that 'Mr Blair swore that he would Ruin him and reduce him to beggary' and that 'It is a well known fact in this quarter that Mr Blair has been jealous either of Mr Dow or the growing prosperity of Blairgowrie . . . His partiality, I am informed could be traced to Coupar Angus where he has a Relation of his own a creature of his own creation whom he wishes to support, to the prejudice and at the expense of this district.' Coupar Angus weavers apparently preferred Blairgowrie because of its bullish cloth market – a charge also recorded in a report on the controversy made to the Board of Trustees for Linen Manufacture. This report also sets out specific allegations against Mr Dow:

> One of the pieces of coarse linen on which he had affixed the national Stamp, was so very ill and unequally manufactured, that Mr Blair thought it absolutely necessary in presence of as many weavers as nearly filled the office, to cut the piece, and upon a certain portion of the inside of it, which was fully a penny per yard worse, than the outside, he caused affix the stamp *Faulty*.

The report adds that 'Mr Dow was smelling of whisky' and Mr Blair's own notes on the affair reiterate the drink allegation, though he adds: 'I did not propose to set him aside merely because he smelt of whisky.' One suspects a certain artificiality in this emphasis, for alcoholism was chronic in Scotland at this time (see pages 122–3). Nevertheless John Rattray went to the length of collecting affidavits on the matter of Mr Dow's drinking habits. William MacPherson, the landowner, wrote: 'I am sorry that I can not wholly confirm Mr Scott's account of Mr Dow's character for sobriety, as I have several times seen him the worse of liquor.' But the minister, James Johnston, disagreed: 'To the best of my recollection I never saw him drunk.' The minister goes on to give an ingenious explanation: 'Now I believed it can be proved that Mr Dow had not tasted spirits that day and that Mr Blair was led into his mistake from our postmaster James Bless[?] leaning over his shoulder or being near them – James was nearly if not altogether intoxicated'.

There is no space here to examine the unfolding revelations in this intriguing spectacle of a community strongly divided in its perceptions and self interests. We must however record the eventual fate of Mr Dow, who was not dismissed – on humanitarian grounds, for he had a large family. Instead James Conacher, stampmaster at Dunkeld, was appointed to be his assistant and successor, and to receive half of Mr Dow's emoluments.

This example has been given at some length partly to show that even before the age of the local newspaper, it is sometimes possible to get a detailed insight into the struggles and passions of a local community; and partly to draw attention to the fact that sizeable fragments of a dozen or so biographies can be culled from these papers. The source concerned is the archive of the Rattray of Craighall family, one of hundreds of such collections held in the Gifts and Deposits (GD) category of the Scottish Record Office, as well as in local record offices, universities, libraries (especially the National Library of Scotland) and in private hands. The National Register of Archives, administered in Scotland by the Scottish Record Office, holds inventories of all known collections, including business archives and the contents of solicitors' offices as well. Among the occasional accumulations of the dross of estate management, letters such as those in the example above are often vibrant with personality and atmosphere, and make possible the vivid reconstruction of daily life for all periods from the sixteenth century.

Literacy is of course a prerequisite of letter writing but the first known Scottish signature dates from as late as 1443, introducing 'the foreign custom of signing documents as well as sealing them' (Marshall, 1983). It is estimated that by 1500, 60 per cent of Scottish noblemen could sign their names. Letters begin to become frequent in the late sixteenth century, and household books, day books or diaries appear concurrently. Those that survive are among the most valuable of biographical sources, providing as they do that so often elusive historical intimacy, as in the following entry in Lord Montgomerie's day book on the death of his wife in 1725:

> We was fourteen years and five months married. Never two lived more happily together. Never man had so great a loss of a loving, virtuous wife and faithful companion, endowed with the greatest ornament and qualities of body and mind, capable of the greatest affairs, the best counsellor I ever had, indefatigable about any business she was engaged in. (Quoted in Marshall, 1983)

Many of the most vivid diaries and collections of letters have been published by the Scottish History Society and similar bodies (bibliographical details are given in the notes to this chapter), but there are many more gems waiting to be discovered among family papers, in record offices and private collections.

Reconstructing daily life

Diaries, letters and household books can, from the seventeenth century onwards, serve as the core for detailed biographical reconstructions of a local community. The seventeenth century is suggested advisedly, for before that time records are somewhat sparse and the researcher will also have considerable difficulty with the handwriting. That century has in fact recently been used in just such a reconstruction, in Helen and Keith Kelsall's *Scottish lifestyle 300 years ago: new light on Edinburgh and Border families*, published by John Donald (1986). Household account books (of four surviving examples kept by women in the seventeenth century, three are Scottish), day books and letters of a group of inter-related families are supplemented by public records such as hearth and poll tax returns (see Chapter Three). It must be said that the fortuitous survival of the core records from related families is an exceptional coincidence for this period (matched perhaps only by the Hope family), but the same technique can be applied to later periods. One will be seeking what the Kelsalls call the voices of the people:

> They will be telling us what they ate, what everything cost, how they got from place to place, what they wore, what illnesses they had and how they were dealt with, how marriages were arranged, what weddings and funerals were like, what they did in their spare time (if they had any), the songs they sang and the games they played, the books and newspapers they read, their gardening interests, the way politicians behaved, about the prevalence of quarrelling, stealing and superstition . . .

As an introduction to the sort of records that could be used, we can turn again briefly to our example of the town of Blairgowrie around 1816 – in itself a convenient date, neatly sandwiched as it is between the two *statistical accounts* compiled for each Scottish parish in the 1790s and the 1830s. Statistical accounts are described in many other publications, for example in Moody (1986) and nothing further need be said about them here. Sasines have already been mentioned in this book – they give a complete picture of heritage or local landownership. Their counterparts are the records of the transmission of *moveable* property at death. These testamentary matters were administered before 1823 by special courts called commissary courts (CC) and thereafter by commissary departments within sheriff courts (SC); most of these records are kept in the Scottish Record Office.

A testament has been defined as 'the writing or decree by which an executor is appointed to administer the moveable estate when a death has occurred . . . . In a wider sense a testament is a will, the formal declaration in writing as to the final disposal of one's property; and the term may denote the inclusion, in a single document, of testament, will, legacy and inventory.' (Barclay, 1977.) If a will exists, the process is known as *testament testamentary*; if no will exists, as *testament dative*. In both cases the executor (nominated either by the deceased, or failing that by the court) pays any outstanding debts, settles taxes etc. and distributes the estate (after an inventory is made) according to the directives of the will or by the rules of intestate succession.

The testament traditionally had five sections: the name, date of death, and details of spouse, children and executors (of obvious genealogical value); an inventory of moveable possessions (of equal value to the social historian); debts owing; debts owed; and finally a declaration by the court ratifying the document. Commissary jurisdiction corresponded approximately to the dioceses of medieval Scotland, so that an initial problem for the researcher is to establish in which jurisdiction any particular village or parish lies. Hamilton-Edwards (1983) appends a list taken from Keith's *Historical Catalogue of the Scottish Bishops to 1688*. A further problem is that the option of recording a testament from any region in the Edinburgh Commissary Court was available until 1800. Printed name indexes for every commisariat up to 1800 have been published by the Scottish Record Society. Various other indexes cover the next 80 years; for dates thereafter an annual index has appeared.

One must not expect to find a testament for every ancestor: there was often little left to be inherited, even in recent times. As T.C. Smout (1986) observes:

> As long as three-quarters of the population lived in houses of three rooms or less and three-fifths in houses of one or two rooms, as was the case before the First World War, there was little space for the accumulation of carpets, knickknacks and all the paraphernalia of the middle class.

The first major possession of many may well have been a radio purchased in the 1930s. This is a far cry from the inventory of the property of Colonel Allan MacPherson, father of one of the protagonists in the stamp master affair in Blairgowrie, who died around 1815. His inventory runs to many pages, with items ranging from 'carriage and carriage horses' and '2 feather beds' (valued at £16) to '3 pieces of old carpet' (5 shillings).

Sasines, testaments, deeds and similar legal documents are excellent for establishing the economic and social context of biography. Detailed wills such as that of Colonel MacPherson will also tell us something of the individual's taste. But on the whole, such records will be less informative about personality. To investigate this aspect one can turn to two groups of archives – *court records* and *parliamentary investigations*.

The precognition of Margaret Martin (1821) asserts that 'within a house situated in Allan Street of Blairgowrie, then occupied by David Martin, labourer in Blairgowrie [you] did bring forth a child, and did conceal your being with child during the whole period of your pregnancy, and did not call for and make use of help or assistance in the birth, and the said child has since been amissing.' (Concealment of pregnancy was made a criminal offence by an act of 1690, after a spate of court cases concerning the murder of newly-born children. A modified act of 1809 is still in force.)

Sworn witnesses include William McPherson, J.P., Thomas Whitson, writer, and the Reverend James Johnston, minister (all of whom we have encountered in the Rattray family papers). Her brother David Martin stated that his sister was 36 years old and that the first he knew of the pregnancy was a visit from the kirk beadle desiring her either to 'file or clear' herself. David Syme, the Blairgowrie surgeon, recalled a visit when 'Martin was then sitting at her wheel spinning and from her appearance she seemed considerably advanced in pregnancy', but he added that she did not come to her full time. The minister James Johnstone supplied the information that she had had a natural child before. Several neighbours testify to her state of pregnancy and incidentally illuminate various domestic details – that for example a disabled sister, Elizabeth, also lived in the house and was unable to write. One also notes, as in the stampmaster controversy, an extraordinary degree of inconsistency in the perceptions and interpretations of different witnesses, a feature which the biographer must constantly bear in mind. For he or she is, in turn, in the words of Sigmund Freud, 'committed to lies, concealments, hypocrisy, flattery, and even to hiding his own lack of understanding, for biographical truth does not exist, and if it did we could not use it' (quoted in Nadel, 1984). Margaret Martin's own testimony was that she was with child four months, before suffering a miscarriage: 'she was delivered of her pregnancy on the road from Creuchies to Glenballoch'.

Precognitions are the evidence collected for the lord advocate's department by procurators fiscal – on the basis of their findings a decision is made whether to bring a criminal 'prosecution'. This distinctive feature of the Scottish legal system has recently been adopted in England. Precognitions are held in West Register House and access is greatly improved by a comprehensive name index on cards. If a 'prosecution' is to follow, an *indictment* is served on the accused; these records are also held in West Register House, though they usually add little to the information found in precognitions, apart from place and date of trial. Trials take place either in the sheriff court or (in the case of more serious offences) in justiciary courts, with different circuits covering different parts of the country. Once again the records are mostly held in the Scottish Record Office. Margaret Martin's fate was to spend seven months in Perth toll booth, having pleaded guilty to concealment of pregnancy.

Blairgowrie, like many other semi-rural communities of early nineteenth-century Scotland, was dominated by hand-loom weaving. A figure of 84,000 has been suggested as the number of weavers in 1838 and 'throughout the whole of the 1790–1850 period [they] . . . were plagued by frequent bouts of unemployment . . . At such times starvation itself was only averted by the voluntary intervention of some local authorities, charitable societies and interested individuals, acting singly or concertedly as *ad hoc* relief committees.' (Murray, 1978).

A personal face to this suffering can be seen in the minutes of evidence taken before the parliamentary Select Committee on Hand Loom Weavers, 1834. No Blairgowrie weaver was interviewed, but several from nearby Perth and Dundee were. James McEwan, a weaver from Perth, assessed the necessary weekly wage for the support of a husband, wife and two children at nine shillings and threepence – this to cover the purchase of two and a half pecks of oatmeal, three and a half pounds of barley, three and a half pounds of beef, as well as vegetables, potatoes, milk and house rent. The following dialogue then ensued:

'You do not include bread?'
'No, the potatoes serve for bread.'

'Have you included there anything for drink?'

'No.'

'What do you do as to drink?'

'If I drink I must take it off the food.'

'Suppose you had the means of purchasing beer, or something to drink, how much would that add?'

'We might take 1d a day for beer, provided we could buy it.'

'That would be about 10s a week [as the necessary weekly wage]?'

'Yes.'

'There is no tea or sugar or tobacco?'

'No.'

'There is no article of clothing included in that?'

'No.'

'Nor anything for extra expense for medicine, or the lying in of the wife?'

'No.'

'About what are the weekly earnings of hand loom weavers in the present time?'

'I have classified them here. Weavers under 16 years of age 5s 9d weekly, deducting 1s for the loom, making 4s 9d. Above 16 and under 55, 8s 9d, deducting 1s for the loom 7s 9d. Ditto above 55, 6s deducting the same.' [Looms were the property of the merchant entrepreneurs who lived mainly in Glasgow and Paisley, and were leased by the weavers for use in their homes.]

This graphic account, when set against the evidence of local testaments (one example from Blairgowrie shows a moveable estate of £2500 being left to three daughters, one of whom was married to a man as lowly in the social scale as a baker) helps to explain the radicalism of hand-loom weavers. As Saunders (1950) says:

Some could retreat into a religious intensity which helped to feed the undercurrent of Victorian pessimism. Many emigrated, carrying their radicalism with them. But others produced their own analysis of their plight, and their ideas, heavily charged with protest, passed outwards to feed the growing anti-capitalist criticism of the age.

There are other points of interest in the Perth weaver's testimony which cannot be explored here, for example the domination in the Scots' diet of oatmeal and potatoes – a fare that is in fact highly regarded by the nutritionist. It was certainly superior to that of the later nineteenth century when cheap imports led 'many poor families [to shift] from porridge to white bread and tea' and the 1930s when 'Scottish consumption per head of syrup, treacle, jam and marmalade was nearly three times the English average' (Smout, 1986).

Select Committee reports and minutes of evidence are part of a group of records of the utmost value to family and social historians. There were (and still are) committees of Members of Parliament of either House appointed to inquire into areas of public concern, be it social conditions, financial management or legal reform. Royal Commissions are similar, although they differ in that their members are specialists from outside Parliament, and in their more widely-based prestige. Also many Select Committees are permanent or standing; most Royal Commissions are appointed for a single occasion. Royal Commission reports are often presented to Parliament as command papers, but are sometimes published under the direct authority of government departments. Papers presented to Parliament (which also include Select Committee reports and bills) are collectively known as *sessional papers*, or, more popularly, 'blue books'. Non-sessional papers include some annual reports of government agencies, statistical series, departmental committee reports presented to the minister concerned, research papers and findings of consultative committees whose remit is to supply technical expertise for the minister. 'The advisory body', says Ford (1972), 'has become one of the chief media for keeping ministers in touch with outside opinion', and the historian is similarly benefited.

The great Royal Commission and Select Committee reports of the nineteenth century included vast quantities of oral evidence from a wide cross-section of the population. In our own century greater reliance has been placed on a different methodology – the analytical techniques of social scientists. The presentation contains three parts: the report itself with its recommendations, the record of proceedings and the minutes of evidence, the last containing the most detail. Since 1921 a change in the rules has led to a large increase in non-sessional papers, an important consequence being that the minutes of evidence are often detached from the report itself, which alone forms the command paper.

Numerous examples will be referred to in subsequent chapters of this book; and accessibility for the researcher is good, thanks to a huge reprinting project undertaken by the Irish University Press in the 1960s. A thousand volumes were produced, the last appearing in 1971; a further advantage is that the reports were grouped in subject areas. You may be able to borrow any that you wish through your local library; at the very least they should be able to provide reference copies for use on library premises. You can discover the volume titles by consulting the indexes of the *British National Bibliography* in the 1960s (under 'Great Britain. *Parliament. House of Commons.* or *House of Lords.*' and committee title for Select Committees, under 'Great Britain' and commission title for Royal Commissions). A breviate of parliamentary papers has been published in several volumes (details in the notes to this chapter) and there are also general alphabetical indexes, consolidated into decennial volumes. For non-parliamentary papers, there is only one index – the annual volumes of the H.M.S.O. catalogue. Most of these bibliographical sources will be found only in the larger public reference libraries, and the best policy is to ask the staff to assist you in finding the material.

As suggested above, the fragments of a biographical history of Blairgowie in the first half of the nineteenth century have been deliberately chosen to illustrate the extent of biographical reconstruction which is possible for a period before the introduction of local newspapers. Only a few records have been touched on, and many more will be mentioned in the following chapters. Blairgowrie is in no way exceptional – indeed in one respect it is unfortunate, for its kirk session minute books for this period have perished. Later reconstructions will draw increasingly on the best source of all – memory – whilst earlier periods will become progressively difficult. Two very important points to bear in mind are firstly that any work of this kind demands a certain amount of slogging through indexes looking for relevant references (full use should be made of lists and aids compiled by libraries and record offices); and secondly that handwriting does become a problem if one wishes to work back beyond the eighteenth century. Mastering early hands is not difficult, however, and merely demands a little persistence. The best procedure is to borrow or buy a copy of Grant G. Simpson's *Scottish handwriting 1150–1650*, published by Aberdeen University Press (1977, reprinted in 1986) and to get hold of a facsimile of a document from the period in a museum or record office reproduction. The latter can be studied in detail and each word written in above as it is deciphered.

Techniques of biography

This chapter has introduced several variants of biographical technique, and the family researcher will need to exploit every one of them given the restrictions of material available. The earliest form of historical biography, claims Edmondson (1971), is genealogy, for 'it is in this borderland between epic and myth, chronicle and legend that biography is born.' From this root hagiography or panegyric evolved; this in turn influenced the nineteenth-century tradition typified by the works of the Scot, Samuel Smiles, who 'satisfied Victorian England's need for heroes who rose to greatness on the morals of good behaviour' (Nadel, 1984). Smiles wrote the biographies of industrial innovators, a good proportion of them Scots, in *Lives of the Engineers* (1861–2), *Industrial Biography* (1863), *Men of Invention and Industry* (1884) and *Life and Labour: or Characteristics of Men of Industry, Culture and Genius* (1887). Singing the praises of one's subject is one style of biography ('I prefer to have all lives written by persons who sympathize with the subjects' wrote Leslie Stephen, editor of the *Dictionary of National Biography*) but some family historians take the principle too far – seeking a vicarious glory in ancestors whose deeds or status barely justify it.

A nineteenth-century reaction to the Smiles approach, which has remained influential, views the biographer's task not as that of interpreter, judge or admirer, but as that of exhaustive collector of facts. Such an approach is strongly influenced by scientific technique, though basically it misunderstands it. 'Facts relating to the past' said Lytton Strachey, the biographer of 'Eminent Victorians', 'when they are collected without art, are compilations: and compilations no doubt may be useful, but they are no more History than butter, eggs, salt and herbs are an omlette.' Many others have echoed his words: 'a fact is like a sock which won't stand up when it's empty' said Pirandello. Family historians have been particularly guilty of producing socks which won't stand up – worthy, detailed and dull compilations ranging from full-length monographs of families or clans to lifeless genealogical articles in family history magazines.

'No biographer merely records a life; every biographer, no matter how objective he declares himself, interprets a life' argues Nadel (1984). Such interpretation involves identifying an image or perception of the person concerned, which the poet W.B. Yeats called the 'one myth for every man, which if we knew it, would make us understand all that he did and thought'. The flow of life as all of us experience it has no meaning or pattern in itself, moral or otherwise, except that which we and others choose to construct. In this respect it has been said that the biographer is as much a storyteller as a novelist. Family historians too should take story-telling seriously.

This view of biography is consistent with what sociologists call 'social interactionism' – the theory that labels, symbols, legends and myths are part of the very essence of how we understand ourselves and others. Techniques of social interaction are being employed when we compare the wages of hand-loom weavers with the level of contemporary affluence shown in testaments. For instead of treating the subject in the traditional manner of social history – by a general study of the plight of hand-loom weavers in Scotland or the United Kingdom – one tries to imagine what were the perceptions of individual weavers within their own community.

On the basis of these general principles, three different biographical approaches are pursued in the succeeding chapters. Firstly there is the investigation of *intimacy*, which has been called the twentieth-century's idea of moral good, in the same way that Smiles' 'public service' was the moral good in the nineteenth century. We tend to judge men and women, not for their public deeds, but for the effect their deeds had on their families and friends; and we are suspicious of ideals, which we even see as variants of bullying. The strength of intimacy as a moral force is perhaps a principal cause of today's interest in family history, and there is great opportunity to investigate previously neglected areas such as private and domestic life, sex and childhood – subjects which at one time were either taboo or regarded as of little importance. Yet intimacy was recognized as important long ago, by the Roman biographer and historian Plutarch when he wrote: 'A slight thing like a phrase or a jest often makes a greater revelation of character than battles where thousands fall.'

The second biographical approach is the *group biography*. 'A consequence of the intimate society, where personalities rather than objects dominate, where motives rather than acts are important, is the emphasis on community, which is the formation of a collective identity' writes Nadel (1984). Families are at the root of community identity and feeling, and researchers can make intriguing studies of the way in which social groups develop out of the relationships which unite families.

The third biographical approach is *contextual* and views lives through a study of the wider social scene. In such a biography the individual loses much of his or her personality, but our argument is that for the family historian there is often no alternative, one's freedom being crippled by lack of specific information. But some interpretations and judgements are still possible, even of personality. For example the intimacy of motive applies not only to the domestic sphere, but also to the social and political arena. Thus, in talking of a nineteenth-century philanthropist (as pursued in Chapter Five), his or her personal kindliness is one judgement, and one which we may very well not be able to establish one way or the other. But another judgement must be of the social and political antecedents and consequences of philanthropic behaviour. The phenomenon was distinctively nineteenth-century, and associated with a specific economic system (that of capitalism), and has been seen as a logical development of capitalist society. So the Victorians, who have been called the inventors of social compassion, can also have their behaviour interpreted in a very different way. The two judgements do not contradict one another: they can co-exist because they belong to different planes, in different contexts. It is the multi-dimensional nature of existence or the structuring of existence which provides the opportunity of pursuing biography from many different angles.

Chapter Two

WORKING LIVES

Of the basic data that one is likely to be able to establish about an ancestor the most consistent is that of his or her profession. It is given, for example, in demographic sources such as census enumeration books and some parish registers and in poor law records. One's profession indeed was so much of an automatic epithet that in many cases it became fixed as a surname. This chapter introduces the subject of the context of working life; one can confidently recreate the working environment of an ancestor from a knowledge of the general conditions of the time and circumstances in which he or she lived.

Life on the land

'During the early Middle Ages,' it has been said, 'the rural dependants constituted the vast majority of the population. Apart from them, there were only, as against the landed aristocracy, small freeholders . . . and town dwellers, merchants and others, also not numerous' (Fourquin, 1976). True of Europe during the Middle Ages, this statement was still true of Scotland up to the nineteenth century. Smout (1986) suggests that two-thirds of Scots were engaged in rural occupations in the 1840s. Even within living memory, Littlejohn (1963) talks of a Berwickshire parish in which 'nearly all the food eaten was produced in the parish itself. Apart from tradesmen, two or three retainers of the Duke of Garvel, the minister and the schoolmaster, everyone in the parish was attached to a farm . . . Every family kept chickens and many a cow while most cultivated a garden of vegetables.'

This apparent continuity, however, conceals a radical transformation of farming practice, beginning in the second half of the eighteenth century. Before that time, a high proportion of rural inhabitants still had a direct foothold on the land – albeit in many cases a mere fragment so that they 'had no option but to seek work in adjacent larger farms to obtain a full subsistence. Grinding poverty was the lot of many sub-tenant families . . .'

(Devine, 1984). Sub-tenants, crofters, cottars, cottagers, grass-men – all fell to a greater or lesser extent within this category (their status relative to each other can be judged by reference to the table below).

None of the above actually owned the land which they farmed, and like the later highland crofters of our own century, the concept of ownership would not have held much significance to them. As in the case of the kindly tenants just above

Social stratification in seventeenth-century Scotland

RURAL		URBAN	
		Burgesses (Freemen)	Non-burgesses
Landowners			
Nobility		Merchants	Advocates
Highland chiefs		Craftsmen	Writers
Barons		Maltsters	Notaries
Lairds		Cordiners	
Wadsetters		Weavers	
Portioners	Ministers	Bakers	
Bonnet-lairds		Hammermen	
(mainly Galloway)		Coopers	
and west)		Skinners	
		Wrights	Unfreemen
Non-landowners		Fleshers	Chamberlains
		Masons	Respectable
Tenants		Bonnetmakers	widows
Tacksmen		Dyers	Clarks
Bailies		Surgeons	
Factors		Apothecaries	(Stratification
Tenants		Skippers	not clear)
Kindly tenants			Journeymen
Sub tenants			Servants
Crofters	Teachers		Common labourers
Cottars			Drovers
Grassmen			Carters
Landless			Coalmen
Taskers			Alesellers
Landless labourers			Milk vendors
Indoor farm			Fishermen
servants			Seamen
Vagabonds			Prostitutes
Beggars			Thieves
			Vagabonds

Table reproduced from Larner (1981) by permission of the Estate of the author and Chatto & Windus them in the social scale, their tenure was based upon custom rather than law, though some of the latter had moved into the class of small landowners or 'bonnet lairds' when the church and some impoverished magnates had sold off quantities of land in the sixteenth century. Another relatively recent group were 'wadsetters', described by Cheape (1983) as 'semi-owner/occupiers between lairds and tenants, those who as creditors occupied land as a security in return for the loan of money and received the rents.'

Working life on the farm before the agricultural revolution of the eighteenth century is difficult to reconstruct. Cheape speaks of farm servants as having 'little opportunity to express themselves enough for the history books to take any notice; they were after all unenfranchised until within the last hundred years . . .'. Communal labour was necessary for working the heavy old Scotch plough drawn by a team of horses and oxen, and the various communal, seasonal tasks can be studied in the surviving records of two local rural courts – barony courts, presided over by the local landowner or his bailie (agent), and birlaw courts, consisting of the tenants of the estate. Some of these have been published by the Scottish History Society.

Specialization of farm labour began to occur as farms increased in size. The barnman, for example, also known as the 'tasker' or 'lotman' 'threshed the grain from the straw with the wooden flail on the clay or wood threshing floor of the barn' (Cheape, 1983). But the main effect of farming improvement was to sweep away the sub-tenants – at least in the lowlands. Their place was taken by the farm servant or 'hind' – whom today we would call a farm labourer. He was and is expected to know 'everything belonging to husbandry and should also be able to perform all and every manner of work relating thereunto: As to plough, to sow, to stack, to drive carts etc.' (Firth, 1899). He may well have been *able* to perform all of this work, having progressed through the hierarchy of farm labour organization, but once having achieved the aristocratic position of ploughman (a term which later became almost synonymous with hind) it seems that he would not always have been *willing* to perform it. 'A Lothian ploughman,' writes Barbara Robertson (1978) 'would feel insulted if asked to pull turnips; any ploughman would refuse to allow another ploughman to work his pair of horse; most ploughmen would refuse to do any byre work . . .'. Some indeed even formed a semi-mystic society called the Society of the Horseman's Word. Carter (n.d.)

explains that 'the promise of the word for a loon [lad] was control of two sets of unruly creatures – women and horses.' A theme which we shall meet repeatedly in this book is the society of man, more or less ritualistic, formed from the insecurity of those a step or two above the bottom levels in the social scale. Those below them have nothing to lose, and those above them have no fears of losing what they have.

Aristocrats of the farm-steading they may have been, yet the work of the ploughmen was far from easy, as Gray (1984) describes:

> The ploughing itself usually started at six or seven a.m. and continued without interruption for five hours; then followed a meal break of two hours in which the ploughman and his team would return to the steading, and finally a further four or five hours in the fields. The working day, however, was much longer . . . The ploughman might well have to thresh his horses' feed for the day, starting at four a.m. or even earlier; then as well as the tasks of yoking and unyoking and the trek to and from the fields, there was evening work in the stables grooming and 'suppering' the horses.

Each hind had to supply the labour of a farm servant, which in the Lothians was often a female servant, known as a 'bondager' – most often a wife, sister or daughter. In the nineteenth century, 46 per cent of the Lothian farm workforce were women. This labour was supplemented by workers hired by the day from local villages, and cheap, mainly female, seasonal workers from Ireland and the highlands. These temporary workers lived in 'bothies' or 'chaumers', the latter being lofts above the stable or byre. 'No artificial heating was provided, and frequently the "room" was neither wind- nor water-proof' writes Gray (1984) 'Bothies' he says 'were perhaps more likely to be weather-proof and might have a fireplace, but its ineffectiveness is indicated by the fact that men often preferred to sleep two to a bed for warmth.' The homes of the hinds were the now-familiar rows of stone-built cottages set apart from the farmhouse; even the cottage garden was often missing, for the cottages could be fronted by an open grass space, only latterly turned into 'traditional' cottage gardens now that the homes have been sold off to middle-class commuters. Facilities in these cottages were primitive; the workers were much less grandly housed than the valuable horses in their stables adorned with the motifs of classical architecture.

Farm workers were a vulnerable group: their isolation from each other and from town life, their dependence on their employers for accommodation and their long working hours made collective self-protection difficult. Economic depression caused enormous suffering; and as a result the researcher has many blue books at his or her disposal to gain a detailed insight into farming life. A few examples are the *Select Committee Report on Agriculture* (1833), the *Report of the Royal Commission on the Employment of Children, Young Persons and Women in Agriculture* (1867–70) with its volume of Scottish evidence (1870), the *Report of the Commission of Inquiry into the Conditions of the Crofters of the Highlands and Islands of Scotland* (1884) and the *Report of the Royal Commission on Agriculture* (1896). In addition, the interest in and enthusiasm for agricultural improvement in the eighteenth and nineteenth centuries generated a considerable literature, sources of which are indicated in the notes to this chapter. We also have what is missing from earlier periods – the articulate farm worker, such as Alexander Somerville, who wrote his *Autobiography of a Working Man* in 1848. This brings us to the wealth of oral material recorded whilst the patterns of pre-mechanization farming were still remembered. 'It is a most difficult thing to get people to consider farm workers as citizens,' said Joe Duncan, champion of the agricultural labourer in Scotland. Some small amends can now be made by listening to their story. Duncan was instrumental in forming the Scottish Farm Servants Union in 1912, though wages and hours of work were not standardized until the Agricultural Wages (Regulations) Scotland Act (1937).

Trades and professions

In the traditional rural economy, there were few job opportunities apart from working the land itself. The displaced, landless labourers in particular had no choice but to move away if there was a shortage of farm work. For, in the words of Sprott (1984):

> the old-style farmer built and thatched his own house, found his own fuel, and devised his own harness, tools and transport. His wife span wool from his sheep and made most of the family's clothes. What tradesmen there were often subsisted on a part-time basis. Before the mid-eighteenth century the furnishing of rural houses was so sparse, often making use of the fabric of the building for seats and beds, that there was little or no trade of that kind for a skilled joiner.

Nor any work, one might add, for a baker, butcher or tailor. The only openings were for domestic servants: even small lairds in the seventeenth century had households of up to twenty servants (though probably no beds for them to sleep in). Domestic service of course remained an important source of employment until well into this century, female servants recording a high level of illegitimate births as they succumbed to the advances of the 'master' or his sons. Sources for studying the status of servants are discussed on pages 52 and 190.

Growth of rural trades occurred only in the eighteenth century, owing to a combination of factors. One was the introduction of iron manufacturing. Sprott likens its impact to that made by plastics in our own time: 'iron started to replace timber in countless small details – hinges, nails, latches, locks and household utensils, as well as important developments in mills and farm implements.' Changing social aspirations also contributed to this process. The laird's wife now 'went to the theatre, mingled with friends of both sexes and read new ideas in recently published novels and journals' (Marshall, 1983). Such a lady of fashion was not going to spend time weaving cloth for clothes. The rise of rural trades can be monitored in the statistical accounts of each parish of the 1790s and 1830s, by which time one finds the ubiquitous village smithy, in this century often transformed into a country garage or small firm of agricultural engineers.

The traditional rural parish boasted perhaps only two individuals pursuing a profession that was not directly linked to agricultural production or processing: the schoolmaster and the minister. As can be seen from the table on page 38, the status of the former was not high. He was certainly not regarded in awe by his pupils, who, though leaving no later than the age of thirteen or so (at which age they would go direct to university), were not at that or even earlier ages regarded as immature. One reads, for example, of incidents in which scholars occupied their schools with pistols and swords when they were displeased. The Statistical Account for the Parish of Urr speaks of a parish school as 'a temporary employment for some necessitous person of ability, or a perpetual employment for some languid, insignificant mortal hardly deserving the shelter of a charity workhouse.' His payment often took irregular forms: a regulation of the town council of Dumfries in 1725 stipulated that 'the under teacher keep the door and exact not more than twelve pennies Scots from each scholar for the benefit of bringing a cock to fight in the schoolroom.' Such an income was supplemented by employment as registrar of births, marriages and deaths, as clerk to the kirk session and even as beadle and gravedigger. Schoolteaching has never achieved a high status within the middle-class professions; and after the introduction of a state system of schools after 1872, it became dominated by women (70 per cent by 1911) of whom Smout (1986) says that they 'predominated because they were cheap to employ, willing and plentiful'.

Information about school teachers before 1872 can often be found in the minute books of kirk sessions and of the heritors, for it was the church which was responsible for the administration of schools and the heritors who were responsible for their funding. Both these sources are held in the Scottish Record Office. After 1872 records are relatively plentiful, in the minute books of school boards (based on the parish) and the log books kept by individual schools. After 1918 education became a responsibility of county authorities, which inherited the archives too. They are now held by Scotland's regional councils (locations are discussed in Chapter Seven).

The status of a profession can be linked to its economic and political importance; its cultural value comes a poor third. This helps to explain the low status of the school teacher and the higher regard in which the clergy were held. For clergymen were responsible for many matters which are today the province of the state: registration, the administration of testaments, poor relief and education – functions which originally derived from an essential skill (from the state's point of view) held exclusively by churchmen, the ability to write. The humble parish priest of pre-Reformation times, who was more often than not a vicar, i.e. a poor paid stand-in for a distant dignitary, was not, however, the main beneficiary. Dowden (1910) refers to the 'inveterate habit of medieval ecclesiastics, of all grades, of getting other persons to do their work, while they themselves pocketed the main part of the profits.'

In fact, the church was perhaps one of only two or three careers with a definite career structure and an opportunity for 'getting on'. The sociology of professions has identified various characteristics of dominant groups of this kind: one would expect to find, for example, a tendency to form a closed élite and an unscrupulous disregard for values – the latter tending to be a preserve of the impotent. One is not surprised therefore by descriptions of widespread nepotism among a supposedly celibate profession. As Dowden (1910) notes:

What we have to remark is that dispensations for illegitimacy were granted [by the Pope] on so lavish a hand that it is certain that a considerable proportion of the clergy in Scotland, not only among the rank and file, but perhaps in even still greater abundance among the dignitaries and high officials of the church, was drawn from the offspring of irregular connexions.

Such careerism is much less noticeable in the post-Reformation calvinist church, and from this one can draw conclusions about the declining usefulness of the church for the maintenance of the state, and the growing power of the laity in rural life.

In the last chapter it was noted that biographical record sources for churchmen are particularly rich. Archive material is equally extensive; one can for instance study the hunt for the accumulation of benefices in the four published volumes of Supplications to Rome (see notes for details). All surviving post-Reformation records of the Church of Scotland are held in the Scottish Record Office, and provide a wealth of information.

From the top of the rural social scale – landowners and ministers – we can turn briefly to those at the very bottom – the numerous vagabonds and beggars, the names of whom are the least likely to be immortalized in historical records. Not that they were not talked about: from 1424 a series of acts (in 1425, 1449, 1455, 1477, 1535 and 1574) established that no person between the ages of 14 and 70 should be allowed to beg, except for the 'crippled, sick, impotent and weak folk . . . unable to maintain themselves except by begging'. The concern (which was financial as much as anything else) reflects the scale of the problem. Cage (1981) notes that 'it was commonly believed at the time that once a child was taught the art of begging, he would always resort to that means of gaining a livelihood (indicating perhaps that it was a profitable occupation)'. Despite the interest, it is rare to find named individuals in the records; beggars were seen rather as a *collective* threat to social order, or, where personal compassion prevailed, as poignant, anonymous entries in kirk session minutes as receipts of relief.

In these circumstances, such first-hand accounts as John MacDonald's *Memoirs of an Eighteenth-Century Footman*, published by Routledge in 1927, are especially interesting. MacDonald was one of a 'large number of children who escaped or were expelled from a formal family structure' (Beveridge, n.d.). When around eight years of age 'he took to leading a blind beggar who taught him to play the fiddle. After one wedding they had played for near Roslin, he was the cause of the beggar's cask of beer being spilt, for which he was severely beaten "so as

I had got two shillings at the wedding in my pocket, I left my master, the ass and the fiddles, and ran as fast as I could into Edinburgh"'. What might be surprising to many is that this nomadic life led by children was still prevalent in the late nineteenth century. In William Cromb's *A Modern Miracle: the Life Story of John Brown*, for example, published in 1898 by John Cossar, one reads: 'I travelled through England and the south of Scotland and made my living by singing, begging, and sometimes carrying in a cart load of coals for people.' The shock caused by Richard Hughes's novel *A High Wind in Jamaica* is mainly due to the speed with which we have forgotten very recent yet very different attitudes towards childhood.

Urban employment

Until the eighteenth century, given the rigidity of the structure of rural life, the ambitious born to a lowly station had little room for manoeuvre. Flitting to the town was only beginning to become an option, for most towns were extremely small and scattered; today we would hardly call them villages. Besides, social organization there was as rigid as in the country, with a division between, on the one hand, merchants and craftsmen, and, on the other, the urban outcasts, described by Fox (1983) as 'a varied group including night-soil carriers, leather-workers, midwives, prostitutes and lepers – all trades, occupations and human conditions, in fact, regarded as "unpleasant".'

Merchants and craftsmen covered a wide spectrum, from the princes of trade in the four major burghs (Aberdeen, Dundee, Edinburgh and Glasgow) making fortunes, for example, in the tobacco importing business, to the humble ale-maker in the smaller, complementary towns. Trading was hedged about with innumerable regulations: the ale-taster for example was supposed to 'stande in the middis of the streyt before the dur [of the tavern] and send an of thar falowis [fellows] in with the bedal [beadle] that sal chese of what pot he will tast the whilk he sal present till his falowis' – this according to the instructions of the chamberlain ayre's court, a royal court held in the burghs. From the eighteenth century free trade came to dominate, a process paralleled by changes in burgess and guild controls. There was a decline in the length of apprenticeships as well as a decline in their number; and burgess title became increasingly a mark of distinction rather than a necessary qualification for the prosecution of business. It was estimated by Devine (1983) that in 1784 at least 135 Glasgow merchants were not burgesses or guild brothers.

The family historian nevertheless has reason to be grateful for the old system, for it has bequeathed a large number of detailed records of the inhabitants of burghs. There are minute books of merchant guilds and trade incorporations, burgess rolls and minute books of town councils and dean of guild courts, plus a range of miscellaneous material. A glance through one of the inventories of town council records held in the Scottish Record Office will give some idea of the scope. All these records belong now to district councils, but many, particularly the older ones, have been deposited with the Scottish Record Office for safekeeping.

Apart from the merchants, the other upwardly mobile group in early modern Scotland were the lawyers, who supplanted the ecclesiastics as the guardians of the written word. Priests had originally filled the posts of notary public, created to authenticate documents (particularly charters) after 'confidence in privately executed deeds had been shaken by the success with which forgers imposed upon the courts' according to Thomas Craig, lawyer-author of the seventeenth-century *Ius Feudale*. Notaries public drew up *instruments* confirming that transactions had taken place, and 'the privilege accorded to such instruments was that they required no further proof [unlike charters which relied on witnesses and seals] and therefore formed the basis of public records and registers' (Robertson, 1977). In these circumstances it is not surprising that some lawyers rose into the ranks of the Scottish nobility.

They obviously remain an important group. As property ownership spread, the profession expanded into every small town, servicing the needs of home-buyers (still the major source of their income), both in conveyancing and in the administration of trust funds for property development with 'little bundles of capital from small businessmen, professionals and their widows' (Smout, 1986). Building societies have now taken over this latter area, but lawyers still make a living from mercantile transactions. Commercial law has evolved with ever-increasing complexity since the introduction of the humble bill of exchange in the seventeenth century. Given the nature of lawyers' business, there is a high survival rate for their records – many papers are deposited in the gifts and deposits sections of record offices, and many solicitors' offices, if one could but obtain access, are treasure houses illustrative of the history of the profession.

Many other professions appeared as adjuncts to the commercial and industrial revolution, such as banking and accountancy with their revolutionary ideas about the function of money. Of equal status were professions requiring technical and scientific skills, whose members' services were increasingly valued as their successes followed one on the other. Doctors were certainly prized; engineers perhaps have been less appreciated in our culture. All these men formed part of what we would call the upper middle class, but the lower middle classes also blossomed in the urban environment. Retailers and shopkeepers first appeared among the non-merchant burgesses in the late seventeenth century. 'They plied the trades of small shopkeeper, pedlar, hawker and packman, and were usually concerned with retail services in the burghs or in the buying of goods from greater wholesale merchants for distribution in the surrounding countryside' (Devine, 1983). These more traditional lower middle class representatives were joined by two other groups: self-promoted journeymen such as shoemakers, an independent breed surviving in Scotland (though less so in England) well into the twentieth century, and a growing army of clerical workers, the human typewriters of the industrial revolution. There were 2,685 commercial clerks in Glasgow in 1861; in 1891 there were 12,982.

A soldier's life

The common men and women of Scotland possibly had little chance to join these middle-class professions. However, if they wanted escape and adventure, they could turn perhaps to the army, which at least provided an opportunity to see something of the world. Conversely, the quartering of troops in a locality caused a great stir among the population, particularly the girls. 'During the militia gathering,' wrote an eye witness (MacDonald, 1893), 'the band of the regiment plays in the park, and the number of tents containing the men is so great as to attract civilians to the spot, thus making the park a favourite promenade.' Thomas Hardy's novels, *Far from the Madding Crowd* and *The Trumpet Major*, also recreate the atmosphere of excitement in small communities when troops were abroad.

Scotland, being an intensely poor country, was unable to maintain a standing army before the seventeenth century, but the Scots, undaunted, went off to serve as mercenaries in continental armies. What records there are of its own armies are scattered among state papers such as the published *Calendar of State Papers Relating to Scotland 1547–97* published by H.M.S.O. between 1898 and 1952, the *Register of the Privy Council* (volumes covering 1545–1691) and the unpublished archives of the Scottish Treasury and Exchequer deposited in the Scottish Record Office. Four thousand eight hundred muster rolls for a single year (1650) and lists of the army establishments during the Restoration are useful for genealogical purposes. Graphic accounts of soldiering life include the English soldier Patten's memoir of the campaign of 1548–9, culminating in the Battle of Pinkie, and many archives from the Civil War and Jacobite rebellions (see notes for details).

The records of the armed services after 1707 are untypical in that they are mostly held in London, mainly in the Public Record Office (published inventories are listed in the notes). There are also important collections in the National Army Museum with its 'documents illustrating the daily life of the British soldier from enlistment to discharge and retirement', the Central Army Library, the Naval Library, the Imperial War Museum and the National Maritime Museum.

Scots have made a disproportionate contribution to the British armed services; over 100,000 for example were killed in the First World War. For records in Scotland, one can turn to those held by regimental museums (listed in the annual *Museums and Galleries in Great Britain and Ireland*), and by the United Services Museum in Edinburgh Castle. Also held in Scotland are the archives of volunteer and militia forces. Militia forces were formed by the compulsory enlistment of civilians for home defence; volunteers, especially the yeomanry (cavalry) tended to be drawn from the better off. These regiments were initially raised in response to the threat of invasion by Napoleon, but during the social unrest of the nineteenth century, they were more often turned against their fellow citizens. Lieutenancy records are the main source, apart from surviving papers of the regiments themselves. The former are part of county council archives, whose location is discussed in Chapter Seven. Sheriff court records contain background information.

Labour and industry

The factory economy familiar to us today is of recent origin, and what we would call the working classes are no older. It is true that there were industrial enterprises – mainly coal-mining – from the early Middle Ages, but the scale was small, the 'black stones' being gathered from surface mines very much as one would gather firewood. Ancillary industries were pottery manufacture (exploiting the clays dug out alongside the coal seams) and salt-panning, which used the poor quality 'small coals' for evaporating sea water. The development of pumping and other technical equipment led to deeper mining in the seventeenth century – and to the appalling conditions vividly described by Hugh Miller in *My Schools and Schoolmasters*, as quoted by Johnston (1929):

> the collier women, 'poor overtoiled creatures', carried all the coal up a long turnpike stair inserted in one of the shafts, and it was calculated that each day's labour was equivalent to carrying a hundred weight from the sea-level to the top of Ben Lomond. No wonder they 'cried like children under their load'; no wonder a 'peculiar type of mouth . . . wide, open, thick-lipped, projecting equally above and below . . . like savages' was developed.

Equally graphic are the descriptions gathered by the Commissioners appointed to Report Upon Employment of Children in Scots Mines in 1840. More information about mining life can be found in estate papers, for it was Scotland's landowners who remained the principal movers in the industry. The Scottish Record Office has collected together an inventory of mining records from different parts of its collection in one of its typed source lists, available for consultation in the historical search rooms. After the 1850s (when major changes in company law were made) many limited liability companies were formed, in mining as in other areas of industry; records of those companies taken over by the National Coal Board after the Second World War are contained with the archives of the latter, also in the Scottish Record Office.

The progress of industrialization in Scotland has been frequently charted, from the domination of textiles (first linen, then cotton), through iron, mining and engineering to ship-building, and then to decline (often attributed to the narrowness of Scotland's industrial base). There are numerous sources for investigating working conditions in these different industries, with parliamentary reports, such as that of the Select Committees of Hand-Loom Weavers cited in Chapter One, being especially useful. Of importance are the reports of the *Royal Commission on the Depression of Trade and Industry* (1886), the *Royal Commission on Labour* (1892–4) and the *Commission of Inquiry into Industrial Unrest in Scotland* (1917–18). Among the non-parliamentary series are the annual reports of the Chief Inspector of Factories and Workshops. Governmental interference in employment conditions stemmed from Althorp's Act of 1833 which stipulated that nine should be the minimum age of children working in mills and appointed inspectors to enforce the measure. The Mines Act of 1842 prohibited the labour of women and children underground, establishing a separate mines inspectorate which produced its own series of annual reports. Ashley's Act of 1847 restricted the employment of women and children aged between 13 and 18 to ten hours a day in mills – other industries were not brought into the regulatory net until the Factory Act of 1863. A final source of information is company papers, some of which are still held by the companies concerned, and others in various archives; Glasgow University Archives for instance holds a fine collection of Clyde shipbuilding records.

The public face of many of these sources should be counter-balanced as far as possible by those reflecting the viewpoint of the workers, who were subjected to the new forces of supply and demand which dominated the industrial economy, as well as to the cycles of boom and slump which typified its progress in the nineteenth century. It was the workers who invoked the traditional governmental machinery for wage-fixing, without success, for the employers had discovered the advantages of 'free' competition in a buoyant labour market.

Ironically, the machinery in question had originally been established to control the labour market (albeit a predominantly rural market) in the interests of the landed employers, through the office of justices of the peace drawn from their number (burgh craftsmen's wages were fixed by burgh magistrates under powers granted in 1426). An act of 1617 authorized the newly established justices to set the wages of non-burghal workers, labourers and servants, and subsequent special legislation enjoined them to 'force and compel all loose men and women to serve for competent hire and wages' (Johnston, 1929). Much of this activity was directed towards supplying labour for the pioneering industrial projects of the late seventeenth century, though it was most effectively enforced in the traditional rural situation, where, in the words of Malcolm (1931), 'masters were at liberty to pay their workers as little as they pleased . . . [but] were forbidden, under penalty of fine, to pay more than the sum fixed by the Justices.' Justice of the peace records are held in the Scottish Record Office.

As noted above, by the nineteenth century different ideas were in the ascendant, and the act fell into disuse. 'The workmen would not set its machinery into motion' says Johnston (1929), 'since the Magistrates and Justices who were to fix the wages were the employers, and the employers, for their part, were in strenuous competition with each other and relied upon great armies of hungry unemployed to keep the wages' rate low'. An interesting parallel development was the abolition of slavery in the mines, which had been introduced at much the same time. The enfranchizing of the serfs was no humanitarian measure; rather it reflected the coalowners' perception that serfdom encouraged a closed shop system which pushed up wages.

Tom Johnston's view in this, as in other matters, was coloured by his political radicalism, for it was in fact after a test case brought by hand-loom weavers seeking to fix wages from falling below a certain level that the acts governing wage controls were repealed (in 1813). With this failure of state controls, notes Marwick (1967), 'union action had henceforth to rely in the main on industrial pressure to maintain or improve wage standards.' The task was by no means an easy one, for the employers had two powerful advantages. Firstly, large-scale immigration from the highlands and Ireland provided a surplus of labour, which came to be regarded like any other commodity, to be bought and sold. Smout (1986) refers to the 'knee-jerk reaction of proposing wage cuts or sackings in any position of competitive difficulty.' The workers had further to contend with cycles of boom and slump such as the first great depression of 1875–8 caused by the onslaughts of foreign competition. In a similar crisis of 1907–8, 16,000 men were said to be on the verge of starvation. A lot of labour was also seasonal. For example, in the early 1900s 'there were 30 per cent more labourers needed in Glasgow Corporation Gasworks at the midwinter peak than at the midsummer trough, and the brickmakers and sawyer's labourers who were laid off in bad weather made for the gas works in December and January' (Smout, 1986).

A second hazard for the working class was anti-trade union

legislation. Freedom to combine was restricted partly by the maze of 'master and servant' legislation; it was not seen to be convenient to repeal restrictive legislation which benefited the employer. In addition there were the Combination Laws of 1799 which, it was originally thought, did not apply to Scotland. Many early unionists found to their cost however that Scottish courts were increasingly disposed to make use of them, a subject which can be studied in the justiciary records of the nineteenth century held in the Scottish Record Office. (A famous case was the breaking of the officials of the Glasgow Cotton Spinners' Association in 1838.)

Legal recognition was not granted until the Trade Union Act of 1871. The Conspiracy and Protection of Property Act of 1878 allowed peaceful picketing; whilst the Employers and Workmen Act of 1875 replaced the hated Master and Servant Acts. It gave to lower ranking members of society 'a tacit acknowledgement that they were no longer pieces of property and objects of servitude being paid mainly in kind, but were the co-partners in a more rational, cash-nexus-based relationship of employer and employee' (Robertson, 1978).

In some ways, the unions that arose were similar to the old burgh incorporations, particularly, Marwick (1967) finds, 'in their insistence on craft regulations and attempts to enforce a monopoly of labour, and in their provision of "friendly benefits".' Less traditional were the 'banners and bands, cultural trappings of class consciousness . . . [which] symbolized communities which were finding a unity and identity, although they had been thrown together so hurriedly and carelessly during the previous two decades' (Wilson, 1978). The overall tone however was conservative. Marwick speaks of the trade union leaders at any rate as thoroughly 'respectable figures, frequently active churchmen of temperate and puritanical habits, with a high degree of literacy, attested, for example, by the literal readability of their copperplate calligraphy, and appearing in their photographs in typical Victorian garb.'

Such conservatism is understandable, for industrialization brought to many working men unprecedented opportunities for self-advancement. Smout (1986) speaks of the chances of masons, joiners and engineers to become small employers or sub-contractors, though towards the end of the nineteenth century much downward mobility resulted from mechanization. In the building trade, for instance, the introduction of stone-cutting machinery led to a reduction in the number of

masons. Mechanization also brought into being a new animal –
the semi-skilled worker – in the shipyards for example.

One reflection of the conservatism of Scottish unionism was
the distinctive development of bodies known as trades councils.
These were based on geographical areas (mainly the bigger
towns) and consisted of federations of small craft unions of the
likes of tailors, potters, shoemakers and bakers. Their rise is also
partly attributable to the relative isolation of Scotland's industrial towns and their degree of specialization (notably in
Dundee). The trades councils attempted to 'give a voice to and
make a movement from the weak, but fiercely independent,
Scottish unions' (Fraser, 1978). In 1924, only one-third of
Scotland's labour force was unionized. The councils were
instrumental in setting up the Scottish Trades Union Council in
1897, representing at that time 55 organizations and 40,000
members. The reports of their annual congress are a useful
study source. The trades councils persisted, in many cases
fusing with burgh labour parties to form bodies with names
such as trades and labour councils. Their minute books are
another important source for the historian; that of Edinburgh
between the years 1859 and 1873 was published by the Scottish
History Society in 1986. Other trade union records are listed in
the bibliography by Ian Macdougall: *A Catalogue of Some Labour
Records in Scotland and Some Scots Records Outside Scotland*,
published by the Scottish Labour History Society (1978).
Information about strikes in the first part of the nineteenth
century is contained in court records; thereafter, newspaper
accounts will give the most detail. Radical journals were
numerous but not always long-lived: the *Liberator* ran from 1832
to 1838; in the twentieth century there was the famous *Forward*
of Tom Johnston.

Chapter Three

LIVING, DYING, MOVING HOUSE: THE STUDY OF DEMOGRAPHY

Demography has been defined as 'the study of the size, territorial distribution and composition of populations, changes therein, and the composition of such changes, which may be identified as natality, mortality, territorial movements and social mobility (change of status)' (Cox, 1976). At first glance the definition may suggest a predominantly statistical and somewhat dry subject, with more points of interest for a biologist than a historian, but the local and family researcher would do well to pause before passing on to other areas. Few if any demographers limit their studies to demography alone: rather it provides one vantage point from which to study human problems – the sufferings of starvation, disease and death, or the stresses of the search for work and well-being, perhaps among alien or unsympathetic communities. A few examples will illustrate this: mean ages of marriages are figures which may reveal a range of interesting questions about the composition of households or the availability of land or jobs; fertility rates may appear of purely biological significance, yet they are linked to many other topics, psychological, social and economic; birth rates may tell a story about the social pretensions of different groups in a community. To sum up, it is the questions asked of statistics that provide the stimulus for the historian.

The core study of demography – the measurement of size and growth of population – encompasses three constituent elements: births, deaths and migration patterns, the numbers of which are in turn directly affected by rates of fertility and mortality. The starting point, therefore, for a demographic study is the analysis of data on these subjects. Fortunately for the family historian in Scotland, an exhaustive study of the sources has been made and a great deal of preliminary analysis carried out in a major project organized at Edinburgh University, the results of which are published in Flinn (1977). A brief description of these sources follows, though any researcher interested in following through a local project is recommended to consult the detailed assessment in the above work. Incidentally, most of these same records are the principal sources used by Scottish genealogical researchers, and these students too will find the book the most accurate and valuable they could have at their side.

Demographic records

Demographic studies in Scotland are virtually impossible to carry out for periods before the beginning of the seventeenth century, and even then the only major source is the parish registers of births, marriages and deaths (in most cases more accurately described as registers of baptisms, banns and burials), of which it has been said '. . . their paucity and relatively poor quality imposes a severe limit to their capacity to yield generalizations of an acceptable standard of reliability' (Flinn, 1977). The parish registers were kept by the church, and the first mention of them appears in a fourteenth-century synodal decree enjoining parish clergy to keep lists of those who had died in the parish. The General Provincial Council of the church in 1552 required all parishes to keep particular (i.e. local) registers of baptisms and proclamations of banns, and in 1565 the reformed church recommended that a register of burials should also be kept. That little was done in practice is confirmed by a General Assembly act of 1616, later endorsed by the Privy Council, in which the same worthy ideals were propounded, though this time with somewhat more success.

The problems involved in using the old parish registers (or 'OPRs' as they are familiarly known) are manifold. For the early period in particular, there is uneven geographical distribution in the surviving series; record-keeping was not always good, especially in the case of burial registers; and where these records were kept, they may refer to burials only in the churchyard, and not in additional burial grounds that may have been established as a result of changing patterns of settlement in a parish. At the heart of the problem is the fact that in the Scottish church neither marriage nor burial was a sacrament. So called marriage registers are more often registers of proclamations of banns, which, incidentally, could be made in the parishes of both partners – an advantage for the family historian but a disadvantage for the statistician. The registration of marriage itself often involved a disciplinary aspect, for the couple deposited 'consignation money' which was returned later if no birth took place within nine months. Because of this moral consideration, marriages are sometimes recorded in the kirk session minutes rather than the registers. But there was no necessity on the part of the couple to go to the kirk session in the first place: so called 'irregular' marriages could be cemented by means of a simple public promise followed by intercourse, or even by referring to one's partner in public as one's spouse. There also existed marriages 'by cohabitation and repute', cohabitation counting in Scottish law as proof of an intended contract. Birth alone led to a sacrament, that of baptism, but after the frequent and often bitter schisms within the Church of Scotland, the secessionists would often no longer be recorded. A particularly bad period is between the years 1783–92, for in addition to the problems outlined above, there was an additional one of the imposition of a stamp duty on registration.

The parish registers of births, marriages and deaths are mainly deposited in the General Register Office in Edinburgh. A few, mostly recorded in Flinn (1977), remain in the possession of churches; and a few more are hiding in the offices of local registrars and possibly elsewhere. The collection in the General Register Office includes some 'graveyard books': in the towns in particular, registers of burials are usually the records of interments in burial grounds under the control of paid officials of the town councils. Nothing need be said here about using the General Register Office, as the subject is dealt with extensively elsewhere (see notes to Chapter One). In any case, you may well find that microfilmed copies of local registers form part of the local history collection of your library authority. Use of them there should be preferred: public demands on the facilities will be less intense.

The late seventeenth century provides a sudden harvest of demographic records, in the shape of the hearth and poll tax returns of the 1690s. All householders (referred to as 'possessors') should have been listed for the hearth tax of 1691, though the sub-collectors did not provide uniform data and the individual names are omitted in some areas. In others, by contrast, returns are quite detailed, as in Wigtown, for which the following are listed: name of head of household, residence, proprietor, number of hearths in the house and any kilns, smiddies, furnaces or salt pans. At the very least it gives:

> a minimum number of hearths for most Scottish parishes. For Lowland Scotland it gives the names of the majority of householders. It is obviously useful to the genealogist. It can also be used to discover the distribution of names: this in turn is of value to demographers as one indicator of population mobility . . . (Flinn, 1977)

The hearth tax can also be used to give a fairly confident population estimate for each parish and the relative densities within it; likewise, it can be used to give some indication of the distribution of social classes, as houses with numerous hearths were in most cases the residences of the more wealthy. Such research ideas could provide the stimulus for many local history projects, both for this period and later ones in which even more detailed and accurate information is readily at hand in the form of sources such as census enumeration books (discussed below).

The records of the poll taxes of 1693, 1695 and 1698 (the last applying only to the rich) have in the main been lost; the surviving records are held in the Exchequer records in the Scottish Record Office, as are the hearth tax returns, and possibly also in a few private muniments, still undiscovered. The poor, as well as persons under 16, were exempt; children over 16 who lived with parents appear to have been recorded irregularly;and others are listed under the categories of ordinary people, tradesmen, servants, merchants and richer tradesmen, tenants, heritors, gentlemen, professions, aristocracy and the rich. Designations were not always consistent from area to area, however.

In the small towns with populations of a few hundred or one or two thousand (which represent the extent of urban growth at the time) town council records can sometimes yield considerably more data than even the hearth tax and poll tax records. In Linlithgow, for example, the council minutes refer to seven censuses taken between 1679 and 1695, plus a permanent roll of householders, a roll of house proprietors and the minister's examination roll. Church examination rolls, also known as visitation lists or catechismal rolls, were drawn up by ministers and included all parishioners old enough to be 'examined' on the catechism, the examinable age varying from five to 12. Lists of communicants were also made. Such rolls were used by Alexander Webster to compile Scotland's first population census in 1755. Equally random in their survival are bills of mortality, which were a particular feature of developing urban areas in the early nineteenth century.

By the time we reach this date, demographic sources begin to multiply. There are many more private family papers (which often contain lists of tenants and cottars); there are newspapers; there are town and estate maps, sometimes recording the inhabitants of all buildings, and there is material from the hospital and dispensary movement. Parish registers are much more extensive too, as are kirk session records.

The state conducted its first population census in 1801. Only a global figure for each parish was returned, based on a simple count. The succeeding decennial censuses up to 1841 retained the same format, though in 1811 the enumerators were asked to answer questions on population trends since the preceding census (the manuscript returns are held by the British Library). In 1841 the census was expanded to include a complete listing of all inhabitants, with details of employment, age and household composition also provided. The 1851 census went even further – parishes of birth were recorded for each individual – and in 1861 the number of rooms and windows in each dwelling was included. These valuable lists, known as *census enumeration books*, are held in the General Register Office, but your local library authority or record office ought to have microfilm copies. Confidentiality is maintained for 100 years; thus the years 1841–81 are the only ones currently widely accessible.

Of course, as well as enumeration books, a census includes published analysis of the findings, on both a regional and a national basis. Up to the time of local government reorganization in 1974 the data was broken down by county, burgh and parish (civil and ecclesiastical). Parish tables included the number of families, number of houses, size of family and numbers speaking Gaelic. County and burgh tables recorded the number and nationality of foreigners, ages of inhabitants, ages at marriage, disabilities, education, birthplace and a detailed breakdown of occupation. From 1911, all the local statistics were brought together in a county report, now (since 1981) supplanted by a regional report. Your library should have copies of these. From 1961 ten per cent of the population has been asked extra questions, providing details of occupation, workplace, recent changes of address, standard of education and technical qualification. This information forms the basis of reports on subjects such as housing, migration, economic activity, transport to work, education and fertility.

Another landmark in Scotland's demographic history was 1854–5, when civil registration of births, marriages and deaths was introduced. The introduction had taken place in England in 1836, but in Scotland it was opposed both by the church (who saw civil involvement as an erosion of its traditional powers) and by the burghs (on grounds of cost). However, the Disruption of 1843 made the church's position untenable – one single institution could no longer pretend to act as the nation's guardian in morality and ritual. An ambitious scheme was started (too ambitious in fact) and the amount of information required was reduced in 1856. Of the 1855 data '. . . the greater part remains without analysis, awaiting the detailed attentions of the modern researcher in the original registration books.' (Flinn, 1977.) Subsequently, the information recorded has included the name and occupation of parents, as well as addresses, and causes of deaths.

The remainder of this chapter explores demographic themes which could profitably be pursued by family historians. Some care is needed in the choice, however, for the following reasons. First, pure demography is principally a study of generalities – quite the opposite of what the local family historian is setting out to do. Secondly, pure demography is impossible without comprehensive data, which is only available for the last hundred years or so. Thirdly, such analysis as can be made with limited material has already been made in Flinn's book. Finally, the family historian should beware of duplicating the work of professional demographers. For example, a detailed examination of census enumeration books for purposes of statistical analysis is a waste of time if the same analysis already appears in the published census material.

Demographic technique

In demographic studies, some knowledge of the relevant terminology is advantageous. The basic data is divided into two categories: *enumeration* or *stock data* representing the state of affairs at a given moment (e.g. by a census), and *flow data*, which records occurrences (such as births). Statistical analysis of the former is often represented by a proportion, and of the latter by a rate (usually expressed per thousand head of population).

One very important tool is the *life table*, which records two essential features: first, the existence of a group in a defined status or condition; and secondly, changes away from this status which deplete the group. The table shows the number remaining at any stage. The nature of the departure from a particular status may be simple (as in the case of death) or multiple (for a group sharing the status of bachelor, both marriage and death are departures). Life tables can be used to understand and plot the life chances of different groups in a local community, and to see their behaviour patterns in the context of the biological and social pressures of the life of their time.

A *cohort* is a group of people whose age increases at the same rate at which time passes (e.g. a group of women married in a particular year). If the history of a cohort is followed through time and from the passage of one state to another, a life table can be used to exhibit the results. The ratio of those dying to those living at any age is the *mortality rate*. The most important term from statistical theory is the *arithmetic mean* which is found by dividing the sum of a series of observations by the number of observations. It must be distinguished from the *median* which is found by arranging observations in order from the smallest to the largest and then choosing the middle observation (or half way between the two middle ones if there is an even number of observations). *Sampling*, which is an essential tool for any researcher faced with any quantity of data, is achieved either by use of processes which are truly random (such as drawing numbers out of a hat) or by adopting a system of stratification based upon a complete list of the possibilities. In other words, if the stratification system chosen is one based on occupation, one must be careful to include examples of all occupations to be found within the group, and in the proportion in which they occur in the group.

Studying the family

The fact that the sacrament of baptism often excluded members of churches other than the Church of Scotland from registration in parish registers renders these registers of limited use in pure demographic studies. The researcher therefore would do best to concentrate on periods covered by census material and the annual reports of the registrar general. The study of family size would be an interesting project, which could be researched even in the context of a single house or tenement. Households between 1841–81 could be checked in census enumeration books, and later years through a combination of valuation rolls or electoral rolls (to provide householders' names) and data on births from the indexes in the General Register Office. Some additional work could be done in the assessment of living and sleeping arrangements; internal household organization would have been affected by changes in family size and by raised expectations of comfort and sanitation.

Fertility (which measures all factors influencing the birth rate) must be distinguished from *fecundity* (the measure of biological potential solely). Fertility rates can be measured by the age of parents (for example the number of births to fathers aged x divided by the number of men aged x) or by the duration of marriages set against the number of children per marriage. There are four determinants: the sex ratio, the age structure, the proportion of women who marry, and the age of marriage – variables which can be studied in detail only from 1861. Some surprising discoveries can be made: for instance that women outnumbered men (the sex ratio) by up to 20 per cent, the cause being their longer life span allied to their reluctance to emigrate. Social factors influencing fertility include war, desirable size of family, religion, social status and domicile (urban or rural). Any of these themes could be made the subject of a study in a local community. Up to 35 children in one family have been recorded.

One example of a study of this type would be to look at the influence of land availability on fertility. A late age of marriage tends to be a feature of traditional communities where family plots of land were not the usual pattern of cultivation. Indeed, one could propose as a general hypothesis that the strength of marriage as an institution is directly related to the importance and availability of land in the local economy. It could be argued that dominant groups used marriage as a means of restricting the acquisition of land by those outside the favoured group, and would (consciously or unconsciously) attempt to divert attention from economic reality by an emphasis on the ritual and morality of the institution. Whether these values were accepted by the other orders of society would depend in part on whether their own interests would be similarly served.

Where there is pressure on land resources the age of marriage would tend to rise (an example often cited is France after the Revolution, when inheritance by the eldest son was abolished in favour of a shared succession by all the children). The phenomenon can be seen in many Scottish rural communities too, though here the reasons for land shortage would be different. Marriage in one's late twenties was the norm in the eighteenth century for example, one consequence being that few men and women ever knew grandparents (life expectancy was then 50–55 years); whatever the truth about extended families in traditional communities, the extension must have been horizontal, not vertical. Once the marriage had taken place in these circumstances, there would be an additional tendency to restrict the number of children. Family size control has often been motivated by economic considerations. To give another example, it has been claimed that the early efforts of the middle classes to rise in social status (in the seventeenth and eighteenth centuries) led to a decline in the number of (costly) children. This thesis could be tested in a local study. Economic factors have also been blamed for the decline in the birth rate in the 1870s. In a time of economic recession, children ceased to be a financial asset; and became a positive burden after the passing of the Factory Acts (prohibiting child labour) and the Education Acts (which meant compulsory school attendance – for which parents were charged). Such are the various influences governing fertility rates, and the consequences too could be far-reaching. For example, family limitation in rural areas will curtail the kind of population pressures which have been important in industrialization and large-scale migrations.

Illegitimacy is a subject that was dominant in the minds of the church – page after page of some kirk session minutes deal with little else – and also a subject which has provoked considerable controversy among historians. Two measures of illegitimacy are used: the *illegitimacy ratio*, which gives the number of illegitimate births per 100 live births, and the *illegitimacy fertility rate*, which describes the number of illegitimate births per 1000 unmarried women of the fertile age group 15–49. In Flinn (1977) it is suggested that a better measure than either would be an *age specific illegitimacy fertility rate*.

The considerable regional variation in bastardy has already been mentioned. In 1855, for example, 'a teenage girl in Banff was more than 20 times as likely to have a bastard as one in Ross, and even for girls in their twenties, the likelihood of becoming an unmarried mother was between four and six times greater in Banff than in Ross' (Flinn, 1977). Another interesting point is that rural illegitimacy was higher than that in towns, despite the image of the town as a den of vice. Both these examples are a good illustration of the value of demography to the historian. It brings to light the surprising anomaly, or poses the interesting question. The answer may be one provided by the historian, or by the demographer, or a combination of the two. In the case of differential illegitimacy in different counties, the problem was and still is hotly debated, a debate exacerbated and confused by contributions from moralists. The differential has been ascribed to overcrowding, to the bothy system, to the sex ratio (surplus of women) and to the high age of marriage. None of these theories are substantiated by the available statistics – an illustration of the way in which an historian is set a problem from demographic data, and is able to check his or her proposed solution against the same data. More recent theories point to the influence of different courtship patterns; for example, a tradition of bridal pregnancy to which no stigma was attached. There are possible economic and social causes too: in some areas a farm worker was hired on the understanding that he provide family labour on the farm. Pre-marital pregnancy would be seen as an insurance policy against infertility. With such explanations we move out of the realm of demography into that of social and cultural concepts, and even more so in the idea of an 'illegitimate subculture' with standards of its own. One could study the stigma of illegitimacy itself, its strength at different points of time, or the social class and profession of those who enforced the view of the shamefulness of bastardy.

Pure demography is concerned with birth and death. What has been traditionally regarded as a third decisive threshhold in life – marriage – differs in being a cultural, not a biological phenomenon. Nevertheless, marriage patterns have an immediate influence, as we have seen in the example of fertility rates. Possible themes of study include choice of partner (by class, occupation or location), marriage rates for populations of a particular age, disparities in age between partners and the proportion of a local population married, unmarried and widowed. Such studies will give insights into the functions which marriage serves and into the relative status of men and women at different times and the way they viewed each other.

Where an institution is strongly sanctioned, as marriage was by both state and church, it is particularly instructive to look at the circumstances surrounding its dissolution. These are likely to provide important evidence of its underlying rationale as well as an insight into personal relationships in former times. Separation and divorce can be studied in the processes (i.e. cases) of a central court known as the Edinburgh Commissary Court, which alone had jurisdiction in this area. It later passed to another central court, the Court of Session, and only recently has it been possible to obtain divorce in the local sheriff court. The relevant processes of the central courts are known as consistorial (they include other family matters too, such as illegitimacy) and the records are held in the Scottish Record Office. There is a published index of individuals involved in the processes: *The Commissariot of Edinburgh: Consistorial Processes and Decreets 1658–1800*, published by the Scottish Record

Society (1909). Special terminology used in consistorial law can be studied in law text books. It includes quaint concepts such as the *declarator of putting to silence*. A *declarator* in Scots processes is a declaration made by an injured party (called the 'pursuer'). This particular declarator ordains a person to refrain from putting it abroad that he or she is the declarator's wife or husband. *Declarators of marriage* are another common result of the vagueness of Scots marriage law. Other processes enforce *adherence* (cohabitation) – the wife was obliged to follow the husband wherever he went. *Aliment* is the term in Scottish law equivalent to the more familiar 'alimony'. The evolution of legal ideas about the roles of spouses can be followed up in the many reprints of classic texts published by the Stair Society. One example is David Hume's *Lectures 1786–1822*, Volume One (Stair Society, 1939). Your local library will be able to give you a full list of Stair Society publications.

Mortality

Three broad groups of influences affect mortality rates: innate differences, the effects of particular events in life (such as accidents) and environmental factors (in the broadest sense, these include climate, soil, occupation and levels of nutrition). Two common types of tabulation are the analysis of mortality by various characteristics of the living – age and sex for instance – and analysis according to cause of death. Occupational mortality investigations combine both types.

Studies of causes of death in the seventeenth and eighteenth centuries have been made from parish registers, but use of records is hampered by lack of a standard nomenclature for causes of death; an international standard was only established in 1893 (it has been periodically revised since). National tables appear in the annual reports of the Registrar General, and local findings can be judged against them. Another difficulty is that causes of death are often complex, particularly among the elderly, but usually only one 'cause' is recorded on a death certificate. The main groups of causes used today are industrial accidents, road accidents, infectious diseases, organ impairments and cancers. Another system of categorization distinguishes between deaths caused by the environment and those caused by the body wearing out.

These can be contrasted with the main causes of death in the seventeenth century – famines, wars and infectious diseases (often in the form of epidemics). Wars caused the deaths of more civilians than soldiers, for armies lived off the land, which led to famine, and they also helped to spread disease from their insanitary camps. Eye-witness accounts of famine speak of:

> . . . death in the Face of the Poor that abound everywhere; the Thinness of their Visage, their Ghostly looks, their feebleness, their Agues and their Fluxes threaten them with sudden Death . . . Some Die in the wayside, some drop down in the street, the poor sucking Babs are starving for want of Milk which the empty Breasts of their Mothers cannot furnish. (quoted in Flinn, 1977)

Famine brought the starving from the countryside into the burghs, partly because the burghs alone were in a position to organize importation and distribution of food through their ports (ports were a burgh monopoly). The resulting tensions can be investigated in the surviving town council minutes of the period and in the records of the privy council (both published sources). In Aberdeen for example:

> the provost, baillies and counsell taking to their consideratioun the great number of beggaris abounding within the brughe and speciallie extranieris com from all pairtes of the countrie; thairfour the counsell ordaines William Scott, wright, to mak ane number of ticketis with Abirdein and the yeir of God, and to be delyverit to thair awn poore, and nane to be estemed thair awin poor but these quha has stayit sewin yeiris within this brughe; and immediatlie eftir the delyverie of the seidis ticketis, the drum to be sent throu the haill streitis of the toune commanding and chargeing all extranier beggaris to remove themselffis presentlie . . . (Aberdeen, 1872)

Failure to comply often led to some gruesome punishments.

Epidemics, the third major source of demographic catastrophe in the seventeenth century, also led to draconian preventative measures. The social consequences can be studied more profitably than the medical causes. Even in later periods, when contemporary material assigns specific 'causes' to death figures, 'great difficulty arises in assigning most of these to meaningful medical categories' (Flinn, 1977). A flavour of medical attempts to come to grips with the mysteries of disease can be followed in papers and monographs by doctors and the Edinburgh College of Physicians (*Essays and Observations Physical and Literary*, 5 volumes, 1733–44). Epidemics were still a feature of the nineteenth century and studies from this period can draw on a considerable amount of local comment, interpretation and reaction. It has been claimed that Scottish Calvinism severely restricted the movement for sanitary reform

For, 'when cholera made its appearance, few doubted that its presence was anything other than yet another demonstration of God's omnipotence, and both lay and medical opinion were to a large extent in line with the clergy' (Maclaren, n.d.).

Class attitudes could also be studied. In middle-class minds Maclaren sees a belief that:

> certain life styles or behavioural patterns predisposed one to contract epidemic disease and these predispositions were rooted in an irreligious proletarian culture . . . This was particularly the case with 'excesses of any kind' – all manner of which laid the individual open to attack. It was essential to eat regular and proper meals, and to avoid going out after dark and keeping untimely hours.

Cholera is interesting to study because (unlike typhus) it struck at the whole community, not just those living in unsanitary areas. How would class prejudices accommodate this fact? Some very strange (to our way of thinking) theories circulated; and, paradoxically, it has been claimed that class perceptions were strengthened rather than weakened. For when all are threatened, the search for convenient scapegoats intensifies.

Another aspect of the study of nineteenth-century epidemics which could be pursued is the rise of holiday resorts. Tourist guide books proliferated from Victorian times, and many can be found in local history libraries. Early guides view the holiday in a different light from that prevalent today: they contain, for example, whole treatises on the medical value of fresh air and sea bathing, which took on a ritualistic quality, as the following quotation illustrates:

> *Condition of the bather.* As long as the patient still feels fatigued or any way indisposed from his journey, he should not think of bathing – the day after his arrival ought to be devoted to rest; frequently even he will do well to wait for a few days before he bathes, for the bracing sea air has always a powerful effect upon nervous and debilitated organizations. (Ferrier, 1873)

It is difficult for us to understand the atmosphere in which the distinct possibility of imminent death haunted the rich and poor alike.

The framework of the history of epidemics is set out in Flinn (1977); the family historian can study his or her area within this context, mindful of the observation that in early periods they 'struck randomly and, for the most part, briefly. During such visitations mortality could rise in a parish or town tenfold . . .'. Some useful work therefore can be done in a detailed local study identifying the specific local pattern, though it will often be the case that the parish registers are too incomplete for a worthwhile project to be undertaken.

Infant mortality is an interesting topic. Where possible one should try to distinguish between deaths due to inborn defects and those caused by external factors. The level of the death rate in the latter category has been seen as a litmus test of existing social welfare and health services. For whereas at older ages each person is to some extent responsible for his or her own survival, the young child's life is entirely dependent on the care of others. A local study could look at a community before and after some key development in health care – perhaps the introduction of a philanthropic nursing scheme, or an act of parliament such as the Public Health Act of 1867.

Studies of miscarriage, abortion and infant murder illustrate changing perceptions of women's role in society and attitudes towards the family. Abortion, of course, was illegal until very recently. Useful in such studies are precognitions – the signed statements from witnesses, from ministers to nosey neighbours, collected as a basis on which to judge whether a criminal offence had been committed. (An example was shown on page 29.) They are held in the Scottish Record Office among the papers of the Lord Advocate's department. Kirk session minutes, with their frequent and tenacious exploration of sexual habits, would also be a valuable source.

Other ideas related to mortality studies can be briefly mentioned. Social class mortality rates could be compared – interestingly, class differences are very small when mortality is very high (epidemics take poor and rich alike) and also when mortality is very low. Attitudes towards death can be studied in various sources – mourning cards and remembrance notices in newspapers, and funerary monuments, both their architecture and their inscriptions. Transcriptions of tombstone epitaphs in many areas of Scotland have been made by members of the Scottish Genealogy Society. Discussion and interpretation form the subject matter of Betty Willsher's *Understanding Scottish Churchyards*, published by Chambers (1985) and, for those interested in a fieldwork project, the companion volume, *Recording Scottish Churchyards*, published by the Council for British Archaeology (1985).

Migration

The movement of people, temporarily or permanently, as individuals or in groups, is a many-sided subject. Archaeologists, social historians and family historians alike have sought answers to questions such as 'Why have whole peoples uprooted themselves from their homes and moved in a body to new ones?'; 'Why have some lived an itinerant existence within a settled economy (such as tinkers and the displaced clans)?' and 'What has motivated men and women to leave a rural existence and seek work in an industrial town?' Alternatively, attention could be centred on the experiences of the migrants. How, for example, did emigrants from the Scottish highlands recreate their social and cultural outlook in their new homes in Canada and Australia? Or, concentrating on the reverse process, what problems have been faced by immigrants to Scotland? Can we detect recurring patterns in the treatment of Huguenots in the eighteenth century, Italian restaurateurs in the nineteenth century and Indian shopkeepers today? It will be evident that the study of migration encompasses the whole gamut of social studies, from the statistical and economic to the psychological.

The movement of whole peoples appears to be a phenomenon as old as mankind itself, and most significant migrations appear to have their roots in economic conditions. Stone Age groups followed each other into Scotland, and the trails they left can be studied in the volumes of the *Proceedings of the Society of Antiquaries of Scotland*, the *Scottish Archaeological Review*, and the *Scottish Archaeological Gazette*. In protohistorical times the most significant movement was that of the Celtic peoples, who originated in central Europe and spread out over a large area of the west, they themselves being part of a more ancient group – the Indo-Europeans of central Asia, whose language is the ancestor of nearly all European languages as well as Persian and the Indian languages. The Indo-Europeans possibly owed their expansion to the development of horse riding, which led to the growth of the first pastoral nomadic economies. An interesting contrast can be drawn between pastoralism and agriculture: the latter forms a barrier against migratory tendencies and fosters values sanctioning immobility – strong community loyalty, a social system in which status and rewards are earned for long residence or service, respect for property and a hostility to strangers – with a resulting problem for immigrants, as will be seen below. Pastoralism was to figure largely in the Scottish highland economy, though in a modified, non-nomadic form. Still, interesting comparisons can be made between society and culture in lowlands and highlands which stem in part from the different life styles.

One system of modified nomadism is 'transhumance', wherein cattle and sheep are driven to the high moorlands during the summer months. Another migrant group lived in huts called bothies, and their life is described by Saunders (1950):

> The botheymen often changed from place to place until they became semi-nomadic and these 'bohemians of agriculture' acquired an unenviable reputation as disturbers of the peace and corruptors of the parish morals. They were accused of being extravagant in dress – it was about the only permanent property they could possess – and of being addicted to drink, cards, 'bothy ballads' and nocturnal adventures; sometimes the strain of living in this fashion led to bullying and fighting.

Bothy ballads have been collected and discussed in John Ord's *Bothy Songs and Ballads*, published by Gardner in 1930 (and reprinted by John Donald 1974). The songs are one example (Saunders mentioned others such as dress) of a cultural response which can be equated with a distinct style of living. The relationship with local settled communities to which Saunders refers can be investigated in kirk session minutes; and the tensions and fights in newspaper reports and in local court records (burgh, justice of the peace and sheriff courts).

The bothy system is one example of the persistence of an older, sometimes ancient, way of life. Societies can be thought of as an assemblage of elements, some old, some new, some almost fossilized, existing together – a living museum in fact, the historian's task being that of unravelling and identifying the different parts. Thus the bothy way of life could perhaps be seen as an adaptation of a purely pastoral society (such as that which built the ancient enclosures on Scottish hillsides) to a later agricultural, and finally industrial, civilization.

In historical times the movement of these pastoral and other peoples becomes easier to plot and it is possible to give firmer answers to a question which has long taxed prehistorians – whether change occurs by invasion or diffusion (i.e. successful new ideas and technologies being transmitted from one society to its neighbours until finally their cultures become indistinguishable). The obvious answer is that both processes occur. That Celtic speakers indubitably ended up in Scotland suggests that migrations and invasions did take place, and we also have evidence from the works of Caesar to that effect. At the same time, small numbers of immigrants could in certain circumstances have an influence out of all proportion to their numbers. For example, the Anglo–Norman barons who colonized Scotland in the early Middle Ages, though few in number, changed the political and social structure to a considerable extent. The Picts have similarly be seen as a native people with a thin layer of Celtic aristocracy on the top.

This process raises a large number of interesting questions which can be pursued by the local historian. For instance, just how much *does* life at the local level change in response to the larger movements of history? It has been claimed that even upheavals such as the Reformation did not significantly affect local church life and religious perceptions. In one sense nothing ever changes; human behaviour remains similar at the micro-level of daily life; and some men and women adapt to new ideas more than others, so that a residual cultural lag remains a feature of all societies. Yet innovation is constant, and the local historian is faced by the need to study local communities on various continuums simultaneously. He or she can also try to examine just how minority élites are able to impose their new political structures, their culture, and even their language, on the majority. Is it that their systems are economically superior and hence are eagerly adopted, with the complete cultural package being a necessary adjunct in the way that Coke follows American capitalism around the world today? Or are the mechanisms of domination – social, military and political – which the élite have learned too sophisticated for the natives to fight?

Different classifications of migration patterns have been proposed: for example, those involving a change in culture (one country to another, or from a rural to urban environment) or within the same culture; those which are voluntary and those forced; and those which are temporary (as in transhumance or membership of harvesting bands) and those which are permanent. Classification can also be made according to the impetus involved: ecological (for example in times of famine), political (resettlement by the state or proprietor) and voluntary (especially associated with rural to urban migration and with movements of groups motivated by utopian or religious ideals).

Since the seventeenth century, from which time detailed local studies are possible, all of the above categories have been well represented in Scotland, a fact which has caused much rethinking about traditional rural society. Once, the local historian may well have carried in his or her mind an image of the local community as introverted and unchanging, formed of family groups with deep roots in the area. Now this appears to be much less the case, and migration studies are central to the investigation of the matter.

The basic sources for such study include the parish registers of births, marriages and deaths, hearth and poll tax returns, and the census enumeration books and published census material. Census enumeration books from 1851 are particularly useful in that they list parishes of birth, and these can be tabulated to give a general prospect of movement in and out of the locality. An accurate count of the extent of migration into or out of an area can be made by comparing successive census counts, after discounting the intervening births and deaths by establishing birth and mortality rates. Thus, if at the census of 1841 the number of men aged 30 was A, and if in 1851 the number of men aged 40 was B, mortality rates can be worked out from life tables and the net difference between B and A represents the net migratory movement. Of course, such net figures can conceal much more substantial movements if both immigration and emigration are prevalent in the locality.

Local migration

Attempts to categorize different localized migrations have constantly to take account of the discovery of new patterns as detailed local studies are carried out in different areas. A few examples can be briefly discussed here.

Rentals from estate papers survive for many areas from the beginning of the seventeenth century. One collection that has been studied in the context of migration is that of the Earl of Panmure in Angus (between Dundee and Arbroath). The study suggests that geographical mobility among tenants operated over limited distances, under ten miles in fact (I.D. and K.A. Whyte, 1983). Identified factors affecting mobility are family structure, extent of capital accumulation, length of lease, the proprietors' rent policies and farming conditions. The founding of new villages by the proprietors appears to have been a response to more fundamental structural changes in the Scottish economy. In fact villages as we understand them only made their appearance in Scotland during the eighteenth century, and in a large number of cases were deliberately planned – they are usually instantly recognizable by their straight streets, uniform building style and village greens on the English pattern. In some cases the tenants were forcibly resettled, in others inducements were offered, and in others again relocation may indeed have been an attractive proposition.

The latter may have been the case in the borders which, like other upland areas, had 'the reputation of being sectors of economic retardation if not backwardness, stubborn refuges for old practices, institutions and values' (Dodgshon, 1983). When the Agricultural Revolution came to such areas (in the late eighteenth century) the changes made were twofold. Firstly the commercialization of the agricultural economy introduced new concepts: a marketing strategy and conversion of rents in kind to those in cash. The extent of commercialization in a local economy can be studied by the researcher through measuring the degree of self-sufficiency within that economy (farm size in other words), as well as investigating the proportion of land acquisition by outsiders and the proportion of the production marketed outside the local economy. The second change brought by the Agricultural Revolution was the introduction of innovations such as crop rotation, specialization (sheep in the case of the borders and highlands) and the removal of multiple tenancies (small hamlets farmed by a number of tenants, often family groups).

The result of these changes was depopulation and the abandonment of upland settlements; these were the first victims of the decline of a subsistence economy. The worst consequences were avoided (or perhaps the process would never have occurred otherwise) by the rise of a part rural, part urban phenomenon: hand-loom weaving. The number of hand-loom weavers rose from around 8500 in 1792 to 50,000 in 1800 and 84,000 in 1838 – a sizeable proportion of the Scottish population. A large number of these weavers lived in the sort of villages discussed above.

Industrialization took the process a stage further, sucking men and women out of rural communities altogether. Those that stayed were affected too, for they tended to gravitate nearer the towns where wages had been forced up by competition for labour. Four factors have been said to have had an effect on the scale of migration to towns: the degree of proximity of the town; the nature of agricultural development; the survival or growth of non-agricultural employment such as hand-loom weaving, and the rate of natural increase of population. The strength of the pull to towns, seen from the viewpoint of the individual, is difficult to measure but attempts have been made to do this by using objective signs such as the size of the towns, the variety and number of jobs, the level of wages and the proximity of rural sources of labour. Another topic of study could be the experiences (which could be quite traumatic) of urban immigrants from rural areas. Urban living was quite a new experience for the majority:

> Some established themselves as in a wider parish, and found that hard work, frugality and honesty still earned the expected rewards. Others were struck by such impersonal factors as an economic crisis or an epidemic; then the conflict between inherited values and urban experiences broke down the exposed and unsupported personality (Saunders, 1950).

The initial rural to urban migration during the Industrial Revolution did not put an end to subsequent movements. In fact, it made mobility easier for all classes of society, such that 'every county of Scotland had evidently been sending its migrants to every other part of the country and every county received some from sources just as widespread' (Gray, 1983). For the professional classes, mobility would then as now be a response to new opportunities for promotion: the Industrial Revolution spawned a whole series of new professions. For the agricultural labourer, now tied to his employer solely by contractual obligations, the phenomenon of 'frequent flitting' arose and was noticed and frowned upon by nineteenth-century observers. 'Frequent flitting' is in some cases difficult to study; the domicile of labourers can be compared between two censuses, but one cannot follow the movements from farm to farm and parish to parish in the intervening period. More comprehensive research is possible where testimonials have survived. These were 'certificates of good behaviour [which] were issued by the minister and kirk session of a parish to those wishing to move elsewhere and were designed to show that the individual or family mentioned was free from church censure and had lived peaceably with their neighbours' (Houston, 1983). In effect they were an attempt 'to keep the mobile elements of the population under the control of the church's moral discipline'. The movement tended to be localized and many reasons for it have been adduced. One of the most obvious is that the workers 'may actually have enjoyed moving around as a way of meeting new people and expanding their range of work experience' (Houston, 1983). The bi-annual hiring fair with its bargaining between master and men worked in this respect – often to the advantage of the latter.

Immigration

The causes and consequences of immigration are another fascinating pursuit for the family historian, and also a chastening one, in that one can learn to understand our current problems and prejudices towards the integration of outsiders. The scale is now global, but it is possible that our treatment of Asians and West Indians mirrors that formerly meted out to Europeans – and, before that, perhaps to the incomer from the next county or village. Anthropologists and sociologists might claim that the cohesion of any group of settled people – family, community or nation – depends upon the exclusivity of its boundaries and the deliberate fostering of hostility towards those outside the favoured group.

Studies from various periods of Scottish history can be made, and interesting comparisons drawn between the groups under consideration. Some immigrants were welcome; others were not, the reasons for their arrival probably affecting their reception. As an example one can contrast the position of Huguenots and gipsies in the eighteenth century from the minutes of the justices of the peace in Lanarkshire. The Huguenots received the following welcome:

> . . . wee have thought ffitt, and by her Majesties speciall command do hereby earnestly recommend it to you at your nixt Quarter Sessions and other meettings of the Justices of the Peace within your shire, to consider the best wayes and methods for disposeing of any number of the said distressed Protestants within the said shire in such manner as they may be enabled by their labour and industry the better to contribute for the support of themselves and their ffamilyes and by your own examples to invite and encourage your neighbours, especially the cheif magistrats of the corporation within your shire, to afford them all countenance and assistance as ther shall be occasions.

Yet in almost the next breath the justices are vowing:

> . . . haveing receaved certain information that there are considerable numbers of vagabonds, sorners [ruffians], louser [loose] and idle persons, both men and women, and particularly those commonly called Egyptians gathered together in companies and are passing through the country armed with swords, guns, pistols, durks [staves] and other such lyke wapons . . . notwithstanding of the laues and Acts of Parliament of this realm . . . commanding the vagabonds, sorners, and common

theives, commonly called Egyptians, to pass furth of this Kingdom and remain perpetually furth therof . . . it shall be leisom [lawful] to all his Majesties good subjects, or any ane of them, to cause take, aprehend, imprison, and execut to death the saids Egyptians, men & women as common and notorious theives by ane asyze only to be tryed, that they are called knowen, repute and halden Egyptians . . .

Other immigrant groups can be identified through a study of town council minute books, but statistical information is quite inadequate before the mid-nineteenth century, from which time the decennial census reports have included tables of immigrants (from 1861 the nationality of immigrants was also noted). The annual record of movement of peoples through the ports dates only from the late nineteenth century, and is difficult to use as Scottish ports are not tabulated separately from the United Kingdom as a whole.

The best documented immigration is that of the Irish, which took place on a large scale during the first half of the nineteenth century. In the census of 1841, 126,326 Scottish residents born in Ireland were enumerated (a figure probably exaggerated by the presence of seasonal harvesters). It is instructive to read what observers said of the Irish in Glasgow; the following was written by no less than a professor of law at Glasgow University:

As a rule quite unprosperous they have in some places displayed special abilities. Thus in Glasgow, they are fast developing a monopoly of the priesthood, the pawnshops, and the public houses . . . They are responsible for most of the crime committed in Scotland, which otherwise would be the most law-abiding country in the world. Wheresoever knives and razors are used, wheresoever sneak thefts and mean pilfering are easy and safe, wheresoever dirty acts of sexual baseness are committed there you will find the Irishman in Scotland with all but a monopoly of the business. (quoted in Wood, 1978)

Irish immigration is particularly well documented because in the wake of the potato famines, the Irish census commissioners collected returns of Irish passengers from masters of emigrant ships leaving Irish and other United Kingdom ports. The information was collated and published annually in parliamentary papers between 1876 and 1920. The complexity of migratory movements is particularly illustrated by the fact that these large-scale immigrations were taking place at exactly the same time as large-scale emigrations, especially from the highlands. Comparative studies could be made on the motivations behind these contrary movements.

Later in the nineteenth century, the main thrust of immigration came from Eastern Europe (the immigrants mainly Jews) and from Italy. Immigrants from the latter developed an occupational specialization in the shape of the first 'fast food' businesses – chip shops and cafés. There can hardly be a small town in Scotland that does not boast an Italian establishment, and the cultural shock felt by an unsuspecting visitor to a remote highland settlement can be quite considerable. The researcher could look into the causes of the immigrants' success and ask whether the occupational specialization was the result of imported skills exploiting a previously unidentified need, or the reflection of a desire on the part of the immigrants to preserve their unity as a group in their new home. The Italians certainly aroused hostility, as newspaper reports of the time will show. Such reports considerably enhance the understanding which today's local historians can have of the psychology of racial feelings.

As an example, one can look at a controversy reported in the *Musselburgh News* in March 1912. The ostensible object of attack was the town's café. At a meeting of electors, the Reverend J.A. Nicholls declared:

> . . . the ice cream shop was far worse than the Sweetie shop. The seeds of moral ruin had been sown in them . . . These places were mostly kept by foreigners. Their ways were not our ways neither were their thoughts our thoughts. Their ideals of morals were much looser, much broader than ours, and he often wondered if morality ever entered into their calculations at all.

Another speaker opined that 'a friend of his, closely connected with one of the sheriff courts of Scotland told him that ninety per cent of the illegitimacy cases had something to do with ice cream shops.' These (to us) innocuous institutions were also accused of being the 'mustering ground by young people on the Sabbath day who indulged in the worst of language, shouting and bawling and every form of disorder.' Chip shops did not escape either: Bailie Kelt remarked that 'people had to put their fingers on their nostrils when passing such shops.'

Points of interest which the local historian might wish to pursue are the strong language of ministers (today the church would probably take a broader view of morality, and a more charitable one), the recurring cultural phenomenon of the older generation lamenting the behaviour of youth (a phenomenon seemingly firmly embedded in the structure of our society) and the development in the new towns, following the Industrial

Revolution, of new recreational patterns among friends rather than families. As one speaker laments: 'He had spoken to one gentleman . . . who said to him – "Why, the young people have no other place to go to". He said – "What about their homes?" "Many of them", the gentleman said "had only a butt and ben to go to", but he [the speaker] considered that some of the greatest men that Scotland ever produced were brought up in a butt and ben.'

Emigration

Sources of information for emigration form a distinct group of demographic records. They are complex, but three phases can be distinguished, emanating respectively from the customs commissioners and Treasury (1770–1840), the Colonial Land and Emigration Commission (1841–72) and the Board of Trade (1873 onwards).

In 1773 the Treasury sought from its commissioners of customs in Edinburgh 'an Account of all persons who shall take their passage on board any Ship or Vessel to go out of this Kingdom with a description of their Age, Quality, Occupation, Employment and former residence; and an Account of to what port or place they propose to go, and on what Account and for what purpose, they leave this country . . .' However, many vessels left Scotland without the knowledge of customs officials, so the lists, while probably accurate in themselves, will not be a comprehensive record of emigrants. These records are preserved in the Public Record Office in London (PRO T 17/20) together with another series from 1772–3 based on lists collected by sheriffs from ministers in the highlands (PRO T 47/12).

The American War of Independence brought emigration westward to an abrupt halt, and the colonies being lost, listing was not resumed (the impetus behind the projects had been fear of infectious republicanism). Listing commenced again only in 1803, the motivating force now being alarm at depopulation and at the condition of emigrant ships. The Passenger Act of 1803 required customs officers at every port in the United Kingdom to procure from the captains of departing ships complete lists of their steerage passengers. Cabin passengers and those who worked their passage were excluded from the act (they were not recorded until 1863). Likewise the act did not apply to emigration to Europe, a situation which remained the case until 1890, and even then Mediterranean port destinations were excluded. Even steerage passengers' lists for the colonies may be deficient, for 'the owners of emigrant shipping had a strong economic incentive to evade the controls of the Passenger Acts [and] it is likely that in the early decades the statistics underestimate the extent of emigration quite substantially' (Flinn, 1977). Few of the early statistics have survived, however: some passenger lists compiled between 1801 and 1803 are held in the Public Record Office (PRO HO 102/18; typewritten transcripts are held in the library of the Scottish Genealogy Society in Edinburgh) and a list for 1808 is also preserved (PRO CO226/23).

Family historians, statisticians and economic historians alike have chafed at the inadequacies of these records, which are only partially remedied by retrospective listings. The first of these was prepared for Parliament in 1830 by the Inspector General of Imports and Exports and covered the years 1821–9. The return was subsequently made annually, and a specifically Scottish series from 1825 was produced in 1833. A further retrospective for the years from 1815 was published in 1853, though Scottish figures were not abstracted for the years 1815–24. The collection of statistics had been taken over in 1841 by an *ad hoc* body, the Colonial Land and Emigration Commission, who in turn were supplanted by the Board of Trade under the 1872 Merchant Shipping Act. The records from 1825 form part of the series of parliamentary papers which have been reprinted in the last twenty years, so the researcher should be able to requisition items through his or her local library from bibliographical details obtained from the indexes prepared by Percy and Grace Ford (see notes to Chapter One).

Where the United Kingdom statistics and lists are deficient, the records of the recipient countries can sometimes help. Annual immigration data was collected by the United States from 1820 and Canada from 1829. These and similar records are listed in A.H. Lancour (1963) and Frank E. Bridgers (1962).

The demographic records that were kept were one response to a high level of public concern, and this concern is manifested in many other documents available to the family historian. Charitable societies were formed to promote or prevent emigration, especially from the highlands. Examples are the Highland Society of Scotland and the Highland and Island Emigration Society. The papers of such societies can be consulted in the Scottish Record Office and National Library of Scotland. But the primary source of information will be government reports, in the early parts of the nineteenth century mainly those of select committees of the Houses of Parliament and latterly those of royal commissions. A selection of the most important is given in the notes to this chapter.

Poor countries like Scotland, on the periphery of European civilization, have always suffered from an export of talents, and the recently identified gravitation of economic activity towards the centre of the Common Market is but the latest manifestation of this trend. From the Middle Ages onwards, Scots found employment as mercenaries in European armies, and the incongruous presence of General Macdonald in Napoleon's forces is only a famous example of a common occurrence. Trade too drew them abroad: the Scottish merchant community in Rotterdam at the beginning of the eighteenth century numbered around a thousand. At the same time there were said to be between 500 and 1000 Scots hawkers in England, this when the total population of Scotland was little more than one million. Incidentally, emigration to England and immigration of the English into Scotland was (and is) sustained and substantial, though given the absence of border controls, the phenomenon is impossible to quantify before the middle of the nineteenth century.

Colonial plantation began in the seventeenth century, in Ulster and Nova Scotia, giving the government the opportunity to export its problems as well as its talent. In 1665, for example, permission was given for the transportation of 'strong and idle beggars, gipsies and criminals, to Jamaica and Barbados' (quoted in Donaldson, 1966). Of course, the major emigrations took place in the late eighteenth and nineteenth centuries, especially from the highlands. The human and social factors in the clearances have been well documented, and can be studied in the government papers discussed above. Attention has more recently focussed on the wider context in which depopulation took place. It was pointed out as early as 1857 that the decline in the population of the three lowland counties of Haddington, Berwick and Dumfries since 1801 had been 28 per cent compared with 30 per cent in the highlands, yet these counties boasted all the accoutrements of a modern society to the absence of which the highland problem was attributed – large acreages of wheat production, high rents, a large mining population, thriving towns, fertile soils and productive fishing industries (as pointed out in Richards, 1985). In this context highland migration can be seen as part of the process of depopulation of pastoral and non-industrial regions. The pressure came partly from the capitalist spirit itself, which saw that the benefits of specialization were the key to the growth of industrial economies. The danger from the rural regions was that they threatened to swallow up the surplus capital generated by the new methods to pay for the relief of poverty; in the highlands demographic crises caused by famine persisted well into the nineteenth century, long after they had vanished from England. Equally seriously, the pressure of population growth in the highlands threatened to cut off food supplies to the industrial towns, where for the first time the majority of the population contributed nothing to food production. To avoid this situation it was imperative that marginal regions themselves adopted modern production strategies by specializing in the kinds of agriculture for which they were physically and climatically suited – a far cry from the old subsistence economy. In the case of the highlands, this meant specializing in kelp, wool, fish, meat and the provision of sporting facilities. Such a development demanded a redistribution of population, but it must be remembered that lowland agrarian counties suffered in the same way from these rationalizing principles.

Population geography

Population geography is the study of the *spatial* aspects of population, and can be distinguished from demography in its emphasis on distribution patterns rather than on the nature and behaviour of populations. Local historians of course need to be particularly conscious of spatial concepts, for their subject more than other types of history is intimately bound up with the specific geography of an area.

Five factors are listed by Zelinsky (1970) in assessing why people live where they do. First, there is the direct impact of the physical environment; secondly, the workings of the local economy; thirdly, the general cultural configuration of a society; fourthly, the impact of physical and social disasters; and finally the influence of specific social and political decisions (the latter was obviously of great importance in the setting up of planned towns and in the work of institutions such as the Highlands and Islands Development Board). These features could be assessed one by one, though judging their relative importance is more difficult. There are complicating factors too. For example, 'the main reason that a population of a given size dwells in a given area is that the bulk of it was there in the immediate past – sometimes with, but often without, much economic justification' (Zelinsky, 1970). Similarly, cultural features such as marriage patterns, which may at one stage have been a response to certain economic pressures, often continue to exist by force of tradition and 'for lack of any compelling reason to abandon them' (Zelinsky, 1970). A point emphasized elsewhere in this book is that a local community is like a museum of living elements from the past, some ancient, some more recent, and that the local historian's job is to try to disentangle them.

The researcher interested in a study of this kind could initially try to compile a simple description of the location of populations in his parish or county from the seventeenth century, and the characteristics of these populations by age, sex, employment and so on. Any studies of earlier periods can depend only on estimates derived from archaeological investigations. From the time of the detailed censuses (1841 onwards) more sophisticated studies will be possible, using information on residence, occupation, place of work, marital status, housing, class, income, educational status, reproductive history and migrational history. The study could proceed with a comparison between neighbouring rural and urban areas on any of these counts. In urban areas, different residential sectors can be identified (based on class or occupation) and questions can be asked as to how and why the pattern came to be formed.

Chapter Four

KIN, CLAN AND COMMUNITY

This chapter investigates the family and its important role in history. It looks too at those ways in which family structures and values have been extended to embrace wider groupings of people not necessarily related by blood, such as clans or working communities. Anthropology is a science which has developed techniques for looking at such close-knit groups in detail. These varied perspectives can provide an effective starting point for those interested in genealogy and family history.

Genealogy

The current widely-shared enthusiasm for genealogy and family history has been denigrated by some historians. G.W.S. Barrow (1978) has highlighted the objections as follows:

> Some modern historians profess to despise the art, or science, of genealogy. They may object that the minute investigation of the family relationships of individuals chosen arbitrarily and pursued regardless of the eminence or distinction of those involved can have little or no historical significance or, on the other hand, that subjecting a handful of the eminent to genealogical study is meaningless.

Part of the difficulty is that genealogy has never enjoyed very high scientific credentials. The same writer for example refers to the dubious practice of inventing illustrious genealogies for royalty and the nobility from unlikely figures such as Charlemagne or Julius Caesar, and the fact that this unfortunate habit is resuscitated whenever a comparative commoner marries into royalty.

These difficulties apart, the student of genealogy is faced with other problems. Firstly, the subject has a superficial simplicity for the non-historian, which is no doubt a contributory factor in its present popularity. Yet as Barrow again says: 'Although I cannot claim to be a genealogist, I have been in the game long enough to realize that genealogy is fraught with difficulty. To construct a pedigree which will convince even a jury of genealogists, let alone a court of uninstructed yet intelligent and sceptical critics from outside the genealogists' world, is no easy matter'. The point being made here is that black and white judgements are often no more appropriate in genealogy than in other areas of historical study, and this applies equally whether the period in question is Barrow's own period, the Middle Ages, or the eighteenth century. Enthusiastic amateurs are inclined to overlook this fact, and, of course, once a single unsubstantiated relationship has been glossed over, the whole edifice of a genealogy becomes threatened. The quite unwarranted assumption that individuals sharing a surname have, or ever have had, any blood relationships with each other is a pitfall to be particularly avoided.

A second serious difficulty is that from the time of its very foundation genealogy has been compromised by ulterior motives – pride, snobbery, covetousness – all of which have been and are an encouragement to misrepresent, whether conscious or unconscious. In the words of Anthony Wagner (1975) 'claims to unsurpassed nobility and antiquity are the natural foible of genealogists'. He might have added that this has been the case for a long time. In a work published in 1890 the great historian of the highlands, W.F. Skene, wrote in relation to the early clans that:

> competition between rival interests and rival races would lead to the gratification of vanity becoming the ruling motive, in order to maintain a *quasi* superiority, and likewise, when the exigencies of their position required it, to a falsification and imposture in order to enable the clans to maintain their ground . . .

The warning is clear: do not always believe what is written in genealogies, however eminent or old they may be. Fake clan-pedigree makers from an early date raided better preserved Irish manuscripts such as the *Book of Ballimote* (1383) and the *Book of Lecain* (1407), and a manuscript known as MS1467 (NLS Adv Ms 72.1.1) which was edited by Skene in 1839 in *Collectanea de Rebus Albanicis* (Iona Club, 1839 and 1847) and again, more reliably, in his *Celtic Scotland*. The later portions of these pedigrees are relatively accurate. A fourth manuscript source, Donald Monro's *Genealogies of the Clans* (1549) has recently been published (Monro, 1961).

The roots of genealogical preoccupations are ancient, as Wagner (1975) notes:

In the kind of society we call tribal the claims of kinship were and are paramount for rich and poor alike. The unity of the kindred, whether expressed in the blood feud, in the rules of inheritance or exogamy, or in whatever way, was a fact of life which made it necessary for each to know who he was, so that children, from Tartary to Polynesia, from Judaea to Ireland, were taught in childhood to recite their pedigrees, or else a bardic class was maintained, among whose duties it was to preserve a pedigree of all the tribe.

Some of the anthropological themes touched on in this passage will be taken up later in the chapter. Here we can note the existence of a Scottish bardic class – the sennachies of the highland clans – whose significance is outlined by Skene (1890):

In considering the genealogies of the Highland clans we must bear in mind that in the early state of the tribal organisation the pedigree of the sept or clan, and of each member of the tribe, had a very important meaning. Their rights were derived through the common ancestor and their relation to him, and through him to each other, indicated their position in the succession, as well as their place in the allocation of the tribe land. In such a state of society the pedigree occupied the same position as the title deed in the feudal system, and the sennachies were as much the custodiers of the rights of families as the mere panegyrists of the clan.

The genealogical function of the sennachies is remembered in the post of High Sennachie of Celtic Scotland held by the Lord Lyon, in which capacity he acts as judge in matters genealogical and maintains the Public Register of Genealogies.

The bardic genealogies of Celtic tribal chiefdoms became increasingly irrelevant as personal authority was replaced by authority vested in land – the so-called feudal system. Another feature of feudalism was primogeniture (inheritance by the eldest son) which had not been the case in the tribes, and this, together with an equally important feature of the feudal system – the establishment of a title to property by means of a written charter – gave a quite new significance to genealogy. It became documentary support for rights of succession to lands and titles.

The new interest in genealogy coincided with and was an integral part of the development of heraldry, which served to emphasize the status of a noble. The coat of arms, of which the earliest known Scottish examples date from the late twelfth century, was a visible symbol of this status. Medieval heraldic practice can be traced in inventories of furniture and monumental effigies, but the main source is the collection of armorial seals, 3000 casts of which are held in the Lord Lyon's office. They are described in Henry Laing and W.R. Macdonald's *Scottish Armorial Seals*, published in 1904. The use of seals on deeds, charters and leases demonstrates the functional value of a system of heraldry in a semi-literate but hierarchically structured society. It was necessary to know at once '*who* you were and *what* you were' says Innes of Learney (1956).

In 1672 a Public Register of All Arms and Bearings was instituted, similar in concept to the recently instituted Register of Sasines, which had proved very successful. Arms indeed came to be viewed in law as a form of heritable property like land. Their use too was quite widespread, Innes of Learney calculating that upward of 10,000 Scots (or one in every 45) were entitled to display arms. Their numbers included not only 'peers and lairds, but professors, lawyers, merchants and businessmen [who] have continually registered arms as a matter of course, by descent if proved, otherwise under new grants. Our Scottish burgesses did not hesitate to decorate the picturesque old houses in which they both lived and carried on their trades with their armorial symbols . . .'.

The Register of All Arms and Bearings is the responsibility of the Lord Lyon, a judge whose court of heraldry and genealogy is still in daily operation in Register House, Princess Street, Edinburgh, where its records are kept by the Lyon Clerk. All arms matriculated (i.e. enrolled in the register) prior to 1903 can be found in James Balfour Paul's *An Ordinary of Arms contained in the Public Register of all Arms and Bearings in Scotland*, published by W. Green (1903).

Under the Lord Lyon are three heralds and three pursuivants. Heralds originally performed the function of recording genealogies as a preliminary to matriculation. The Public Register of Genealogies, also maintained by the Lord Lyon, contains two distinct forms of record. The *birthbrieve* sets out 'the descent, nobilitary status and all such matters relating to the social, feudal or tribal position of the petitioner as may seem useful at home or abroad . . .' (Innes of Learney, 1956). In medieval times it was frequently obtained from the local town council or under the king's great seal and used as a form of passport in foreign cities. Some burghs kept their own burgh propinquity books, but these have been superseded by the statutory Lord Lyon registers. Unpublished examples will be held in burgh archives. Birthbrieves recorded under the great seal will appear in the published volumes of *Registrum Magni Sigilli*, 11 volumes, 1882–1914, recently republished by the Scottish Record Society

(1984). A birthbrieve contains information as to the nobility of all sixteen great-great-grandparents where possible and of subsequent generations. It differs from a *lineal pedigree*, which is the second type of record held in the Public Register of Genealogies, in that the latter pursues a single line indefinitely. It is used in confirmation of birthbrieves.

The value of genealogy in historical research has been variously expressed. G.W.S. Barrow (1978) sees a particular importance for it in the study of medieval times where 'in a comparatively simple, homogeneous society . . . ancestry, parentage, marriage and offspring seem to be always in the forefront in every class and in every community.' Wagner (1975) looks more generally at history as a 'tournament of combining or competing families, whose subtle interplay and manoeuvres, never wholly to be understood, we can only begin to grasp by first analysing and clarifying their genealogies.'

Those interested in researching aristocratic genealogy have a large number of sources at their disposal (some are listed in the notes to this chapter) as well as the existing biographies of specific aristocratic houses. Among the latter are almost fifty volumes written by Sir William Fraser (1816–98) who has been described as the greatest of the family historians of Scotland. But far more popular today is the compilation of the humble pedigree, especially that of the researcher himself or herself. The motivation for this is usually somewhat different: such a genealogist is unlikely to be staking claims to property and arms, and equally unlikely to find a proud ancestry of which to boast. This is not to say that the humble genealogist is not open to temptation, as the *Encyclopedia Britannica* of 1957 sagely notes in its references to 'a vast number of genealogies, many of which combine the results of laborious research . . . with extravagant and unfounded claims . . .'. A very common error is to assume that sharing a surname with a Scottish aristocrat constitutes a degree of affinity with him. The error arises from a misunderstanding of the origin and use of names, so the next section outlines the history of names and the proper use that can be made of them.

Surnames

Donaldson (1981) warned against 'casual assumptions or guesses about kinship and descent based solely on surnames [which] are no substitute for serious research into ancestry.' The unwarranted assumption to which he refers is that individuals sharing a surname have, or at some time had, blood relationship with one another. The mistake sometimes arises from a misuse of a famous work – George F. Black's *Surnames of Scotland*, New York Public Library (1946) – the mistake being to regard it as a work of genealogy where it is in fact a study of *etymology*, the origin and meaning of names. Etymology is not a study to be neglected. 'Our names preserve a record of the government, industries, habits, beliefs and fancies of our ancestors' said Donald Mackinnon, and W.F.H. Nicolaisen (1980) points out that 'surnames, when tied to place-names, can give us information on migration, while other types of names reveal occupational histories and patterns of kinship. The very act of naming has both communal and personal importance and can yield significant socio-cultural data.' Such studies, however, must be clearly distinguished from genealogy, and Black's lists of occurrences of names are not lists of members of the same family.

Surnames have been divided into four classes according to their origins: whether from place-names, parents' christian names (patronymics), occupation, or personal characteristics. Those derived from place-names are probably the oldest and are first recorded in Scotland around 1100. Territorial designation was a natural feature of the feudal system because of its emphasis on land 'ownership' as the source of political, legal and military authority (the so-called barons had these powers devolved to them from the king along with the grant of estates). Among the highland clans territorial designations were used as second surnames to distinguish among various branches of the clan ('Cameron of Lochiel' for example). A chief was also officially described as 'laird of *x*', though this is not quite a surname in our modern sense.

It is easy to understand how surnames deriving from place-names came to be fixed. The feudal landowner was permanently associated with the place, and his son inherited his territories from him. In time, the men of his estate might also acquire the name, though of course they were not relatives in most cases. Far more difficult to understand is the process by which the other types of surname became fixed. Take patronymics as an example: a man Donald whose father's name was John would rightly be called Johnson. But his son should be called Donaldson (as indeed he still would be in Iceland). At some stage, therefore, patronymics (and likewise occupational names and nicknames) became detached from their descriptive meaning and took on a life of their own as what we call a surname, which was passed from father to son. Inheritance is perhaps the key concept here, for it was the twin pillars of inheritance and kinship which underpinned the feudal system, and how could either be better or more neatly expressed than by a tag which immediately proclaimed the relationship? This situation can be contrasted with that in the clan where individual relationships were less important than membership of the group as a whole. Here there was no need for surnames.

Nicolaisen makes the point that:

> this increasingly semantic opacity or irrelevance eliminated the surname as a viable locating device placing identified individuals in their rightful slots in contemporary society . . . Somebody called *Aberdour* may now have been born in Kirkcaldy, somebody named *Thomson* may have Peter as a father, and somebody bearing the name of *Little* may be of considerable physical stature. When the very occupations denoted by surnames have perished or decayed (Barker, Gosman, Cordiner etc) then the surname becomes nothing but a linguistic fossil useful perhaps in the reconstruction of medieval popular culture but without much direct relevance to the contemporary scene.

In other words, one can use surnames from the Middle Ages in local projects – they can tell us for example about migrations (the man called Aberdour found in Glasgow has probably come from Aberdour) and about local industries and crafts. But thereafter, their use is in genealogy.

As suggested above, highland names are perhaps something of an exception, but there are conflicting views about this. Some have claimed that surnames were not used in the highlands until the sixteenth or even seventeenth centuries. A patronymic system was used, but it included strings of ancestors (akin to the old bardic pedigrees) with the name of the farm occupied or perhaps some personal characteristic tacked on at the end. If a highlander found himself among strangers (migrating to the lowlands for instance) he took or was given a surname. But against this, what is to be made of the evidence of a privy council act of 1603 proscribing the name McGregor because 'the bare and simple name of McGregoure maid that haill clan to presume of their power, force and strength, and did encourage them without reverence of the law or fear of punishment to go forward in their iniquities'? It is similarly hotly disputed whether the surname, once it arrived in the highlands 'was the binding link between the members of the clan' as asserted by

W.C. Mackenzie, (1950) or whether a variety of names could be found. Whatever the truth of the matter, the uncertainties are such that the family historian should be very careful in the use of surnames as evidence.

Genealogical records

If the researcher in Scottish genealogy should at the outset reconcile himself or herself to a likely humble origin, he or she should equally be reconciled to the possibility that little progress will be made in the construction of his or her genealogy. Scots who were born, married or died in Scotland since 1855 (the date of the introduction of civil registration) can be traced with very little trouble from the records held at the General Register Office in Edinburgh; but the period prior to 1855 can prove very disappointing.

The demographic records available to the genealogical researcher have been discussed in detail in the last chapter and many of their omissions and inadequacies indicated, though the General Register Office does maintain a file of names that are known to be missing in the parish registers. However, given the constant refrain of the ministers writing the statistical accounts of their parishes in the 1790s that 'many neglect to get the names of their children entered in the public register', there will be many deficiencies that are never made good. Of course, these very children are the ancestors of some of today's researchers, and for them the loss is very personal – all trace of their family has literally vanished, and it is impossible to pick up at an earlier generation if a single missing link cannot be established. Even if records have survived, the problem may well be to discover *where*, for the fact that pre-1855 demographic records are mostly parish-based means that if ancestors moved one cannot establish whence or whither, short of checking registers for the whole of Scotland. The latter alternative, however, is now becoming feasible, thanks to the work of the Mormon church.

The Mormon church, or the church of Jesus Christ of Latter-Day Saints, to give it its full title, holds the view that children can be 'sealed' to their parents 'for time and all eternity' – and not only living children. One's ancestors, according to the Mormons, can be sealed by proxy to each preceding generation until one ends up with 'what could be considered as the ultimate in the concept of an extended family, from Adam as the progenitor' (Slorance, 1980). For these ceremonies to be performed (and the Mormons are thus encouraged, being exhorted to 'seek out their dead') genealogical data must be gathered, It is stored in the church's Genealogical Society library in Salt Lake City and consists of family group sheets submitted over the years, with information drawn from parish registers, civil registers, census enumeration books and other sources. The names from these family sheets have been transferred to an alphabetical computer file index, published on microfiche as the International Genealogical Index. It is now available in many local history libraries, as well as in special Mormon libraries established in some cities. The latest edition (1984) is arranged by county, whilst the previous edition covers Scotland as a whole.

Use of this alphabetical list can often save the genealogical researcher a lot of time, especially in those circumstances where migration has occurred and the researcher has no idea from whence his or her ancestors came. Of even greater value, when it is completed, will be the Mormon church's Old Parochial Register for Scotland, a microfiche alphabetical listing of all names in the parish registers.

Where demographic records are deficient, the genealogist does have other weapons in his or her armoury. Tombstones are one such source, though 'a searcher should never be optimistic about finding any family's memorial inscription before the mid-19th century . . . ' (Mitchell, 1978). Earlier stones were sometimes 'extensively pillaged' and 'in the terrible times of plague . . . the plague-smitten poor were often taken out of the towns and burned where they died without any memorial at all.' Even as late as 1832, cholera victims were given short shrift. A Musselburgh judge recalled in a Musselburgh newspaper in 1911 how, as a boy of four, he had watched his father working as an undertaker, with 'no separate graves – just one big trench up at Inveresk there, and fires burning day and night – to let men see to bury the dead and to help drive away infection.'

Many transcriptions of tombstone epitaphs have been made by the Scottish Genealogy Society, and a list of these and other transcriptions is given in the *Scottish Genealogist*, 1981, pp. 19–32 and 171–6. The luckiest circumstance for a genealogical researcher is where a family purchased a lair, and all members, parents, children and even grandchildren are commemorated on the same stone.

The absence of a headstone does not conclude the matter, however, for one can also hope for the survival of graveyard registers. Lair registers, also known as lair books, sexton's books, beadle's books or ground officer's books, list owners' addresses, the date the lair was purchased, the cost of interments, as well as the name of the deceased, date of death, date of interment and relationships to the lair owner. Registers of interments are also kept by cemetery officials, and register details of the deceased – usually name, address, place of death, age and occasionally occupation. Current locations of these registers are varied. Some are held by churches, some by local registrars of births, marriages and deaths, some by local history libraries and some in council archives.

Cemeteries are now the responsibility of district councils, usually of such departments as the Civic Amenities Department, the Department of Leisure, or of Leisure and Recreation, though in some districts there is a separate Burial Grounds, or Parks and Cemeteries, Department. Because of their responsibility they will often have inherited older registers, including those of churchyards. Rapid population growth in urban areas often led to municipal involvement in cemeteries at an early stage, the traditional churchyards being much too small to accommodate the rising demand for space. Catholic churches have always kept their own registers; these are located in Columba House with the Catholic archives.

The study of death is an important area for the family historian. Whilst inspecting graveyards he or she might like to note the style of funeral architecture from different periods; in his or her interviews with older relatives, information can be sought about burial customs and rituals and how they have changed. By chance, he or she might also come across a collection of funeral literature, such as mourning cards and letters, which tend to be kept as memorials. Even the remembrance poems in local newspapers can be studied to understand changing attitudes towards death.

Ingenuity can come to the rescue where other genealogical sources fail. In traditional communities (such as are still to be found in the highlands) field evidence can sometimes play a part. Trades and professions are often hereditary, suggesting possible affinities. Even visiting habits (with whom, for example, do people stay when they have to make a journey?) and naming-patterns can be instructive. In the north-west, for example, 'the more usual pattern . . . is to call the first son after the father's father, the next after the mother's father, then after brothers of the father and mother in turn. With daughters, the pattern is the same, but with precedence in the mother's family' (Lawson, 1979). Ingenuity is also required (together with an element of luck) in the use of the large number of records which were not compiled with any demographic consideration in mind – those of church and government.

The family in history

The central purpose of this work is to look at ways of illuminating the lives of our forebears, and it may be asked what contribution the family genealogist can make to this goal. The sort of genealogies produced, unlike those of the medieval aristocracy, are not generally helpful in the understanding of political allegiances or intrigues, nor do they illustrate a period of history when the family was at the heart of economic organization. Even if the wider approach is adopted and a considerable amount of information collected about the individuals featured in the family tree, what use is a product which consists merely of a series of unrelated biographies – a collection of episodes punctuated by *non sequiturs*? It is in this context that criticisms of the contribution of genealogists are often made, so this section looks at positive ways in which historical processes can be illustrated and understood.

There are two broad approaches which may be adopted. One is to see ancestors as representatives of their age and to look at life through their eyes. A standard frame or questionnaire could be used for each generation, with headings such as 'mobility', 'employment prospects', 'beliefs', 'expectations' and 'economic behaviour'. Of course, the individual's peer group could be included, indeed would probably have to be included, in order to obtain sufficient data. A comparative approach of this type helps to overcome the frustrations caused by the frequent paucity of information about individual Scottish forebears, for the individual acquires flesh and colour by reference to the situation of the time. The researcher can contribute to an understanding of change, not as an abstract force, but through the perceptions of a generation. Ideas for pursuing a family history along these lines are investigated more fully in subsequent chapters.

The second approach, which will be dealt with in more detail here, concentrates on the family itself. The attraction of this method lies in its acknowledgement of the significance of the family, which has been regarded as 'the cornerstone of society.

It forms the basic unit of social organization and it is difficult to imagine how human society would function without it' (Haralambos, 1985). Not only would it be difficult to conceive of society without the family, it has even been the case that extended family institutions have been synonymous with society, with no other institution mediating between them and the state.

To understand the advantages of the family as an institution, one can look at the variety of functions it can perform with some degree of efficiency. Five main functions have been identified: sexual, reproductive, territorial, economic and educational. The first two are both obvious and basic: in the case of sexual drives, the family institution is a means of containing and stabilizing a potentially divisive and destructive biological instinct; in the case of reproduction, it has a positive role in extending and formalizing the biological instinct to nurture young. 'Territorial imperatives' are claimed as biological by some psychologists, and whether they are or not, there can be no dispute about the fact that they have played an important role in cultural and historical terms. The family can serve as a focus for territorial drives, particularly as these marry very neatly with nurturing instincts. Territoriality, quite apart from its importance in the study of conflict (from the neighbourhood dispute to the international conflagration) has also had a fundamental influence on the development of law. Early Scots law, like most pre-industrial legal systems, is dominated by problems relating to the ownership and inheritance of property, a theme which is taken up further in Chapter Seven. The economic function of the family derives ultimately from its territorial function: the family as a working unit (young children as well as adults) was commonplace until recent times, and of course still is in many parts of the world. Young children in Scotland guarded the herds on the common pastures or helped their parents for long hours on their cottage hand-looms; the unlucky ones worked in coal mines. The educational function of the family has been particularly stressed by sociologists, who use the term 'socialization' to embrace the different ways parents introduce their children to their culture. The process involves not only what we understand by formal education – learning to read and so forth – but also an unconscious familiarization with the unwritten rules of be-haviour and a conscious familiarization with moral standards. Up to fairly recent times, the family played an even more important role in the educational process than it does today, for the state has appropriated some of the functions once performed in the home. 'Even ways of behaving, formerly thought to be innate, such as aggression, or sloth, can be shown to be learned' notes Farmer (1970).

Because of the multi-dimensional characteristics of family life:

> relationships to ancestors and kin have been the key relationships in the social structure; they have been the pivots on which most interaction, most claims and obligations, most loyalties and sentiments, turned . . . A man's health and security, his very life and even his chance of immortality, were in the hands of his kin. A 'kinless' man was at best a man without social position: at worst he was a dead man. (Fox, 1967)

Scotland was no exception to this rule; indeed, the circumstances of its difficult terrain and marginality to European culture nurtured a very intense and permanent feeling for kinship.

Many so-called primitive societies have maintained a tribal system in which each individual belongs (with or without blood ties) to a clan, which is so much regarded as an extension of the family unit that marriage among its members (known as *consanguines*) is often forbidden. Such an arrangement is known as *exogamy*, and one's in-laws are known as *affines*. Clan membership is allocated in two basic ways, according to whether descent is *matrilineal* or *patrilineal* (also called *agnatic*). In the first, a woman's daughters establish the line, and bring their husbands into the clan. In such a system, a man's own sons will not be his heirs; instead his property will pass to the sons of his sisters. In a patrilineal system, descent is traced through the male. If descent is traced through male *and* female, the system is called *cognatic*.

Economic and social structures will be profoundly affected by the pattern which is adopted by any society, and there is excellent scope for work by Scottish family historians in this field. For matrilineal descent was found among the Picts, and the consequent social organization in the highlands and its very distinctive characteristics may owe something to this. Comparative studies can be made with other matrilineal societies. Extensive fosterage is another feature of highland society. The practice emphasizes the point that blood relationship is not the only factor that determines the social organization of the family. The question for the historian to answer is for what purpose such a custom exists.

Many other traces of tribal organization can be found in the

Scottish clan system. Clans are usually regarded as prevailing where the authority of the state is weak and where the concept of the state is equally weak. The introduction of state responsibility, for law and order in particular, was often only accomplished by distorting and straining institutions and instincts associated with patterns of family organization. The main changes in Scotland occurred during the fifteenth to seventeenth centuries; as this was also a period in which Scottish local records became more substantial, it is ideal for study by the Scottish family historian.

A key feature of these times was the importance of personal retinues: 'what ultimately gave one man more power than another was the extent of his personal influence, the number of dependents on whose support he could count' writes J.M. Brown (1977). A contrast can be made with the eighteenth century, when power was more closely associated with the extent of a man's landholding. In our day, power is more likely to be financial. The essential difference is that the landowner and the financier rely on the power of the state to underpin their authority: the latter provides controls and sanctions through its legislation, it maintains the peace, and it helps to promote concepts which support the activities of these élites. Before the eighteenth century the state performed none of these functions with whole-hearted success, and, indeed, often did not even regard their performance as a very high priority. Realistically, given poor communications and unfavourable terrain, it had very little choice.

One of the consequences of this was that personal power was more important than the power of the state. Personal power lay in followers, for the level of military technology of the day meant effective use of weapons was dependent upon adequate manpower to wield them. The cohesion of this group of supporters around the local laird or noble was perforce based on family relationships, for the very fragmentation of society made any kind of political or ideological commitments rather meaningless. In the words of Keith Brown (1986),

The Stewart monarchy, the Protestant church, and Scots law did create common loyalties and values, but this was still a society in which the locality, even more than the nation, shaped men's lives. The locality was understood in both a structural and an existential sense. The tangible side to it was castle or tower house, baronial court, church, village, cultivated lands, grazing pasture, water and woods. Within this physical environment most people were born, lived and died. It was also where family and friends were, where lord and man formed their bonds, where loyalty was forged and pride was invested.

At the core of the local power system was the kin group, to whom were attached other men by extension of the principles of loyalty and trust in family relationships. These various others were described in a standard form of words: 'kin, freindis, allya parttakaris tennentis servandis and dependaris'. Wormald (1985) explains this phrase as follows: kin referred to men of the same surname within the lord's locality; tenants were those who rented his land; servants and dependents were the permanent members of his household 'from his gentlemen servants to the cooks and scullions'; friends were social equals, perhaps related; whilst the 'allya' and 'partakers' – those who would take his part – belonged to the lesser gentry, who might be a distantly related cadet branch of his house. There is obviously much matter here for detailed local study by genealogists and family historians.

Extended families, like those of the Mafia of southern Italy, could be a force both for good and for bad. While enforcing loyalty between lords and men and keeping the peace among tenants and followers, they also encouraged the existence of private armies and the forging of links with bandits of the rural underworld, such that 'some Scottish noblemen, especially in the highland and border regions, presided over extensive criminal networks involving protection, blackmail, terrorisation, raiding and murder' (Keith Brown, 1986).

Two aspects of the family-based society have been highlighted recently: the *bond of manrent* and the *bloodfeud*. Bonds of manrent, by which a laird bound himself to serve a lord, have been described as 'the most effective method of complementing and adding to the kin group and imposing on those who were not of the lord's kin the obligations which bound those who were' (Wormald, 1985). The bonds (800 or so have been identified, mainly from the sixteenth century) served the mutual interest of both superior and vassal. The former extended his power base in his locality at a time when 'the local community [had] more practical meaning than the national one, and where men [relied] on mutual help within their social groups' (Wormald, 1985), whilst the latter was guaranteed protection by his powerful neighbour. Without a police force and with courts of justice of only limited authority (and that authority usually the partisan one of powerful families), seeking a lord to whom to bind oneself was rational behaviour, and indeed, behaviour recognized and even encouraged by the state itself. Under the feudal system, power, both administrative and judicial, was deliberately devolved upon local magnates, who 'stood in for' the king. Loyalty, therefore, was to men, not to institutions or ideas. In these circumstances the values that predominated were those associated with family relationships, local territoriality and the establishment of petty dynasties. The local and family historians' contribution to this study would be to identify these values and to see how they permeate relationships among the extended kin and local society as a whole, and, as a further stage, to see to what extent they continued, and still continue – albeit in modified form.

The bloodfeud has been seen as one important manifestation of kin-based society – an extension of the nexus of emotions associated with protection of offspring. The key connecting ideas are: blood/protection/loss/honour/revenge/blood.

At first glance, the bloodfeud might appear to be a totally negative and destructive process, but the truth is more subtle. For a start, the word itself does not mean that the feud was bloody, rather that 'the escalation of bloodshed [was] halted by settlement and compensation' (J.M. Brown, 1977). 'Assythment' (compensation) was the means of atoning for crimes, together with elaborate ritualistic procedures of homage and humiliation (such as wearing sack-cloth) to ensure that honour was satisfied. 'Honour and shame' societies are a particular category identified by anthropologists; they often exist where personal alliances are more important than institutional ones. The satisfaction of honour took some strange (to us) forms, for example in the insistence that a man marry a woman whom he had raped. Homage was a form of ritualized revenge, in that 'the honour lost in the failure to attain blood vengeance was regained in the public humiliation of one's enemies in the homage ceremony' (Keith Brown, 1986). Ritual, as we shall see elsewhere, is an important tool for resolving conflict and maintaining the cohesion of a group. The 'letter of slains', signed by all four branches of the dead man's kin, guaranteed that the bloodfeud was ended for ever.

Bloodshed only occurred where the process of ritual revenge broke down, and it has recently been argued that it did so less often than might appear. Although Scottish, and especially highland, history, seems bloody and anarchic, one must consider that potential sources of conflict existed in every small locality, and peace could reign in any one for decades at a time. In this context it must be noted that Scotland's kin system was *cognatic*: cognatic systems will tend to encourage compromise because men will have allegiances to more than one kin group (those of both father's and mother's lineage, and possibly a wife's lineage too). It is also true, as today, that good news is no news: a periodic breakdown of order is noticed and reported; peace is not. Of course, local lords usually had a vested interest in peace, for if anarchy reigned in the local community, there would be a drain of their resources and the chances of rival factions emerging would be strengthened. For these various reasons, it was rare for a feud to run its natural course, in which 'revenge dictated that blood be shed in recompense, and ideally the blood of the killer or perpetrator of some infringement . . . but if he was out of reach, then his blood might still be spilled by killing those who shared it, his kinsmen' (Keith Brown, 1986).

It is noticeable from the above account that crime and punishment were not the concern of courts of law. For 'the principle that the head of the kin or the lord of the victim of crime had not only the right but also the responsibility of forcing the man who committed the crime to compensate the injured man . . . was still an entirely acceptable and regular method of dealing with crime' (J.M. Brown, 1977). Similarly, it was expected that the criminal should make reparation to those he had wronged; modern state law by contrast emphasizes punishment rather than reparation.

The family-based society began to disintegrate in the seventeenth century, when 'throughout most of Europe the long-established adherence to lords and kindreds was put under enormous strain as rival churches and self-confident princes claimed that it was to them that obedience was first owed. Church, state, lord and family all had to compete for loyalty' (Keith Brown, 1986). The family's place in this competition for loyalty can also make an interesting study for the historian of later periods. Family feuds, for example, still occur – they can be studied in newspaper reports and criminal court records, and their similarity to the historical feuds assessed.

Generally speaking, however, it has been claimed that in industrial societies '. . . family and kinship groups [no longer] perform a wide range of functions. Instead, specialist institutions such as business firms, schools, hospitals, police forces and churches take over many of their functions' (Haralambos, 1985). Economic factors, on the other hand, appear to have worked in the opposite direction. Traditionally a person's occupation was often determined by that of the father, and it is claimed that resulting 'dynastic' patterns are still noticeable among the upper classes, for since members of the ruling class and élites have an important influence on appointments to top jobs, the retention of family ties makes economic sense. A family historian might like to check the theory with prominent local families, using family papers, wills, newspaper accounts and biographical material discussed in Chapter One. Marriage contracts are another useful source; being legal documents they were recorded in the Register of Deeds which form part of the Court of Session archive held in the Scottish Record Office. The various indexes are discussed in Moody (1986). The property brought by the wife to the marriage including her 'tocher' was often turned over to trustees, whose petitions concerning its administration will be found in the same court's records.

At the other extreme of the social scale, with the very poor, extended family groups have been associated with life in industrial cities; nineteenth-century census enumeration books can be used to investigate this. A reason for the association may be that a high rate of sickness and unemployment made extended families an insurance policy for group survival. Also, among the very poor, matrifocal families are judged to be common (what today we would call one-parent families). Again, an economic justification can be found for this: in a situation of poverty and unemployment, each male wage-earner constitutes a high risk for the family group, and overdependence on any one individual can be harmful to its prosperity and survival.

Clans

A clan has been defined as a unit 'often consisting of several lineages in which common descent is assumed but cannot necessarily be demonstrated . . .' (Fox, 1967). The Scottish highland clans are not at all typical of the anthropological archetype, and this fact constitutes only one of the many problems facing the historian interested in their study. For a start, a knowledge of Gaelic is desirable. Then there is the problem that the clan system of today is primarily an invention of nineteenth-century romantics and astute businessmen bent on the exploitation of a myth (the latter, for example, having no qualms over the promotion of forged documents relating to the origin of tartans). The ensuing confusion is responsible for 'the modern popular image . . . of a body of people related by blood, descended from a common ancestor, inhabiting a clan territory, ruled by a chief who is head of the kin, wearing a clan tartan and all having the same surname' (Munro, 1981). Not a single one of these assertions is entirely true, and some are quite false; nor is the distinction between highland and lowland society as marked as was once thought. Smout (1969) sums up the difference as follows: 'highland society was based on kinship modified by feudalism; lowland society on feudalism tempered by kinship.' In fact, we can best understand the clan system by seeing it as a fundamentally kin-based society with one or two specific accretions – the strong Celtic background, the extent of isolation from centres of government and the nature of the terrain (small pockets of fertile land divided from each other by large stretches of barren mountain and moor).

Little information has survived about the Picts, who were perhaps the earliest Celtic people in Scotland. Numerous sculptured stones are their most lasting memorial, but the main documentary sources which we have are Irish annals (the *Annals of Tigernach*, the *Annals of Ulster*), Northumbrian sources (such as Bede's *Ecclesiastical History*) and Adomnan's *Life of Columba*. These sources suggest that a highly structured tribal system operated, practising matrilineal inheritance, possibly reinforced by polygamy. (In a polygamous society it is difficult for a man to know which of his sons should take precedence.) Matrilineal-ism would not have been tolerated after the Picts' conversion to Christianity (which was strongly patriarchal), and, moreover, the Picts were conquered around AD 850 by the Scots – another Celtic people, from Ireland – who were patrilineal. There is also some evidence that they married, divorced and kept concubines at will, much like the Old Testament patriarchs, practices barely conceded in some clan genealogies.

In the Celtic system 'the principle of government and of the social order was personal and the personal status conferred rights of holding land' (Cunningham, 1932). This was certainly not the case in more recent times, however. Land-holding in the highlands required the same documentary evidence as anywhere else in Scotland, although traces of the former practice survived in the attitudes of the highlander, as was noted as late as the 1880s by the Napier Commission:

> The opinion was often expressed before us that the small tenantry of the Highlands had an inherited inalienable title to security of tenure in their possessions while rent and service are duly rendered – an expression

indigenous to the country though it has never been sanctioned by legal recognition.

These clansmen saw themselves as 'kindly tenants', a term used of those who occupied land on favourable terms under a special lease giving hereditary rights. (The word 'kindly' is derived from the root 'kin'.)

Typical of the Celtic tribal system was an aristocratic ruling group, 'heroic' in character in the Homeric sense of the word. Within that group, periodic redistribution of land took place, preference being given to near relations of the chief. The result was 'a tendency for the older branches of a clan to sink into poverty and insignificance, unless any special prowess in war, demanding special acknowledgement, helped to maintain their importance' (Cunningham, 1932). The chief's position of authority was therefore by no means automatic or permanent. If judged wanting, or if misfortune and poverty overtook him, he 'no longer possessed the power of discharging his duty to his people' and could be replaced.

The paucity of surviving evidence makes it difficult to know exactly how the tribalism of the Picts and Scots became transformed into the historical clan system, but the spread of feudal ideas was certainly an influential factor. Feudalism was originally developed within Charlemagne's empire, which was difficult to govern because of its large size. Most of the king's subjects were rural peasants, in whom he had no interest, whether for their health, education or happiness. Lives were short and cheap. It was sensible for him, therefore, to devolve the government of them upon local landowners, a social class which was important to him as a source of funds and of military service. Many of the local magnates already had experience of local administration as possessors of lordships, which allowed them to exact dues and services from their tenants. Feudalism differed in its grand central strategy: to establish a rigid hierarchy by means of written contracts between the king and his barons – recording a grant of land in exchange for an undertaking to supply military and other services (and later money). This contract was known as a 'charter', and without it no claim of land could be substantiated.

The gradual introduction of feudalism into Scotland consti-tuted a potential source of conflict with the Celtic tradition of land tenure. The general view of historians is as follows:

> . . . if the chief of a clan was also the feudal lord of the lands his clansmen lived on, well and good; he concentrated in his hands both personal and

territorial rights, and there was no conflict between them . . . But if the
two types of power did not thus coincide, their collision was inevitable
and touched the very basis of ordered society. (Cunningham, 1932)

Some writers have argued that the historical clan system,
fragmented, isolated, feuding, resulted from this collision,
whilst the larger unit of society – the tribe – disintegrated. When
a new system of government is introduced, it is often the case
that adaptation and assimilation occurs at a local level (that of
the clan); but the superstructure (here, the tribe) is more
vulnerable, being less immediately based on self-interested
accommodation. This theme of continuity on the micro-scale in
history will be taken up again in this work, and is a
phenomenon of great interest to the local historian.

The determination of the government to impose feudalism in
the highlands culminated in an act of 1597 requiring 'that the
inhabitants of the Iles and Hielands shaw their haldings' by
producing 'all their infefments rights and titles whatsoever
whereby they claim right and title to any part of the lands and
fishings within the bounds foresaid.' The result of such moves
was a flurry of spurious charters to match the earlier spurious
pedigrees. These form another potential pitfall for the family
historian.

The adoption of feudalism by highland chiefs made their
position ambiguous: they were often not related to the people
whom they led – the native population which had probably
inhabited the territory from remote times. Even where the
chief's family was not of native stock, however, 'the spread of
junior branches and intermarriages within a compact community would soon strengthen the ties of kinship and common
descent' (Munro, 1981). The resulting clan consisted of an inner
core of kinsmen, the gentry of the clan, or 'daoine uaisle',
known in Scots as 'tacksmen'. A 'tack' is a lease, but these were
no ordinary tenants: the lands they controlled were of enormous
extent and were heritable; they were also responsible for
organizing the clan as a fighting force. In default of 'opportunities of serving their chief at home they sought employment in
the Continental armies – where they were known for their
proud bearing and ferocity' (Cregeen, 1968). In later times they
sometimes emigrated to the colonies, and such being the pride
and loyalty of the clan, the whole community often emigrated
with them. The sources of information about emigration
outlined on pages 193–4 can give considerable insight into the
clan system.

The lesser clan members who accompanied their tacksmen consisted of small tenants (known as 'common tenants' because they occupied a farm in common), together with their sub-tenants and servants, plus other families who had adopted the clan name for protection; this group of clan members also included various functionaries – harper, piper, sennachie, bard, henchman, armour-bearer and purse-bearer, some of whom occupied hereditary posts. Septs were groups of ancient local families too weak to stand alone. Innes of Learney referred to the practice of 'sept-snatching' by clan historians, and remarked that 'it seems to have superseded cattle lifting in clan circles as an acquisitive operation' (quoted in Maclean, 1981).

As dubious a habit as sept attribution is the designation of clan territories. Clan chiefs were political animals who made alliances, waxed strong and waned, and generally behaved like any other aristocratic magnates, highland or lowland. Whether the territories they controlled contained men of their name or blood was a matter of indifference. Thus 'the extension of the Macdonald's power over the northern clans had nothing in common with the old tribal earldoms, but was analogous to the feudal superiorities and jurisdictions, which, at a much later period, the Earls of Argyll held over clans with which they had no connection of sentiment and kinship . . . Feudalism enabled the tribal chief to overstep the natural limits of his power . . .' (Cunningham, 1932). Geography in fact was more important than kinship. The Gordons, for example, who were 'left in the original family holdings in Berwickshire were in no real sense members of the great Gordon kindred in the north-east . . .' (Wormald, 1985).

The clan historian must pick his or her way through the complexities outlined above, avoiding on the one hand a too-ready acceptance of the clan as a group acting as a cohesive unit, and on the other a too-ready identification of the clan with its chief (or seeing a detailed chronological account of his deeds as of local importance, whereas it cannot be understood outside the context of national politics). There is a tendency in clan histories towards too many trees and not enough wood. Today, work could more profitably be concentrated on the structure of the clan itself, studied in relation to a specific geographical area. Thus one could enquire why it was that 'the ordinary Highlanders esteem it the most sublime degree of virtue to love their chief and pay him a blind obedience, although it be in opposition to the government, the laws of the kingdom, or even to the law of God' (*Letters . . . 1726*). To answer, one could look at the highland terrain: in an isolated community, emotions of strong adherence were a necessary survival strategy for any individual, for 'men without kinsmen were weak preys to the "clannit" families' (Brown, 1986). Even ministers were despised, as 'kinless bodies'.

One could look too at the 'lawlessness' of highland life. A detailed study of a local environment would show in many places a soil too poor to support the large number of dependents that was a natural consequence of a society based on personal power; cattle raiding into the lowlands therefore became a basic strategy for supporting the population. One could even speculate on the possibility of excessive inbreeding among cattle in an isolated glen, and see the genetic advantages of a raid. One could ask too why cattle raising was seen as a 'manly' occupation to be celebrated in song and legend, just as it had been among the earlier Celtic tribes and was to be among the American cowboys.

Anthropology and family history

Various points raised in preceding paragraphs have owed something to an anthropological perspective on historical study. Kinship structures are a central preoccupation of anthropologists (and the terminology used in this chapter originates from their studies), but this is not the only area of mutual interest. Anthropologists, like local and family historians, also look in detail at small, closely-linked communities. Their approach is original in its interest in 'the interconnexions of events [and] the structure of ideas, values and social relations' (Lewis, 1968), in short its concern for generalization and problem orientation. It thus asks questions such as 'Why do clans exist?' and seeks the answer in a consideration of the functions that institutions such as clans perform in a local community. Such a perspective aims to lay bare the 'nature and consequence of conflict and competition, relations between secular and mystical power, the implications of different types of authority, of marginality or the social concomitants of the division between the sexes . . .' (Lewis, 1968).

Historians, on the other hand, tend to look for unique factors in any given situation, concentrating on the individual actors, their particular responses and initiatives, not types of response and initiative. The historian considers each event in its own right, whereas the anthropologist seeks a pattern. The latter can and often has been criticized for underestimating individual actions; after all, actions, cumulatively, are the main causes of change – of history. Anthropologists, in their emphasis on functions, can behave as if change does not take place. Their science has even been called an 'epiphenomenon of colonialism', reflecting the desire of imperial powers to see their subject peoples as men and women without aspirations, in perfect unchanging harmony with their surroundings. As Redfield (1956) notes:

> . . . these primitive communities could in fact be registered without reference to anything much outside of them; they could be understood, more or less, by one man working alone. Nor need that man be a historian, for among these non-literates there was no history to learn.

The past so viewed is 'the product of the present and may be treated to a considerable extent as myth' (Lewis, 1968). There is a lesson here for local and family historians, for they too have been guilty of romanticizing the permanence and harmony of traditional society.

All communities, however isolated, have a past; no men today are inhabiting lands which they have inhabited since the dawn of mankind. Upheavals, migrations and revolutions have been their lot. Anthropologists, recognizing this, have attempted in recent years to place small societies within an historical context. One fruitful outcome has been the idea that even traditional European communities have passed through set stages of development, during which they conform to a greater or lesser extent to certain patterns, the sort of patterns the anthropologist is trained to recognize and investigate. One such stage is that of the peasant society, and Scotland from the early Middle Ages up to around 1800 has been regarded as an example of this type.

Four essential criteria of a peasant society have been proposed. These are that the peasant family farm is the basic unit of social and economic organization, that agriculture is the principal means of livelihood, that a traditional 'culture' exists and that the peasantry is governed by an élite which is divorced in many ways from the local community. Other features, while not essential, are typical. They include a strong personal attachment to land, often celebrated in a mythology of an Arcadian past, a conception of marriage as an economic transaction, a practical view of sex, patrilocal residence, descent in the male line, and a high value placed on reputation and social solidarity, gossip being the weapon used to bring the ambitious down to size.

A peasant society is intermediate between a tribal and an industrial organization, and its fundamental tension is that between the self-sufficient neighbourhood and the imposed superstructure of a ruling élite with a national economic strategy, involving the 'relationships of the more and the less educated, of the townsman and the countryman, of the national institution and the local and traditional institution' (Redfield, 1956). This dichotomy can be clearly illustrated in the lives of the great Scottish barons. In the Middle Ages, for instance, at a time when the local community was possibly the widest horizon of most inhabitants of Scotland, men such as Roger de Quincy had properties in Perthshire, Fife, Lothian, Berwickshire and Galloway:

> His English lands were mainly in Leicestershire, Northamptonshire and Huntingdonshire, but outlying properties spread as far north as Cumberland and as far south as Dorset. Indeed it was possible for Earl Roger to travel from Perthshire to the English Channel, and, except for a stretch of about a hundred miles in the north of England never to be more than thirty or forty miles at most from some piece of land in which he had an interest. (Simpson, 1985).

Of another Anglo-Norman aristocratic family, the Morvilles, it has been said that distance and frontiers occupied no place in their mind. It was no different in the eighteenth century: Scotland was a peasant society still, yet its aristocratic leaders such as the Duke of Argyll lived in style in London houses, speculating on the newly formed Stock Exchange.

Local historians of an earlier age who regarded the biography of these leading individuals and families as tantamount to the history of the locality missed an important perspective on local life. The anthropological approach, on the other hand, takes as its starting point the local peasant community, leading families being considered only in the context of their impact on the society and economy of that particular neighbourhood. For the local and family historian, the latter approach has much to commend it, for the effort of understanding is concentrated on that which is best known – the local environment – and the historian is not required to develop a knowledge of national and international affairs, which would be necessary if he or she were approaching the subject from the biographical angle. The next section therefore looks in greater detail at concepts of community that can be useful in this respect.

Community

Before 1800, as suggested above, Scotland was overwhelmingly rural in character; it has been reckoned that no more than ten or fifteen per cent of the population lived in towns. Even villages were a rarity, and roads were almost non-existent. The bulk of the people were thinly spread among innumerable hamlets, known as 'farmtouns' (or 'fermtouns'), many of which survive today only as farm-steadings or in local place-names such as 'grange', 'milton', 'mains', 'kirkton' and 'muirton'. Some settlements have totally disappeared, and are known only from locations marked on old county and estate maps. The farmtoun was approximately of the size that could be cultivated by one plough with its team of oxen or horses – the so-called 'ploughgate' of about 100 acres. (This was divisible into two 'husbandlands' or 'merklands', or eight 'oxgates'; a 'davoch', a measure found mainly in the east and central highlands, was equal to four ploughgates.)

The personnel of the fermtoun varied. A tenant, known as a 'husbandman' or 'gudeman', could rent the whole area and work it with subtenants (crofters and cottars) together with servants and landless labourers. Tenants were quite significant men in the rural hierarchy; their successors were the independent tenant farmers of the nineteenth century. Alternatively, joint tenants, each with their own sub-tenants, could share a lease. In parts of the highlands, joint tenants cultivated the land in common – a genuine form of communism; elsewhere the land was divided into 'rigs' (strips), with each tenant farming scattered plots. A third possibility was the consolidation of each tenant's share into separated blocks of land ('rundale'). The situation was often further complicated by joint ownership of rig farms ('runrig'). Whatever the system adopted, communal activity was a prerequisite:

> Peasants holding runrig or rundale had to decide on a common crop, a common rotation and common dates for sowing, reaping and cultivating their scattered and intermingled strips: they had also to contribute animals to draw the community's plough, and to do much else by general agreement. (Smout, 1969).

The cohesion and isolation of the farmtoun make it an ideal subject for detailed anthropological scrutiny, particularly as a great deal of research still needs to be carried out, both on the organization of the farm and on the interrelationships of the personnel. To what extent, for example, was the joint tenancy a kin-based system? Rental books and copies of leases (or tacks) will help to give the answer. Surviving monastic rentals have been published, as have some collections of tacks in family muniments (for details see the notes to this chapter). Many more, especially from the seventeenth and eighteenth centuries, await study in estate papers held in record offices and country mansions. Survival will be patchy, as leases would often be thrown away after their expiry.

The essential elements of a tack or assedation (lease, in modern parlance) were a fixed rent in cash or kind and a fixed term of expiry. Short terms were the norm in the Middle Ages, and were the subject of unfavourable comment from agricultural improvers; so, progressively, 19-year leases were adopted. A tack could be ended before its expiry by the tenant submitting a letter of renunciation, but for him, security of tenure was guaranteed. At the end of the term he could be removed by the issue of a precept of warning (at least) 40 days before the expiry date. This precept could subsequently serve as a basis for obtaining from a local court a decree of removing, and, if the tenant still did not budge, letters of ejection under the royal signet or a precept of ejection from a court could follow. Examples of the forms of all these documents are given in the *Formulary of old Scots Legal Documents* published by the Stair Society in 1985; any researcher embarking on a study of the type outlined above will save a lot of time and effort if he or she studies these samples beforehand.

Leases will tell us about tenants; they will not tell us about the sub-tenants and landless workers of the farmtouns. Patient work will be required to elicit relevant information about the latter, and it may be that nothing at all can be found out about certain communities before the time of census enumeration books. In some cases, inventories of estate personnel may have survived among family papers. The parish registers of births, marriages and deaths can also be consulted.

In a society where cooperation is necessary for economic survival, there can be little place for individuality; and one would expect to find mechanisms to reinforce community and restrain personal ideals. The researcher can look for these in religious attitudes (sermons for example), in living arrangements and in rituals and festivals. One observer quoted by Alastair Orr (1984) recalled:

. . . the whole household constituted one family, which looked to the gudeman as the natural and patriarchal head and considered his interest as in some degree connected with their own. The words *our hairst* and *our crops* were commonly used to express those of their master. Only a vestige of this relationship . . . survived in the tradition of the harvest supper or 'kirn' . . . the symbol of human and class cooperation in labour.

The peasants' emotional attachment to their land and their community can likewise be seen in novels and memoirs.

Some communal rituals still endure in the highlands. In the lowlands, they probably only exist in the memories of older residents, now all but supplanted by a new generation of middle-class commuters. The local and family historian can do useful work interviewing and recording the memories of these older people before it is too late, comparing their recollections with the new rituals devised for today's needs.

Fundamental change first took place in the middle of the eighteenth century, when agriculture came to be understood as 'the art of rendering the earth as productive as possible and converting that produce into money.' The result was that:

the celebrations of the older world – May Day, Midsummer, Harvest Home, Hallowe'en, the play of the masked Gyzarts with their drama of death and resurrection – faded and became silly or a nuisance. The new régime centred round the Feeing Fair, the Plowing Match, the Cattle Show as the year's landmarks, and the tension of the year's work tended to find a more violent release on these occasions of urban contact. (Saunders, 1950)

Ritual bonding did not altogether disappear. The sociologist James Littlejohn, who made a detailed anthropological study of parishes in the Borders in the early 1960s, noted ceremonial elements in the ostensibly rational institution of the clipping band: 'Apart from the communal meals eaten throughout the day, the men did not turn up in their dirtiest working clothes, as one would expect for a job like sheep shearing, but in newly cleaned clothes . . .'. The local historian can look for similar customs in his or her own rural community.

In most respects, however, Littlejohn found the community spirit eroded by the economic aspects of production: 'each farm is a productive unit on its own, a business from which the farmer tries to make a profit. There is little cooperation in work among them.' In such circumstances, kinship bonds consisted of little more than 'a claim to priority consideration in the way of invitations to weddings, funerals, of hospitality and of protection against depreciatory judgements by non-relatives.' Littlejohn did note, however, that 'below a certain size . . . farms have to be worked on a subsistence basis. Where this is the case the family farm is the basic economic unit and any community of such farms will be characterized by numerous kinship ties and by a high value placed on neighbourliness.'

It will be evident that the resolution of conflict was of the utmost importance in communities which depended on economic cooperation, and equally evident that the possibility of squabbling was ever-present given the interdependence of its members. Neighbourhood disputes occurred over land, boundaries, ownership of teinds and conditions of lease. Women who inherited land (a regular occurrence in the absence of male heirs) were particularly vulnerable. Local resources such as water, peats and even church seating could also be a source of friction. Keith Brown (1986) discusses the case of Andrew Wood of Largo and Robert Lundy of Balgony who 'feuded over a seat in Largo Kirk for over a decade, during which time Largo destroyed the seat installed by his rival, both men defied the presbytery and the crown, and church life was so disrupted that the congregation was unable to meet for worship . . .'. Many of these neighbourhood disputes arising from the irritations of proximity will be quite familiar today, and a current edition of any local newspaper would make an interesting comparison with the records of the barony courts which thrived from the Middle Ages until the mid-eighteenth century, and to which neighbourhood disputes were brought. There are several published examples. Another rural court was the 'birlaw' or 'boorlaw' court. More serious disputes were taken to the sheriff courts. (Archives for the latter may be found in the Scottish Record Office.)

In other cases local irritations were symptoms of, or excuses to pursue, wider power struggles. However, the 'pressures of common residence' served to mitigate the excesses of local feuding (as did threats of eternal damnation, or punishment by the state). The emergence of a strong state was nevertheless a mixed blessing for the local community, for it led to a third source of conflict – a localized spin-off of power struggles within the royal court, where 'major policy decisions were made, wealth and office could be acquired or lost, and patrons or clients were cultivated on a scale which went beyond the parameters of a man's own locality' (Keith Brown, 1986).

Disentangling local and national elements, kin allegiance and patriotism, superstition and religion is the fascinating task facing the social historian. The relevance of such study today is also important, for there must always be a level of interaction in human affairs which is restricted to the local community, where the ideologies of states, religions and economic systems have to be re-interpreted and cut down to a practical, human scale. This need is perhaps at the core of the appeal of family and local history; the excesses of sentimentality and myth-making associated with the very word 'community' are themselves an expression of the importance of a pragmatic accommodation of people of diverse character.

Of the varied manifestations of this sense of community, that of the traditional rural parish is only one, albeit one of the most significant. (Chapter Five touches on the concept of urban communities or neighbourhoods.) The term 'community' is broad enough to include other connotations too. In the traditional royal burghs, for example, which had a monopoly of trade until the seventeenth century, municipal government was controlled by privileged merchant families who referred to themselves (and were referred to by others) as the 'community' of the burgh. This was not mere rhetoric: the merchants were a closely-knit élite consisting of relatively few families; their ramifications can be followed in burgh records such as the minutes of town councils, guilds and trade incorporations. This community was held together by its allegiance to a primitive mercantile law, by which merchant burgesses were held jointly and severally responsible for the conduct and financial standing of any of the community's members. Typical of the collective perspective that dominated their economic thinking is the ancient law from the *Statuta Gilda* that 'whatsoever burgess shall buy herring, all his neighbours who were present at the buying of the said herring shall have for the same price at which he bought, without any fraud'. Merchants could even be seized abroad if another from their town had unpaid debts.

It is interesting to note that the virtues espoused by the burghal communities – exclusivity, restrictive practice, kinship alliances – were identical to the vices for which burghs were condemned in the eighteenth and early nineteenth centuries and which were investigated by the Royal Commission on Municipal Corporations (reporting in 1835). Their type of market organization had become out of date and the associated values were judged accordingly. The new economic system – that of free trade – had its own myths and values, including the principles of equal opportunity and democracy.

The new industrial society which resulted in part from free

trade capitalism was not lacking in community spirit, however, though now this tended to be prominent at the bottom of the social scale, among those who were made more vulnerable by their new circumstances. An example is given by two recent writers:

> There was, too, the isolation of the mining communities, confirmed both by the miners' own exclusiveness and the unwillingness of others, for example farmers' daughters, to associate with them. Thus could develop very close communities, bonded together by the fight against the dangers of the seams and the demands and manipulations of the employers. The bonds were all the tighter because of the work dangers of the men, and the shared fears of the women day by day and when they stood together at the pit-head when the seams had entrapped their men folk. (S. and O. Checkland, 1984).

Fishing communities were similar to this in character. They sometimes formed enclaves within larger towns – a group of close-knit families with only a few surnames among them. Shared ownership of boats and gear dictated marriage patterns. The women, who were left ashore to process and market the fish, made an important contribution to the household economy, and were unusually independent for the times. As within mining communities, there were shared dangers and fears, and the same hostility and suspicion from outsiders. 'A large number of the children are of the poorest class, wretchedly clad, dirty and offensive in their persons, and apparently ill-fed and neglected at home' recorded a school inspector of fisher children at Dunbar in 1887 (Macdonald, 1893). The cohesion of the fishing community was reinforced by superstitions and rituals, such as the throwing of salt from boats as they left harbour which was intended to preserve them from harm. Local festivals and processions provided an opportunity both for enjoyment and for cementing and celebrating the group's communal identity.

Chapter Five

EXPLORING LOCAL SOCIETY

A hundred years ago, the German sociologist Ferdinand Tonnies suggested that there was a contrast to be drawn between 'community', as discussed in the last chapter, and 'society' or 'association', which he saw as the distinctive mode of social organization in the industrialized city. Daily existence in the city is typically divided into unrelated sections (work, shopping, leisure pursuits and so on) during which one associates with different groups of people; in a community one associates perforce with only one group. Farmer (1970) makes the same point another way:

> In simple societies all aspects of life are related to the family or kinship structure, and the family is the most important unit of social organization. Indeed family and society are synonymous . . . In more complex societies it has less influence, and indeed the greater the complexity of society, the greater the variety of external agencies with which the family interacts.

The city still being with us today, the family historian can feel an instant familiarity with its human problems and social institutions, and can observe the way in which the family has adapted to new roles different from those it played in a kin-based local community.

A fundamental feature of urban living is its population distribution, and the period under consideration has seen a concentration of people in towns and cities where before they were isolated in scattered hamlets. From this concentration other changes ensued, for example an unprecedented anonymity, a loss of the sense of belonging, but also a widening of opportunity for individual talent, enterprise and social mobility. In the words of Saunders (1950) 'each component individual would be enabled to become a person, enlightened, responsible, enjoying a wide range of satisfactions that were independent of such accidents as birth and rank and material circumstances.'

Another consequence of the adoption of urban life was the development of *secondary institutions* (associations, pressure groups, self-help organizations, philanthropic enterprises and so on) which can be contrasted with the *primary institutions* (such as the family and the church) which were prevalent in rural communities. We now take for granted the association of men and women in groups based on common interests and ideals, but such organizations are of relatively recent origin in our history. Haddington, a representative small Scottish town, boasted in 1900 five societies of the masonic or mutual benefit type, 12 sports' clubs, six associations based on common interests (such as ornithology, music, cycling), four philanthropic societies and three political associations. In the eighteenth century and before, even in those few towns with a population comparable to that of Haddington in 1901 (3800) these types of institutions would have been inconceivable. Common interests were seen in terms of family, religion and perhaps politics, and the idea that people should mix together on the strength of shared enthusiasms did not occur, partly of course because of the lack of free time to do so.

The towns which made association possible grew up at the start of the nineteenth century. They soon came to differ profoundly from the traditional market towns in terms of their size, functions and buildings, their 'banks and insurance offices, their security and repute symbolized by their impressive frontages, the corn exchange, the subscription library and reading room, the museum and hall of the literary and antiquarian society, the offices of the local weekly newspapers [and] the new churches and schools' (Saunders, 1950). The fabric of many of the towns in which we live today dates from this time, and the buildings that were constructed to serve the burgeoning institutions remain part of their landscape, albeit in many cases long since converted to other uses. The existence of these buildings adds another dimension to the local historian's study, as the function and ethos of the institutions can be better understood by a direct response to their presence. Architectural style is of course a language in itself, which can convey to us the spirit of the organization responsible for a particular building.

Further resources for the study of secondary organizations are the collections of ephemera often preserved in local history library collections. The sort of material you are likely to find in these might include the savings' book of a penny bank, the menu or prospectus of a coffee house, the catalogue of a mechanics' institute library, the annual programme of a lecture society or horticultural club, a broadsheet supporting or opposing the establishment of a public library on the rates, or a petition to the Court of Session regarding the administration of a charitable trust for orphans or the elderly. If you want to go deeper into the subject, many archives of such institutions (containing minute books, accounts, letter books and annual reports) will be found in the Scottish Record Office and local record offices, both in the GD categories (gifts and deposits) and in the records of defunct companies (BT – in West Register House only). (Many philanthropic institutions were constituted as limited liability companies.) Annual reports and other publications of associations should be handled with care by researchers: then, as now, they tended to gloss over difficulties and exaggerate successes.

Self-help groups

Adjustment to the new urban life-style was obviously a painful process for some, and perhaps a liberating one for others. One theme of the nineteenth century is the trauma of adaptation, by the individual, by society and by government. The researcher can expect to find extremes of behaviour and response – an understandable reaction on the part of those caught up by forces they did not understand. As Saunders (1950) puts it:

> The loss of individual worth might find compensation in an old-fashioned religious fervour or in the utopian enthusiasm for the future or, in some cases, in a preoccupation with metaphysical speculation or scientific discovery. For others, resentment against a crushing environment or the perversion of social justice might find relief in the 'atheism' or the anti-capitalism of small groups of protestants. But alongside the visions of the sects were the practical forms of mutual help and support . . . and a practice of associated action that began to achieve results.

Perhaps the most important of such mutual help organizations were the friendly societies, consisting of individuals from a common profession or trade. They were built around two linked ideas: self-help and thrift (both words are titles of popular works by the advocate of nineteenth-century self-improvement, Samuel Smiles). Friendly societies actually date back to the seventeenth century; the United General Box of Borrowstounness Friendly Society and the Sea Box Society of St Andrews were the earliest of these, instigated in 1634 and 1643 respectively. Many of the nineteenth-century societies claimed similar, if not greater, antiquity (in common with many of the equally recent masonic orders), partly to establish their mystique and partly 'due to an anxiety to impart to members and prospective members a sense of the permanence of their institutions' (Gosden, 1973). The records of the early societies are described in a memorandum annexed to the Chief Registrar of Friendly Societies' Report for 1906.

Friendly societies performed several functions simultaneously and it is interesting to compare these with traditional kinship functions. Primarily, they were insurance institutions, operating at a time when there were no state security benefits, unemployment pay or a national health service. Contributions by the members were deposited in a box to open which at least two keys, held by different members, were required. The money was used (to quote a typical constitution) 'for the relief of the distressed widows, orphans and the poor of the fraternity.' Insurance societies such as the Prudential became competitors; they differed in being companies with shareholders, and not therefore mutual benefit organizations.

The friendly society was also what its name implies – a social club, providing a source of companionship for working men. Some even consisted of incomers to the city from a common area and as such they sometimes survived as dining clubs. The meeting house was quite often an inn, indeed the landlord was often treasurer, the members coming together 'in quest of those convivial activities and the enrichment of their impoverished social lives' (Gosden, 1973). One of the drawbacks of these societies was that many spent a considerable proportion of their weekly or monthly contribution on liquor on 'lodge night', with the result that there was often insufficient left to pay benefits. Feast days which became local holidays in smaller communities were another excuse for festivities – and a further drain on funds. Such expenditure could of course be concealed under the title 'management expenses'. Mismanagement of funds was a recurring problem in the friendly societies – many men who joined as youngsters found that when they reached middle age, the society had nothing left for their retirement, because the next generation, rather than join a society of older men who would be a potential burden as they became elderly and sick, formed their own society instead. Even more serious a problem was the tendency to offer benefits which were larger than the contributions could support. Dividing societies, so-called because they distributed most or all of their funds at the end of a set period, overcame this particular difficulty but provided only short-term security (they were basically the forerunners of our Christmas clubs). Also of restricted scope were burial societies, which exploited 'the contemporary abhorrence of the pauper's funeral' (Gosden, 1973). Their willingness to insure infants is said to have encouraged child murder. Two particularly large burial societies in Scotland were the Scottish Legal and the City of Glasgow.

A third function of friendly societies was to impose and maintain moral discipline and self-respect among working men in circumstances where the traditional rural authorities of church and local gentry were lacking. The Rules and Regulations of the Jellieston and Dalharko Friendly Society (1880) are typical. These coal-miners ordained that no member was permitted to be out of his house after ten o'clock p.m. in summer and nine o'clock p.m. in winter, nor to go beyond a distance of four miles from his place of residence without a letter from the doctor or by special permission from the committee. For defaulters, sanctions were imposed:

> Any member who shall have been rendered incapable of following his usual employment through drink or misconduct or by immoral conduct contracting disease otherwise than through the visitation of God, shall not be entitled to any benefit from the funds of the society.

Allied to this moral propriety was a more mystical concept of brotherhood which thrived in the uncertainties and loneliness of Victorian cities. One aspect of this was the sharing of trade secrets, illustrated in one of the rules of the Ancient Fraternity of Free Gardeners of East Lothian:

> if any of the Fraternity betwixt Meetings, finds out or learns any art concerning Plants, for furthering their fruits, he shall publicly and openly reveal the same at the Yearly Meeting in presence of the whole Fraternity then present . . .

Brotherhood often went a stage further, with the introduction of quasi-religious rituals and ceremonies, with their paraphernalia of passwords, handshakes, costumes and banners (examples of which are now often to be found in local museums). Such developments were especially associated with national organizations originally formed by the amalgamation of local societies. The Independent Order of Oddfellows, the Ancient Order of Foresters and the Independent Order of Rechabites (for teetotallers) were three of the largest. (Schisms tended to occur, and the secessionist groups often adopted similar names to those of their parent organizations.) Hearts of Oak was a national society that eschewed the social functions of other societies and acted solely as an insurance institution for small shopkeepers and other 'respectable' tradesmen.

The final function of the friendly society was as a surrogate trade union. In this guise the societies led an uneasy existence under threat of prosecution from the English combination laws. This aspect of the institutions can be studied in many court cases brought against societies in the sheriff courts and the High Court of Justiciary.

There are several other sources of information about friendly societies. Their articles of association (constitutions) and minute books frequently feature in library local history collections, as do examples of initiation certificates for the national associations. Many more archives of specific societies are deposited in the Scottish Record Office (inventory FS). Among the published sources are the *Reports of the Royal Commission on Friendly and Benefit Building Societies, 1871–4*, together with the reports of the assistant commissioners (1874). Societies were given the opportunity to register with a Registrar of Friendly Societies for Scotland in 1829 (an Act to consolidate and Amend the Laws Relating to Friendly Societies). The main advantage of registering was the recognition it gave to the society as a corporate entity, enabling it to sue any members who embezzled funds. An act of 1846 allowed cooperative societies to register, and in 1875 the formerly independent Registrar of Friendly Societies for Scotland became the Assistant Registrar for Scotland within a United Kingdom registry.

Friendly societies were only one of a series of mutual aid institutions. Building societies, whose appeal was more limited (rates of subscription put them out of the reach of most working men) first appeared in the 1780s. Some registered under the Friendly Society acts. The Benefit Building Societies Act 1836 enforced registration, but unlike the friendly societies, supervision after registration was not a condition. Permanent building societies can be contrasted with the earlier 'terminating societies' which accommodated only one initial group of applicants, each having their house built in turn as their names were chosen by lot – a long wait for those at the end of the queue. Permanent societies often became, and still often are, 'mainly agencies for the investment of capital, rather than for enabling the industrious to provide dwellings for themselves' (Gosden, 1973). The Building Societies Act of 1874 placed them under the supervision of the Chief Registrar of Friendly Societies, and further legislation was passed in 1894.

Consumer cooperatives sometimes registered as friendly societies, and the Industrial and Provident Societies Act of 1852 recognized the similarity between them. The Rochdale Equitable Pioneers Society spearheaded the movement, with the simple principle that 'profits are to be divided among all members who made purchases in proportion to the amount they spent.' Most of the societies (nearly 300 by 1900) federated to the Scottish Cooperative Wholesale Society which was established in 1868. A Cooperative Bank and a Cooperative Insurance Society were also founded. Though cooperatives were intended to benefit the poorest members of society, they sometimes virtually monopolized trading in a locality (for example, in mining villages) and in these cases it has been argued that societies could keep prices high in order to increase profits. The very poor suffered, not being in a position to wait for a prospective dividend. The importance of the cooperative society in some communities did however have positive effect: it would often sponsor reading rooms, libraries and lectures. This century has seen the progressive amalgamation of local societies. Records are often still held by the societies themselves; there are also some published histories of the movement.

Savings banks differed from friendly societies and cooperatives in that the trustees, not the depositors, controlled the organization; here the paternalistic and philanthropic elements were to the fore. The trustees usually came from a business background and were expected to make contributions to offset management costs. Motives were not always altruistic however. It has been claimed that:

> in essence, the savings banks were established by members of the influential classes in an effort to provide the means by which the lower orders might come to make provision for themselves, thus achieving the dual aim of lessening the burden of the poor rate and becoming more prudent and sober working men. (Gosden, 1973)

The moving spirit behind these banks was the Reverend Henry Duncan, whose *Essay on the Nature and Advantages of Parish Banks* was published in 1815, by which time he had already established the first bank in his parish of Ruthwell, Dumfriesshire. The Edinburgh Savings Bank followed in 1813 and by 1818 there were around 130 in existence. It is symptomatic of the new opportunities available in industrial society that working men had money to deposit on this scale – or even money at all, payment in rural areas still being mainly in kind.

The main aim of the banks was to attract small sums which a commercial bank would not consider and 'which might otherwise be squandered away, unsafely deposited or lost altogether' (Checkland, 1980). The trustee savings banks themselves invested with the commercial banks on behalf of their depositors. In 1835 legislation set up the legal framework for the banks' development.

Some, however, were still too poor even to use the savings banks. Such people were accommodated by the penny savings banks, of which there were a variety of types: Sunday banks, church banks and local street banks. This movement was initiated in the 1840s and 1850s. The money was usually collected weekly at the door, and by 1881 in Glasgow alone there were 60,000 depositors in over 200 banks. One particular rival was the Post Office, which set up its own savings bank under the Post Office Savings Bank Act 1861, though the main losers were the trustees' banks; many of the smaller ones closed down immediately and transferred their assets to the Post Office.

Philanthropic institutions

As important to the nineteenth-century town as attempts by the working classes to band together for mutual security and improvement was the paternalistic concern of the middle and upper classes to alleviate the worst sufferings. The phenomenon is particularly interesting in that it is the first sustained application to strangers of the obligations associated with kinship. Philanthropy has been called a misfit in the economic structure of modern society, which rests upon principles of exchange (of capital, labour and goods). Capitalism, however, and the market forces which it supported, made philanthropy all the more vital, because men and women could be cruelly exposed in the vast markets that constituted towns. Social idealism was a necessary counterweight to a civilization which eschewed traditional protectionist economics and with it the rigid social hierarchies that to some extent formed a safety net at the bottom of society.

The motives of the philanthropists themselves have been variously interpreted, some generously, others less so. Status certainly played a part; for the rising middle classes, still unsure of their position, charitable work was a symbol of affluence, proclaiming that the individuals involved (mainly women) belonged to a level of society where 'free time was the ultimate achievement' (Checkland, 1980). These people's participation was far from anonymous; on the contrary, it was advertised through the publication of sponsors' names. Another motive for philanthropy was the very proximity of the poor; when better transport made suburban living possible, philanthropy declined. For others the concern was professional: the medical profession in particular were in the forefront of the fight for improved environmental health, housing and hospitals. Of course, professional interest was not entirely altruistic either; status, ego, career prospects and economic remuneration are all areas of self-interest furthered by professionalism.

Political motivations were another force, leading to the involvement of magistrates and town councils in many charitable enterprises. Compassion, idealism, political advantage and the chance to reduce demands on the rates can all be adduced as root causes. Finally, fear of instability and anarchy can be cited as factors. The new cities could be frightening, threatening to unleash unknown powers from the ranks of the concentrated masses. Those who particularly benefited from the new economic system – the middle classes – would naturally try to maintain it by mitigating its worst effects and by attempting to uphold the moral standards which sanctioned it.

The golden age of middle-class philanthropy was in the mid-nineteenth century, when there was an attempt to institutionalize the whole process with the setting up of umbrella organizations such as the Charity Organization Society (a United Kingdom fact-finding body). The Edinburgh Association for Improving the Condition of the Poor was founded in 1868, coordinating charitable work in that city and publishing the Edinburgh Philanthropic Yearbook. Similar bodies were set up in Glasgow and Aberdeen, becoming social service departments after World War Two. Long before that, however, philanthropy as a force had given way to the advancement of the working class which had been feared. When this came it did not result in anarchy and revolution but in the relatively peaceful development of the trade union movement and the Labour Party.

Typifying the philanthropic spirit was the nursing profession, an invention of the Victorian age, offering a girl the popular 'angel of mercy' image based on the concept of 'sublime drudgery'. This, according to Checkland (1980), had the advantage (for men) of reaffirming women's dependence.

Despite the fact that institutions which accommodated the poor were considered unsuitable workplaces for respectable girls, nursing represented women's 'first mass assault upon a profession'. According to the *4th Annual Report of the Association for Providing Trained Nurses for the West of Scotland* (1879), the very poor were treated free and the working class at a moderate fee. By the end of the century there were 92 nursing associations affiliated to Queen Victoria's Jubilee Institute for Nurses. Annual reports and minute books are sometimes held in library local history collections.

Philanthropists also assimilated the moral guardianship that traditionally belonged to church and kin, nowhere more strongly than in the temperance movement. In 1838 the annual per capita consumption of spirits in Scotland was 23 pints; in England it was 7½ pints. The discrepancy is interesting in itself, but it is not one that would have caused much concern at the start of the nineteenth century. It was not until 1838 that the Scottish Temperance Union (later renamed the Scottish Temperance League) was founded. Early reformers held the idealistic view that it would be possible by persuasion to stop people drinking. Later, more modest proposals aimed to alter laws, control licences, fix opening hours and give local residents the power to keep their neighbourhood dry. The Forbes Mackenzie Act of 1853 helped to fulfil the first three objectives; the last was partially achieved in the Temperance (Scotland) Act (1913) which provided for the holding of local polls. Such legislation had been urged by the Scottish Permissive Bill and Temperance Association (founded in 1858), which scored some major successes. In Glasgow, for example, 'when large areas were covered with local authority housing in the inter-war years, no pubs at all were built in those parts of the city' (Checkland, 1980).

Another tactic of the reformers was to provide alternatives to public houses, in the form of coffee shops and the like. One of the hotels in most of today's Scottish towns probably started life as a temperance hotel (with the name proclaimed on old High Street photographs). A search among the valuation rolls from the end of the nineteenth century will provide corroboration of this. Temperance hotels were often constituted as limited liability companies (with names like the '*Such and Such* Temperance Hotel and Coffee House Company'); this means that the names of shareholders can be inspected in the dissolved company records held in West Register House.

Gothenburg pubs were slightly different. Usually formed as municipal enterprises or trusts, they did serve drink, but advocated 'an orderly public house in which drunkenness shall be forbidden, in which the licence law shall be observed, in which no credit shall be given, in which gambling and all immoral accessories shall be done away with . . .' (Rowntree, 1901).

Nineteenth-century philanthropy manifested itself in many other areas: in model housing for the working class, lodging houses for the destitute, and in hospitals and schooling – another traditional function of the family or church. An interesting illustration of this extention of the nurturing instinct is that priority for admission to endowed schools was often kin-based. In Schaw's Institute at Prestonpans, for example, education was to be provided for boys of poor but respectable parents, with preference being given to those with the names Schaw, M'Neill, Cunningham and Stewart, in that order. Responsibility for education of course subsequently passed to the state, but a debate which is still current concerns the traditional rights of kin, as parents, to directly control their schools. This reflects, depending on your point of view, either a reaffirmation of the family or an erosion of a broader and more confident vision of society.

Sociology and family history

'The more sociological history becomes, and the more historical sociology becomes, the better for both' said E.H. Carr (1964). Among the specialisms of historians, family history in particular benefits from a sociological approach in that it shares a common concern with detailed, even personal, analysis. Abrams (1982) indicates the intimacy of sociological history:

> In the year 1250, for example, it was taken for granted that people ate with their hands often from a common dish, blew their noses in their hands or if at table on the tablecloth, spat and belched as the spirit moved them, shared their beds with casual visitors, broke wind, emptied their bowels and bladders in the presence of others and took great delight in mutilating the bodies of those they had overcome in battle.

The almost psychological questions raised here (concerning emotional and institutional barriers to the expression of feelings, and to changing perceptions of revulsion, shame, delicacy and propriety) help to define the difference, which can never be absolutely clear-cut, between sociology and anthropology.

Anthropology looks at a community in its entirety, as an entity or self-enclosed system with all its features contributing to its cohesion. It is strongly influenced by the theory of functionalism; this maintains that all cultural attributes – religion, family, taboos, social relationships – have the primary purpose of ensuring stability. The anthropologist's task is to investigate and explain how these attributes fulfil this role.

Sociology is usually more selective and more personal in its concern; it responds to the complexity of life (particularly modern urban life, where most sociological research is concentrated) by looking at specific elements within it, such as group relationships, status, class, institutions and working habits. Developed as a tool for analysing contemporary society, sociology has latterly been influential for historians keen to understand the mentalities of past societies 'and to explore the history of such unconventional matters as oppression, class formation, lunacy, crime, magic, domestic social relations and generally, people in the mass' (Abrams, 1982). In such historical studies individuals loom larger than they do in traditional history for, again in the words of Abrams, 'we are talking about personal careers rather than about social revolutions, about . . . the child in the family rather than the working class under capitalism . . . '.

Though it deals with the particular and personal, however, sociology is akin to anthropology in seeking generalizations about human behaviour. Sociological techniques are basically comparative, drawing on the experiences of a mass of individuals to make conclusions about humanity as a whole. At its heart is the notion that 'social phenomena cannot be adequately explained by the characteristics of individual actors' (*Introductory Sociology*, 1981).

History, traditionally, takes quite the opposite approach, seeing every event and process as unique and unrepeatable, peculiar to the specific actors involved, divorced, almost, from their background and personal circumstances – as if one's participation in history was a mode of behaviour in itself and not the distillation of a variety of personal behaviour patterns, in one's work, family and social relationships. Sociology, by contrast, is a *distilling* discipline. In the process, 'some things are certainly lost', as B.R. Wilson (1970) says, but the very complexity of modern life has made some kind of conceptualism necessary for all of us:

. . . as the boundaries of community dissolve, as the individual's life is no longer encompassed by concretely known social entities . . . the need for abstraction increases . . . The local cannot be understood without increasing reference to the national or the universal; and so abstract concepts become indispensable to social explanation. (B.R. Wilson, 1970).

The value of history to sociologists is that it provides a concrete and particular restraint against generalization; the value of sociology to historians is that it provides a technique for seeing the past through the eyes of ordinary men and women. (It also incidentally provides them with a refined conceptual vocabulary: B.R. Wilson uses the example of the analysis of status, with its rich terminology – 'ascribed status', 'achieved status', 'role performance', 'status contradiction' and 'reference group'.)

The family and local historian is a particular beneficiary of the sociological approach. This is in part because the traditional narrative style of history ('A happened and then B') is often unsuited to work in the local context, given the paucity of records and the fact that nothing much may actually have *happened*, thereby making the study of local *structures* a more promising enterprise. It is also because the family or local historian is generally interested in a detailed examination of people and their lives rather than with issues of transition to industrialism or even with any other type of large-scale social transformation. Abrams (1982) terms this 'micro-history' and explains: 'History is not of course something that happens only on the larger stage of whole societies or civilizations. It occurs also in prisons, factories and schools, in families, firms and friendships.' History too can look for the *springs* of human behaviour rather than its traditional *consequences*.

Micro-history holds another attraction – that the researcher need not be so knowledgeable about the wider historical context, which involves judgements about major political revolutions and ideologies. In other words, the approach is particularly suited to the amateur interested in his or her own locality or family.

One problem for the historian interested in sociology is that, unlike the contemporary sociologist, he or she cannot go out and collect the data needed for research if it is not available in printed sources. Care therefore needs to be taken in the choice of period and subject. The most potentially fruitful approach is to concentrate on a period within living memory, in which case one can interview the elderly and build up an 'oral historical' picture in much the same way as James Littlejohn did in his absorbing study of Westrigg (1963). For earlier times, one of the best sources for the researcher will be criminal records, which 'bring us as near as we can get to the people in the concerns of their daily lives. They are a reflection of these concerns, usually at the point where things went wrong, and they therefore expose the mechanics of living, which is very close to the heart of history' (Sanderson, 1986). The same author also contrasts the 'micro' and 'macro' scales of history, and examines their juxtaposition at the point where criminals 'are affected by and respond to circumstances which they themselves did not necessarily create but which were imposed on them by the public and political decisions of others.' Some major published collections of trials are listed on page 199.

Sociology of the family

Whereas the anthropological study of the family focuses on its functions as an institution within society, sociology and psychology look at individual members of the family and their relationship with each other. This is the most challenging area of research for family historians, and one which is now receiving a great deal of attention (as a consequence of the current revaluation of the benefits and drawbacks of family organization). The challenge lies in the problem of how to exploit traditional historical material for sociological ends. To take one example, Smout (1986) laments – while discussing the sons of middle-class Victorian families and their proximity to female domestic servants – that 'no doubt many, perhaps most (there is no way of telling) were as chaste as their sisters'. One's individual psychology owes a great deal to one's family relationships, if Freud and his successors are to be believed. Adjustment to the loss of exclusive maternal love is, they argue, at the heart of choices of partner. For example, men may only fall in love with women of a particular status in the sibling order (always an elder daughter say). Such patterns *can* be tested with ancestors in that remarriage was common, given the low life expectancy, and will give insights into their characters.

The key starting point for the study of relationships is the home. The home is indeed the basis of one definition of what constitutes a family: an assemblage of co-residents not necessarily linked by blood or marriage (i.e. a household), as opposed to a house or lineage, an élitist concept defining a group of kinsfolk who do not live together but are related by blood. Families in the latter sense were not found among the poor until recent times. Indeed, even households did not mean a great deal to them, as prior to the nineteenth century their houses were 'so uncomfortable . . . that they lived elsewhere as often as they could' (Flandrin, 1979). The rich were little better placed, for 'their vast residences were crowded with domestic servants and visitors, which prevented them from living in privacy with their wives and children'. Such communal living extended to the sharing of beds with complete strangers – even those of the opposite sex. It is difficult for us to think ourselves into the psychological situation of these ancestors, just as it is difficult for us to imagine the mental sufferings of families who lived (and still do live) in squalid and cramped accommodation. Farmer (1970) blames cramped conditions for the fact that 'home in a traditional working-class area is a place on the whole almost exclusively reserved for family and kinsmen.'

The growth and the prizing of privacy is one of the key elements in the evolution of the modern home, and the root of the sentimental connotation which the word 'home' has for us. The force of his image owes much to its cultivation by the nineteenth-century middle class, for whom the home was seen as a refuge, presided over by a woman, where a man could 'forget the pressures and strains of the outside world, the commercial world, the competitive world, and relax, replenish his spirit, find comfort and solace' (Calder, 1977). The middle-class Victorian home did not accommodate male activities – for those one went to a club. The idealization of women had what Calder calls 'a kind of porous quality of influence whereby simply the existence of the female improved the world'; this was one aspect of a new concept of marriage as a sanctification of a sentimental relationship between the partners. It thus became the decent thing, says Flandrin (1979), 'to mourn one's dead . . . the grief manifested on such occasions was evidence of the love one bore to the deceased person . . .'.

The lesson for the social historian is that behaviour which we might be inclined to attribute to an essential human nature is very much *learned* behaviour, and that this is true even of emotional behaviour. For example, the traditional late marriages in peasant Scotland do not appear to have led to much overt sexual frustration. It is also true that no idealization can take place without a psychological price being paid, and that this price is often paid mainly by the woman. Patrick Fraser, author of the standard nineteenth-century treatise on the law of husband and wife, refers to 'the injury to social order and the evil consequences to the domestic peace of families [following on] the establishment of a right in a wife to resist her husband's authority' and of his right to turn 'the wife or his children out of doors.' In the Victorian era, suggests Calder (1977) 'we can partly attribute the growing clutter of things in the home to the fact that many women had little to do but make great numbers of things of limited use or value . . . It was important to preserve amateurishness'. Such subordination typically involves providing services that 'no dominant group wants to perform for itself (for example cleaning up the dominant's waste products). Functions that a dominant group prefer to perform, on the other hand, are carefully guarded and closed to subordinates' (Baker, 1978). Corresponding subordinate values are those of submissiveness, docility, dependency, loss of initiative, and they can be studied in the lives of Scots wives past and present. As has often been pointed out, subordinates know more about dominants than vice-versa, which makes them ideal subjects for oral recording. Dominant male groups too can be studied; the authority of even fools, bullies and cowards over women has been immense, despite their 'own narrow toe-hold on the material and psychological bounties they believe they so desperately need' (Baker, 1978).

Such psychological relationships can be investigated in imaginative literature (as discussed in the next chapter), in court records (especially in cases of bigamy, rape and assault), in women's magazines, from a study of the legal history of the family and from treatises on morals and etiquette. Beveridge (n.d.) lists several eighteenth-century examples of the latter, such as Adam Petrie's *The Rules of Good Deportment*, published in 1720, and John Mitchell's *The Way to True Honour and Happiness*, 1699.

Social relationships

Relationships between members of a society are inescapable; society would be impossible without them. Psychology studies the most personal aspects of these relationships, the reasons for one's choice of marriage partner say, but even at this intimate level, it is impossible to ignore the presence of larger social structures. The choice of marriage partner is a case in point, for 'as soon as one investigates which people actually marry each other, one finds that the lightning shaft of Cupid seems to be guided rather strongly within very definite channels of class, income, education, racial and religious background' (Berger, 1966). The governing factor in this is that society is experienced by individuals as 'a fact-like system, external, given, coercive, even while individuals are busy making and remaking it through their own imagination, communication and action' (Abrams, 1982). One of these 'fact-like' realities is the social group, which defines and constrains the behaviour of those who are part of it. The individual in history, therefore, whatever his or her personal characteristics and achievements, can only truly be understood in the context of social relationships.

Status is the social position which a person occupies, and his or her role consists of behaving in the expected corresponding way. Yet social roles 'are not just a matter of the way people can be *observed* to behave . . . but . . . [also] the way it is thought they *ought* to behave' (*Introductory Sociology*, 1981). Furthermore, people of different status will sometimes be expected to behave differently. These behaviour patterns are reinforced by the existence of norms (positive values) and sanctions (non-legal methods of punishment, such as gossip, ostracism and ridicule). Study in this area is suited to the historian of the village or rural parish, for 'in small-scale and closely knit communities, where self-respect is very closely tied up with the esteem in which one is held by one's fellows, any sanction of this sort, designed to erode it, is likely to be particularly effective . . .' (*Introductory Sociology, 1981*).

Status is to some extent fixed by one's gender or birth. It is also frequently argued that in traditional societies, status is generally *ascribed*; that is, if one's father was a blacksmith, one would (if male) almost certainly become a blacksmith too; whereas in industrial society, status is increasingly *achieved*. The family historian is in a favoured position to examine this issue, and its corollary, that where the rate of social mobility is low, solidarity and cohesion is strong.

All societies except the most simple appear to be socially stratified. At first sight this is an odd phenomenon since all humans are biologically alike and the social stratification does not correspond to any innate differences in temperament or intelligence. It is caused solely by the existence of society itself. Social class belongs to society as status belongs to kin. Such is its importance that the lives of ancestors cannot be understood without taking it into account. One theory of stratification is that it stems from the necessity for large-scale human groups to be welded together, such groups being too large to be bonded by personal affections. Instead, an appeal is made to common values reinforced by symbols and totems whose function is to provide emotional surrogacy – a sense of belonging in place of the face-to-face familiarity of small groups. Common values, however, imply the ranking of individuals according to the contributions they are able to make to the maintenance of these values. Thus in the capitalist society in which we have lived for the last two hundred years, capital accumulation and investment for profit are more highly regarded than labour itself. Hence the working class is at the bottom of the social hierarchy.

Approaches to the study of social stratification are various, but comparing the outlook of different classes is an interesting starting point. Members of the lowest sub-stratum often have a fatalistic attitude towards life which influences successive generations, thus compounding their difficulties in changing their status. Saunders (1950) points to a corresponding bleakness at the base of society, 'a population of dockers, carters, porters and navvies . . . badly housed, casually employed, ill-paid, exposed to risk and temptation, some bettering themselves and their children, others demoralized, as their inherited standards gave under urban pressures.' Littlejohn (1963) notes some more subtle connotations of class:

> unlike the upper-middle class the working class is not afraid of silence in a gathering and often admits implicitly that there is nothing to say. It is common for friends to sit silently round a fire for long stretches. One old shepherd if he couldn't find anything to say to a visitor simply went off to bed, without saying so . . . this is unthinkable among the upper-middle class.

Just as the outlook of different classes can be compared, so can what is known as their 'life-chances' – the opportunities open to them for education, health, leisure, travel and employment. These aspects can be studied to some extent in census records. The concepts of ascribed and achieved status are particularly relevant in this context. One could, for example, look at one of the many mining or fishing communities in Scotland. Their location was dictated by the presence of raw materials (in the days before sophisticated transport systems); work opportunities as well as specific skills would be handed down through generations in much the same way as occurs in non-literate societies.

Another possible topic is the dissection of the class structure of a community at a frozen moment in the past. The sometimes crude generalizations of nineteenth-century commentators, dividing society into upper, middle and lower classes, have now been much refined by sociologists. One can cite differentiations in the middle classes of the mid-nineteenth century, between *nouveaux riches* free-trade entrepreneurs and traditional merchants, such as have been studied in the composition of the eldership of the Free Church and Church of Scotland in Victorian Aberdeen. Not that the traditional merchant class itself was not fragmented, with, at one extreme 'the petty shopkeeper and packman, at the other the opulent merchant prince and between a myriad army of men of varied social and material standing' (Devine, 1983).

The Marxist emphasis is always on the economic determinants of class. Sub-classes can be identified by a study of wage rates, which in the eighteenth century were set by justices of the peace (whose minute books can be consulted in the Scottish Record Office, Inventory JP). In the nineteenth century, free bargaining was introduced, and a variety of sources must be used for comparing rates of pay, including newspapers, royal commission reports and company archives. Capital accumulation is more difficult to establish, but some techniques for doing so are outlined below. Max Weber put a somewhat different emphasis on class, or rather he pointed to a wider variety of determinants, of which economic status was only one. Some professions, for example, had higher prestige than others, even though they might not be as well remunerated. In other words, people's *perceptions* of class positions in turn affect the *reality* of their class positions.

Closely connected with the idea of class is that of the élite, which has received a lot of attention in recent years. The two crucial factors in the maintenance of an élite are *recruitment* (i.e. the possibility of outsiders becoming members) and *integration* (the forces of cohesion binding the members). These cohesive forces are often closely connected with family networks in business and politics; this is another example of the structural role which the family can continue to play in a society not based on kinship.

Sources of power for élites can be military, economic, political or cultural – or any combination of these. Where there is considerable overlap, what is known as a ruling class emerges. A more specific definition is given by Scott, John and Hughes (n.d.):

> . . . a ruling class may be said to exist where the economic élite is closed, highly integrated and takes the form of a 'class', where the political élite is closed and highly integrated, where there is a high concentration of power within each system and where the members of the economic élite are in large part also members of the political élite.

This work on the theory of élites provides a challenging framework for local studies. One could, for example, look at the distribution of economic power in a locality. Traditionally, land was the major source of economic wealth, and one finds plenty of evidence for the existence of élites based on this: in 1878, 68 persons owned nearly half of Scotland. Sources of information on land ownership are discussed in Moody (1986) and the subject is relatively easy to pursue in that Scotland has maintained comprehensive registers of land transactions (the registers of sasines) since the beginning of the seventeenth century. Printed abridgements are held in some local history libraries and record offices; the complete records are preserved in the Scottish Record Office.

Much more difficult to study are less tangible forms of wealth: capital, investments, directorships and so on. Where family papers have survived they may furnish some clues in the form of share certificates or account books. It is also relatively easy to study the composition of limited liability companies using the records in West Register House, or, in the case of still-existing companies, those of the Company Registration Office in George Street, Edinburgh. Testamentary procedures provide a complete picture of an individual's affairs at the time of death.

As suggested above, economic power is only one of several factors contributing to the establishment of élites. Military power was still a significant factor up until the seventeenth century, after which time the naked exercise of power became a prerogative of the state. Cultural power depends upon the promotion of dominant values, such that 'if the subordinate members of society can be persuaded to believe that those who dominate have a *right* to do so, and that those who have great material advantage have a *right* to it, then they are very unlikely to challenge or threaten the privileged' (*Introductory Sociology*, 1981). 'Deferential traditionalism' is a particular form of subordination which occurs where employees are in direct association with an employer and are not in a position to organize together or to have dealings with the employer in a wider social and cultural setting. The rural farmworker was for centuries in this position. As Littlejohn (1963) reports:

> Deferential behaviour was more constantly and strictly demanded of the
> labouring classes . . . in the form of cap lifting and 'sir-ing'. As the
> blacksmith said, 'it used to be terrible always lifting up your bonnet, you
> barely had your bonnet on all bloody day'. A farm servant who
> neglected to give these signs of his position to any in the class above
> risked being branded as 'impudent' and fired from his job.

In this case, therefore, cultural deference was reinforced by
economic power. It is also interesting to note that the
blacksmith was not willingly deferential. This is possibly partly
due to recent changes noted by Littlejohn: 'the former personal
relation between master and servant has given way to a more
impersonal one – they confront each other more as abstract
administrative categories, employer and employee, whose
relationship is regulated by the two unions and the state.'

Social geography

A town does not consist only of a concrete physical arrangement of building materials, it is also an expression of human
social interactions. The local historian, who concentrates on
understanding history within a restricted geographical context,
can benefit from the study of these social relationships inherent
in the spatial organization of our lives. Space in this sense is
social space – the space created by activities of mankind – as
opposed to space considered as a container.

In the same way as a distinction can be made in a broad
context between community and society, so a town at the
micro-level can be regarded as comprehending two planes of
existence – the neighbourhood and the wider identity that
defines the boundaries of the town itself. The neighbourhood
has been seen as an urban version of the rural community, and
like its rural counterpart it consists of three major elements: the
locality, common ties and frequent social interaction among its
members. These are all moot points, awaiting confirmation or
refutation by local and family historians. Other features of
traditional rural communities – a homogeneous culture, relative
immobility, strength of custom and church, co-operative
endeavour – are arguably less pronounced in towns, though we
have seen how the Industrial Revolution increased the incidence
of the extended family. An exception must also be made for the
traditional occupational communities within fishing and mining

towns. Although cities may have destroyed some of the cohesive elements of society they helped to emphasize others, such as race, ethnic origin and class interest, which became reflected in the spatial groupings of people within different localities. These secondary groupings are commonly imposed more often than they are chosen, and are more significant in social geographic terms than the voluntary associations stemming from shared interests or for mutual benefit considered earlier in this chapter. These latter do have spatial connotations, however: the benefit society with its occupational basis might have a membership drawn from a tightly-knit neighbourhood, as might the charitable association from a middle-class suburb. Furthermore, neighbourhoods themselves are the impetus for the establishment of voluntary secondary groups, for example the community association or the city gang (usually found in the run-down areas near city centres). For these various reasons, the significance of the urban community must not be underestimated; indeed, it is claimed by Jackson and Smith (1984) that 'the experience of urban renewal . . . commonly uncovers an intense identification between people and places, leading those displaced to undergo a profound sense of disorientation . . .'.

The social geographer or historian examines the spatial components of all group activities with a view, first, to establishing a distribution pattern for the group members around the town, and secondly, to discovering the causes and consequences of that pattern. Many groups, as suggested, have a natural derivation from a shared socio-economic status, with its corollary of shared ideas and norms of behaviour. A social group's territorial well-being (measured by nine major criteria – income, wealth, employment, living environment, health, education, social order, social belonging and recreation) can be studied from census returns. This information may be plotted on maps; the resulting lines of demarcation may help to answer the question, 'How is a neighbourhood or community defined or perceived?' Once a sense of neighbourhood is felt by the residents of an area, this feeling will intensify, creating a social space invested with symbolic values. The primary aim of street gangs can be seen as an attempt to give an area ritual definition.

Territories marked out in such ways, however, are neither static nor rigidly delineated. In 'grey' areas, there may be evidence of social stress, which can lead to high levels of migration (census enumeration books will show this up). There may also be overlapping, specialized territories, some perceived as a part of the public domain (shopping centres, for example), others religious (such as parishes) and others considered as home territory, in which each individual will have his or her own individual space. Different social phenomena such as crime or the distribution of disease will have their own territorial patterns. In short, cities 'may be conceived of as an expression of social relations generated by territoriality' (Jackson and Smith, 1984).

As well as the groups themselves, the social historian can look at the relationship among these groups. Conflict (competition for scarce resources) and power (the relative standing of groups within this competitive framework) leads to an unequal distribution of rewards, such that 'the spatial structure would then reflect the distribution of power in society' (Jones and Eyles, 1977). Space in the industrial town is an economic resource (in recent years it has increasingly been viewed as such in rural areas as well). Each plot of land has its optimum use based on the potential income from the site; this might be retailing, wholesaling or housing. And, so the argument runs, its use will gravitate towards that optimum despite attempts (by planning authorities for example) to have it otherwise. This state of affairs has not always existed. At one time space was also a symbolic or cultural resource; that is to say, religious and political structures dominated the skyline in the way office blocks do today. Even in the first half of the nineteenth century, when industrial towns were already growing fast, economic considerations were not predominant; the territorial segregation of classes was consequently much less pronounced. In the words of Gauldie (n.d.):

'House for sale' advertisements in the first quarter of the nineteenth century show the effective neighbourhood-patterning this kind of society had created. Houses for 'genteel families' plus rooms for workers would be advertised and sold as one lot. The genteel families would buy for themselves more room and a better outlook. They had not yet begun to object to having their employees as neighbours.

Another key question here concerns the reasons for the choice of location for development outside the existing boundaries of towns. Why, for instance, was Edinburgh New Town planted where it is? Once a locality has an 'incipient' character, however, the process tends to be self-fulfilling, for 'individuals perceive themselves to be of a certain social standing and often feel that this standing is threatened by the presence of others of lower social position' (Jones and Eyles, 1977). Of course changes do take place, cumulatively, until the whole character of an area seems silently transformed. An often cited example is the inner city, once a fashionable residential area, which has progressively become run-down until, in recent years, it has been swept away.

To conclude this chapter on a more general note, the family and local historian can use social geography to take a broader look at the development of his or her town and its impact on social relationships. Models have been proposed that are worth examining, even where some of the assertions are open to debate. It is argued that the bonds uniting the inhabitants of towns are weaker than those in traditional rural areas, hence social order is maintained by formal institutions rather than by personal contact. Town dwellers are less likely to know each other personally, and it would also be impossible to assemble them all together in the way that a good number of rural inhabitants would meet together in church, where public pronouncements were made from the pulpit. The local historian can look at the development of the local newspaper as a forum of information, as a means of social control and as a substitute for the church. Paradoxically, the rise of the local newspaper coincided with the decline of the local community. It has been argued that an increasing division of labour, with the large enterprise displacing the family firm, was an inevitable urban process. More contentiously, it has been claimed that 'competition and mutual exploitation replace[d] co-operation', and that class structure became blurred because individuals had wide-ranging contacts. As life became departmentalized, so identity conflict probably became more common, and there was less likely to have been a strong sense of attachment to a locality (though, as we have seen, there is some contrary evidence here). As the vast majority of us are now city dwellers, it is appropriate that these issues are investigated. Until recently, most of the contributions to this study came from geographers and sociologists, both of whom tended to neglect the historical perspective; the time is now ripe for local and family historians to assess and amend their hypotheses.

Chapter Six

CULTURE AND BELIEFS

Perhaps the most fundamental – and difficult – objective of getting to know one's ancestors is to determine how their minds worked. What men and women have done, and what has been done to them, is often recorded, whereas what they thought about this has been much less well documented. How did they view themselves and others and the world around them? What were their aspirations, beliefs and values? Without knowing the answers to these questions we cannot truly know our ancestors as living people. This chapter aims to provide some techniques for answering such questions and for probing the minds of Scottish forebears. As in previous chapters, indirect methods of study will have to be employed, for it is the exceptional ancestor who has set down his or her thoughts in diaries, letters or reminiscences.

The first point to bear in mind when studying thoughts, emotions and beliefs is that there is little independence and originality in what we feel; our perceptions are to a great degree made for us, through the agency of our culture. Culture has been called the man-made part of the environment and has been defined as 'any form of behaviour which is acquired through learning, and which is patterned in conformity with certain approved norms. Under it anthropologists include all the customs, traditions and institutions of a people, together with their products and techniques of production' (Bascom, 1965). Artefacts are but one small manifestation of a mental and emotional plan of the world that is our all-pervading heritage, from the most trivial details of daily life – dress, food, manners, games, home decoration – to the questions about existence posed by religion, philosophy and literature. Because of our powerful need for social bonds, and for a sense of familiarity and recognition, we accept this view of existence, modifying and developing it only at the periphery as we respond to changes in ourselves and our environment. This is why we feel uneasy when confronted by foreign cultures; and the more exotic the culture the more uneasy we feel. The study of history can provoke similar feelings. What, for example, would most of us today make of the Highland custom described by Pococke in 1760: 'They spend commonly three days at funerals . . . and this time is spent in eating and drinking very plentifully; and the widow and children danced with others round the Corps till very lately'?

The power of culture and the subordination of independent thought can be illustrated by a simple example: the role of the male in procreation. That the male sperm was necessary for conception (or what is called a 'cultural construct') had been known for five thousand years in our patriarchal societies, yet the sperm's role in procreation was scientifically established only in the nineteenth century. Culture relies upon the power of assumptions, the acceptance of a body of related ideas – some rational, some irrational, some non-rational or ritualistic. Even those areas which we regard as most personal and private are culturally determined, for our feelings are articulated to ourselves by means of silent speech, whose language and concepts are themselves a cultural inheritance, with accretions of meaning supplied by previous generations.

For the historian, the fact that culture is a collective and social expression means that the task of understanding individual minds is made possible, which would not be the case if each created his or her mental world from scratch. As a result, we can talk meaningfully of a 'Scottish culture' or an 'eighteenth-century culture', in the confidence that all who lived at that time will have shared certain common perceptions, irrespective of the distinctive marks of their personality. We can even get glimpses of the latter as well, for a culture holds out a variety of options within its basic framework, and the choices made can signify much about personal psychology. One example investigated in this chapter is that of religious denomination.

Folklore

A folk has been defined as 'any group of people whatsoever who share at least one common factor' (Bascom, 1965). Occupation, religion or language are examples of such common factors. The integrating power of shared beliefs within such groups is a common theme of anthropologists; and one is likely to find 'folk' elements particularly prevalent in 'set-apart' communities such as fishing villages and traditional rural settlements. One argument, now somewhat unfashionable, asserts that folklore reflects archaic modes of thought and belief. For example, the throwing of salt from fishing boats and the related practice in the highlands of placing earth and salt on the breast of the dead, 'the earth symbolizing the corruptible body and the salt the immortal spirit' (McNeill, 1977) is said to reflect a primitive association with ideas of preservation. Such non-scientific modes of thought are with us all, so that just as our towns and villages are in one sense living museums of the structure and fabric of different generations, so too our minds are living museums of associations and beliefs inherited from our fore-bears, reassembled to meet the needs of today. The mental apparatus of even the most intellectual of people consists of pockets of rationality embedded in seas of non-rationality. Folklore indeed has been defined as the 'non-rational', the everyday level of existence, but it is in no wise inferior for that. For 'despite its superficiality, the culture of everyday interaction in all societies bears the imprint of more articulate and critical social myths and ideologies, knowledges and beliefs, whether they be drawn from the institutions of religion, magic, science, politics [or] education . . .' (*Introductory Sociology*, 1981).

This view of folklore emphasizes its currency and perma-nence, and is sceptical of the theories that see its origins in a magic, later superseded by religion. The 'primitive' misunder-standing comes about partly from an undue focus on elements which have left the non-rational sphere to join the rational. A typical charm recorded in the seventeenth century sees a cure for 'those who rage at some Fits' in clapping 'a Bible frequently on their Faces' (Campbell, 1975); and this aspect of folklore is now supplanted by medical science. But there are more areas that do not have and could not have a scientific counterpart. For the field of folklore embraces, in a list given in Dundes (1965): myths, legends, folktales, jokes, proverbs, riddles, chants, blessings, curses, oaths and insults, retorts, tongue-twisters, greeting and leave-taking formulae, folk costume, dance, drama, songs and names. One might perhaps ask what, if anything, the items on this list have in common; to which the answer would be that they are transmitted orally. Written music and literature are thus excluded, as are other aspects of formal or institutional culture (religion for example). On the basis of this definition, anthropologists have identified 'folk-type' societies – simple tribal cultures which maintain magical systems without alternative beliefs which might create conflicts and crises of confidence. When such a group's solidarity is weakened, for instance when it is subjected to wider macro-intellectual systems of religion, the hypothesis is that its folklore becomes less homogeneous and integrated; it becomes 'superstitious', unrelated to a coherent world view.

There is much scope for Scottish research in this context, particularly in the highlands, which has retained many elements of an oral culture up to recent times. Its vitality in fact can serve as a reminder to the researcher that manifestations of folklore are not quaint relics of antiquated ways.

Derick Thomson (1954) sees two artistic strands in the Gaelic tradition, the heroic and its obverse, 'the anonymous folk-poetry which tells of the more intimate and emotional part of the life of the time.' Heroic culture has its roots in the aristocratic pastoralism of tribes such as the early Greeks (who provided Homer with the material for his great epics) and the Celts. The Gaelic bardic tradition (which was partly oral) similarly sang of great chiefs and their noble deeds – a vigorous abstraction from the reality of daily life. For the latter, one has to turn to Thomson's second category, which sings of 'birth, babyhood, love, marriage, disappointment in love, heroism, death . . .' and in which the 'prime common factor . . . is the personal relationship'. These poems were at the same time songs; Francis Collinson (1966) mentions various categories, notably communal labour songs (especially the 'waulking' songs sung while shrinking cloth) but also clapping songs and songs for 'reaping, sowing, the quern, spinning, milking, churning'. All these are distinctively Gaelic in character: 'the Lowland Scotswoman may well have sung at her work as she reaped the corn or churned the butter or spun the wool and flax, or shrank her newly woven cloth; but she possessed no specific songs for the purpose'. Other categories of Gaelic music are the lullaby, the mourning and funeral song and the supernatural song which tells of imaginary beasts or the love of human beings for fairies.

A positive approach to the study of folklore concentrates on the functions which it can perform, such as those of compensation and escape: the fairy tale as a wishful success story has been particularly associated with this aspect. It is also interesting that such stories occur most frequently in peasant societies, as defined in Chapter Four. A second function of folklore is the validation and justification of culture. Bascom (1965) quotes the anthropologist Malinowski to the effect that its role is to 'strengthen tradition and endow it with a greater value and prestige by tracing it back to a higher, better, more supernatural reality of initial events'. In this respect sociologists have noted how belief systems are sustained by a circularity in the ideas which constitute them and a refusal to grant legitimacy to the assumptions on which alternative views are based. Our own scientific culture conforms to this pattern just as much as one that believes in fairies. A third function is education, as found explicitly in proverbs and moral tales. In respect of proverbs, James Kelly noted in 1721 that 'the Scots are wonderfully given to this way of speaking, and as a consequence of that, abound with proverbs, many of which are very expressive, quick and home to the purpose' (quoted in Douglas, 1935). Riddles too have been seen as essentially didactic devices for sharpening the mind, as has much else that belongs mainly to the lore of children. The latter has been described as 'didactic and initiatory, introducing the younger child to the sophistication of the next grade' (Edmonson, 1971).

A final function of folklore is the maintenance of social cohesion. At a basic level greetings, farewells and toasts are 'more or less pure signs of contact and solidarity, supporting and sustaining speech by the affirmation of continued attention' (Edmondson, 1971). Songs and tales are frequently used to express disapproval of certain forms of behaviour, often through ridicule. More subtly, folklore can be used as a safety valve for tension, as in songs of social protest. Bascom (1965) considers that 'to the extent to which folklore contrasts with the accepted norms and offers socially acceptable forms of release through amusement or humour and through creative imagination and fantasy, it tends to preserve [society's] institutions from direct attack and change.'

As already suggested, the study of the functions of folklore has to a large extent supplanted the study of its origins. The latter are sometimes quite transparent, as for example in the highland celebration of the old Celtic festivals of Beltane and Samhuinn (May and November) with their clearly preserved rituals of human sacrifice, or, in the more complex practice noted by Marian McNeill (1977), of tying 'two rowan twigs crosswise with red thread' – a characteristic combination of pagan and Christian symbolism – in order to make an amulet to protect the cattle in the byre. Nevertheless, folklore is predominantly a response and adaptation to contemporary needs. In other words, the origin of the material is irrelevant to the understanding of the way it is now being used, and in fact can obscure its real significance.

The value of the functional approach to folklore can be seen in comparative studies of different types of local community. The folklore of the highlands, for example, has been considered to be quite different from that of the lowlands, and these distinctions go beyond the linguistic divide. Where kinship and tribal traditions are strong, there is emphasis on the legends of the origin and deeds of the clan, 'mythologizing the mystique of family pride' in the words of Edmonson (1971). In the lowlands, with its cash crop economy, the heroic ballad is replaced by the bothy ballad, indicative of a more divided society (particularly in terms of class). As already mentioned, even more radical changes occur when a group's solidarity is weakened by urbanization; in these circumstances much of folklore becomes 'folksy' – a self-conscious imitation of itself based on no coherent belief system.

The study of folklore can be pursued either from existing collections put together by folklorists or by an original fieldwork project. An early survey by James Kirkwood, carried out in the late seventeenth century, has recently been published (Campbell, 1975), and many travellers made incidental references to customs which they came across. A complete list of published tours in Scotland was compiled by Arthur Mitchell (1902). The nineteenth century was a great age for Gaelic folklorists, of whom two, John Francis Campbell and Alexander Carmichael, stand above the rest. Campbell published four volumes of *Popular Tales of the West Highlands* between 1860 and 1862, and another volume, *More West Highland Tales*, was published posthumously for the Scottish Anthropological and Folklore Society in 1940. Stith Thompson's *Motif Index of Folk Literature*, published by the Indiana University Press, (six volumes, 1932–6) is used by folklorists to study the distribution of a particular tale (which can be very wide, cutting across even international boundaries) and for identifying the distinctive local elements of any one version of this tale. The 'age-area' principle states that the wider the distribution, the older the source.

Alexander Carmichael was, in the words of Derick Thomson (1954):

the first of the collectors to realize that in gathering traditional material everything is potentially significant. So he collected not only prayers and incantations, charms and songs, but also accounts of customs and beliefs, descriptions of work processes, season lore, lexicographical material, proverbs – in short, all he could lay hands on.

The collection has been published in six volumes under the title *Carmina Gadelica* (1900 [2 vols.], 1940, 1941, 1954 and 1971; see chapter notes). Derick Thomson suggests that given the destruction of traditional highland lifestyles 'it seems unlikely that anything that can be done now will usurp the pre-eminence of *Carmina Gadelica*'. Nevertheless, fieldwork still continues, notably under the aegis of the School of Scottish Studies whose library of tapes and transcripts is available for study. Some fieldwork transcripts are printed in the School's journal, *Tocher*.

As suggested above, some aspects of folk culture exist in all societies, in children's games, proverbs and in greetings, and it is these intimate aspects of social bonding which can best be studied in contemporary society. Not to be forgotten, too, are the many folk life museums which have grown up in recent years.

Religion

The folk culture which we have been investigating in this chapter has been spoken of as the 'little tradition' as opposed to the 'great tradition of the reflective few' (Redfield, 1956). The latter is characterized by its institutionalized priesthoods and organs of government, sustained by cultural, political and economic élites. Interestingly, the disintegration of this upper stratum can leave 'practically intact the underlying local folk cultures' – the continuum more directly related to the rhythms and hardships of ordinary daily life. It is for this reason that we find ancient Celtic festivals being celebrated in the nineteenth-century highlands and also that the general assembly of the Church of Scotland, 50 years after the Reformation which had supposedly transformed religious perceptions, found it necessary to attack 'those who went on pilgrimage to wells, trees and old chapels, and put up bonfires' (Wormald, 1981).

Nevertheless, it is essential for understanding the mentality and behaviour of any single individual that this intellectual superstructure is considered, for it constantly impinges on the lives of all. As Redfield states:

> . . . the intellectual and often the religious and moral life of the peasant village is perpetually incomplete; the student needs also to know something of what goes on in the minds of remote teachers, priests or philosophers whose thinking affects and perhaps is affected by the peasantry.

Because this influence permeates the structure of mental life, it becomes of less significance that the majority may have been only indirectly exposed to it.

As an example one can take the Church of Scotland. Despite its limited appeal (even in a 'religious' age such as the eighteenth century, the parish churches which were built could have accommodated only a small proportion of the parishioners – proof of the fact that many even then were not concerned with religion) the church 'so construed its position as to legislate not merely for its own congregations, but for those outside its membership' (Drummond and Bulloch, 1973). Thus in 1709 it could even legislate against the liturgy used by the episcopalian church, and a few years earlier could sentence an 18-year-old boy infected with the pantheistic notion that 'God and nature were one' to be 'taken to the Gallow-lee on the eighth of January, between the hours of two and four in the afternoon, and to be hanged' (Drummond and Bulloch, 1973).

In the following sections some of the themes of the Scottish 'great tradition' are considered, together with their interaction with the 'little tradition', for the light that they throw on the mental processes and behaviour of individual ancestors.

Religious denomination

One of the pieces of information that you will often be able to establish about an ancestor will be his or her religious persuasion. Civil marriage certificates record the religious rites employed; besides, the clergyman was usually one of the witnesses. Registration in the parish registers will sometimes, though not always, indicate that the person concerned was a member of the established church. Interpreting the evidence depends partly on date, for which Flinn (1977) provides the requisite background information.

Religious persuasion can give a good indication both of an individual's character and outlook, and of his or her economic and social situation. In the eighteenth century, for example, viewpoints polarized around two clusters of attitudes, that of the moderates, exemplified by the mainstream Church of Scotland, and that of the evangelicals, represented by successive secessions from the main body of the church. The first of these occurred in 1733 under the leadership of Ebenezer Erskine, forming the Associate Presbytery. This church itself split into two further groups, known as the Burghers and Anti-Burghers, in 1747; both of these in their turn split into 'New Licht' and

'Auld Licht' factions. The two 'New Lichts' united in 1820 and in 1847 combined with the Relief Presbytery to form the United Presbyterian Church. The Relief Presbytery was a small secession from the Church of Scotland formed in 1760.

The propensity to schism noticeable in these groups is a phenomenon which sociologists see as typical of those 'of the strongest conviction and greatest respectability' (Drummond and Bulloch, 1973). The same authors compare their village theologians splitting hairs over Calvinist doctrine with groups from industry discussing Marxist-Leninist doctrine in the 1930s. Their fire and passion can be contrasted with the outlook of the moderates, 'rational, tolerant of all except the intolerant, and blind to the strength of emotion in human life'. The moderates emphasized law and order, regarding sin as an error in judgement; they generally reflected the interest of the hierarchy in a stable agricultural community. Crucially, they viewed the church as an arm or ally of the state, and the issue on which much of the secession movement turned was that of patronage – the right of the local landowner to nominate the minister for the parish when the post became vacant. Those who accepted this position would have tended to accept a number of other related ideas: that one's station in life had been ordained, that society was more important than the individual, and that life was to be enjoyed in its own right. As Drummond and Bulloch (1973) observe, such optimism and rationality sprang from 'the security and felicity of the wealthy and educated'.

A secessionist by contrast believed that each man stood before God with no intermediaries, either secular or religious. Independent and egalitarian (seceders tended to support parliamentary reform), he or she would have to some extent lacked the communal support of the parish 'where face-to-face contact was the cement of social relations' (Dickson, 1980). Such self-confidence would often be a reflection of social status: independent tradesmen and hand-loom weavers could have afforded the luxury of integrity more than farm workers in thrall to an estate. In fact, one of the most interesting projects in this area of research is to examine local communities and individuals and to judge the significance of the strength of secession in a locality in the context of the local economy. Drummond and Bulloch sum up the character of the secessionist as one of 'devotion and responsibility . . . obstinacy and total lack of any sense of the communal nature of the Christian church.'

In the nineteenth century, the church once again tore itself apart, and once again the ostensible issue of patronage served to focus differing views of the relationship between church and state. By this time the established church had forsaken its moderate position; the humanism of the eighteenth century had been overtaken by the science of the nineteenth, whose full-scale assault on religious truths led to a new emphasis on emotional and scriptural non-rationality. The church was in retreat, both intellectually and physically, for it was failing to come to terms with the new industrial cities. It was claimed in 1838 that in Glasgow and Edinburgh alone there were 100,000 adults who were not practising Christians. Even in rural areas it seems that the situation was little better: the presbytery of Uist in 1836, with a population of 3000, boasted only 450 regular churchgoers and only 14 communicants. The ground of the argument, therefore, in the church/state debate, had subtly shifted. Supporters of patronage now saw the state as a necessary source of support for a weakened church, rather than the church being a support for the state; while their opponents saw disestablishment as part of the movement towards the liberalization of the state through restriction of its right to interfere in social and economic affairs.

A sociological explanation for this trend is that whereas in a homogeneous peasant culture it is easy for religious leaders to preside over simple legitimating systems, in a pluralistic society such as that of the nineteenth century, religion must perforce 'retreat into an intimate sphere . . . which is relatively less dependent on class and institutional factors' (Berger, 1969). The church's weakness in this situation has in the long run led to a progressive reunification of most of its schismatic elements and to growing ecumenicalism, but in the short term it led to the most substantial secession of all – the Disruption of 1843 and the formation of the Free Church.

The leaders of the new church were the industrial middle classes – the Free Church has indeed been called 'the embodiment of the Scottish bourgeoisie at prayer' (Dickson, 1980). In these circumstances one would expect that the disruption was particularly acute in the cities, which is indeed the case. Paradoxically, however, its appeal was equally potent in the least urbanized areas – the highlands, of which more below. The elders of the Free Church tended to be drawn from among businessmen and other professionals, this in itself 'being regarded as a visible sign of worth in the eyes of God' in the words of A.A. Maclaren (1983); whereas the elders of the

Church of Scotland had been local landowners large and small, known as the 'heritors'. The conflict was thus at its root one of economic and political power in two different types of society, the rural and the urban, with the middle class seceders seeking 'control of patronage in order to establish themselves as leaders of the local state, with control over such important functions as educational provision and poor relief . . .' (A.A. Maclaren, 1974).

Studies of eldership and the composition of church congregations have been made, notably in Aberdeen, and the family history researcher could pursue similar lines of research in his or her locality. The interesting phenomenon of parishes split down the middle (one-third of the Church of Scotland ministers defected, leading to a second parish church being established) can be studied in the kirk session minutes of the respective churches.

A third interesting study of the relationship between church and state, and one which also illuminates the significance of religious denomination, is that of the revivalist evangelical movement which, like the Free Church, made its strongest mark in the highlands and in the industrial cities. The evangelicism of the nineteenth century had no truck with any state institutions at all. In this it can be contrasted with traditional bodies such as the Scottish Society for the Propagation of Christian Knowledge which worked within established authority. It was set up in 1709 to work 'especially in the Highlands, Islands and remote corners thereof, where error, idolatry, superstition and ignorance do mostly abound by reason of the largeness of the parishes and scarsity of schools.' The revivalism in Scotland around 1800, led by the Haldane brothers who built 'tabernacles' and missions in such places as fishing and mining villages, was different, and the established church took their proselytizing amiss:

> they assume the name of missionaries, as if they had some special commission from heaven . . .; they are introducing themselves into parishes, without any call, and erecting in places Sunday schools without any countenance from the Presbytery of the bounds or the minister of the parish.

Later the evangelical sects had even greater successes in the urban sprawls of the mid-nineteenth century – a testimony to their appeal to the destitute.

A sect is typically a small religious group with members

drawn from the lower classes and the poor. Such people reject many of the values of society, replacing them with beliefs which are often at odds with contemporary thinking. Those who have least stake in a society and least chances of making successful headway are those with most to gain by jettisoning its cultural heritage. Max Weber referred to this group as 'a theodicy of disprivilege'. It is a reflection of the desperate situation in the highlands that this region shared the evangelical fervour of the cities, and indulged in a masochistic denunciation of its traditional folk culture. Alexander Carmichael (quoted in Collinson, 1966) recalls a woman in the Isle of Lewis saying:

> the good men and the good ministers who arose, did away with the songs and the stories, the music and the dancing, the sports and the games that were perverting the minds and ruining the souls of the people . . . they made the people burn their pipes and fiddles.

Evangelism has flourished in Scotland up to the present day, and membership of these groups can tell us much about the personalities of the individuals concerned. Different types of sect have been identified, based on different responses to, and philosophies of, the world. For example the conversionist sect (including the Assemblies of God) emphasizes the moral view that the world is corrupted because man is corrupted: if men change, so will the world. One of the ramifications of such an outlook is that social or political reform is unimportant. By contrast, the revolutionary sect (including the Jehovah's Witnesses) awaits the overthrow of the present social order through an eschatological convulsion: its members have less tendency to moralize because they see the course of events as being pre-determined by God. A full typology of sects is given by B.R. Wilson (1969).

Of course not all the urban poor embraces evangelical extremism. As noted above, the flavour of the church as a whole was evangelical in the nineteenth century. The established church through its church extension movement, pioneered by Thomas Chalmers, brought a similar spirit into the industrial suburbs. Its memorial is the now familiar and ubiquitous mock Gothic church sharing its street with the less pretentious mission and evangelical hall. Some of the poor resolved the challenges of the age by rejecting religion altogether (the church no longer had the power to punish disbelief) in favour of political activism (discussed further in the next chapter) or an aggressive faith in science and progress.

Individual theology

More intimate still than religious persuasion is personal theology. Notwithstanding that the complexities of theology are the preoccupation of the few, one-sided interpretations, popularizations and misunderstandings are potent and widespread, and tell us much about the meaning of religious belief for all types of individuals and the effect it has on their actions. The study of this subject in Scotland has centred on Calvinist theology, which appears to have been particularly susceptible to misunderstanding and whose variants have proved far more influential than their source, in areas quite unconnected with religion.

It is the Calvinist belief in predestination which has been seen as the crucial element in its influence – leading to what has been called 'salvation panic' and a 'terrifying anxiety about whether one has been chosen, throwing the believer into psychological turmoil' (*Introductory Sociology*, 1981). This isolation is at a far remove from the community spirit of medieval christianity, with its priesthood acting as an intermediary between God and man. In Calvinist belief, which deeply affected Scottish thinking, all communal support is lacking.

Individuals, in working out their own salvation, began to resolve the crisis of election by seeking for evidence in their own lives that they were recipients of God's grace; this represented a dilution of Calvin's view of the awesomeness and uncompromising might of God. If their lives appeared faultless, so they argued, perhaps they were saved. If they were successful in the world, perhaps this too was God's sign to them that he had made them his elect. Nevertheless constant vigilance was needed: time-wasting, laziness and conspicuous consumption had to be avoided. To such an extent indeed did this moral attitude take root that in the nineteenth century 'anyone who failed to meet his debts in the business world had to cease forthwith from practising as an elder, and a church member could be denied communion until he had satisfied those to whom he was indebted' (Maclaren, 1983). This close association between, in Maclaren's words, 'spiritual and economic destitution' reflects a wider association of ideas and behaviour that has been called 'capitalistic' and which has had a profound influence in the Protestant world over the last three hundred years.

The most detailed study of the seventeenth-century origins of the relationship between Calvinism and capitalism was conducted by Gordon Marshall (1980), who links interpretations of

Calvinist doctrines with:

> such unambiguously modern capitalistic traits as the desire to expand according to rational principles, the closing of less profitable lines of production in order to expand more profitable lines, the continuous estimation of returns and reinvestment in the areas of highest expected yield, the attempt continually to increase productivity and to utilize labour in the most efficient and profitable manner.

In short, self-discipline and vigilance were the qualities capitalists demanded, both of themselves and their workforce, and these were qualities without which a factory economy would not have been possible.

Marshall quotes extensively from the pastoral writings of seventeenth-century churchmen, whose fulminations, such as the following by James Durham, give us a colourful and reassuringly universal picture of human behaviour. Durham condemns:

> sexual looseness, adultery, lusts and wantonness, and . . . such encouragements to sexual licence as obscene pictures, filthy discourse, drunken or bawdy songs, amorous books and ballads [as well as] excessive mirth, laughter and jollity, indecent conversations, dancing, vain clothing and decoration of the body, extravagant fashions utilizing lace and ribbons, decorating of the face and hair, exposing of the body [especially of the neck and breasts by women], and the use of rings and jewels.

The above extract is a good indication of the value to the historian of collections of sermons and other pastoral writings – those unprepossessing volumes which take up so much shelf space in many local history libraries. Yet they were the predominant form of literature up to the nineteenth century, and through imaginative reading one can recreate the impact they would have had on the original congregations.

Church and community

The previous two sections have considered the significance of religion for the individual, but religion also performs social and communal functions only indirectly related to theological ideas. An ideal opportunity for studying this aspect of religious belief is provided in the highlands, where missionary efforts are responsible for the unexpected phenomenon of co-existing Catholic and Protestant communities. Both churches proselytized in this fertile territory, which the Scottish Society for the Propagation of Christian Knowledge acknowledged to have been neglected. The ready success of the missionaries' efforts

illustrates the strength of the 'great tradition' and the suscepti-
bility of folk cultures to the imposition of outside structures.
Protestant and Catholic belief in these areas thus reflects nothing
about the *intrinsic* character of different settlements – it merely
tells us who got there first. We can, however, study whether the
differing concepts of community held in the two churches have
subsequently affected the way they have developed.

A contrast of this kind has already been drawn in the study of
the urban poor, between the Scots and the numerous Irish
immigrants, of whom it has been said that 'a high proportion
. . . were churchgoers, for it was in their religion that they
found identity and comfort, and in their priests that they found
leadership and community' (Checkland, 1984). A church can
thus be a cohesive social force, and this is particularly true where
it is the only church, with a monopoly on 'truth'. Conversely, a
minority church with threatened values will also tend to
emphasize communal aspects of society, forming a close-knit
group cut off from secularizing influences. In urban Scotland,
evangelical sects and the Roman Catholic church have been alike
in this respect.

Traditionally, however, the Scottish church has approxi-
mated to the 'monopoly of truth' model; as we have seen, the
Church of Scotland did not countenance opposition until well
into the eighteenth century, and in this it merely continued the
practice of its predecessor, the Catholic church in Scotland. One
finds, indeed, an unexpected continuity, focussed on that
symbol of rural unity, the parish church, which, next to the
castle, was the only public building in a neighbourhood. As
such, it performed many social functions. Donaldson (1985)
writes that:

> . . . despite periodic legislation to preserve its sanctity, it was constantly
> used for a wide range of secular purposes, from the fairly respectable
> holding of courts . . . and transaction of other legal business, down to
> less reputable games, dancing and worse: to reconsecrate a church
> polluted *sanguinis vel seminis effusione* [by the spilling of blood or semen]
> was a routine episcopal function. In the absence of any other public
> building, the parish church fulfilled functions which today belong to
> broadcasting, the theatre, the newspaper, the local government offices,
> council chamber, law courts and social centre.

Community through the church was reinforced in many
ways; for example in the use of ritual. In the mass a small object
called the 'pax' or 'paxboard' was 'kissed by everyone,
representing a collective kiss of peace' (Grant, 1984). The same

author considers the view that sinful action was condemned, not as it is today for being morally wrong, but for its potential damage to good neighbourliness. Adultery may perhaps be seen as a sin less for sexual reasons than for its capacity to provoke a feud between husband and lover. It has been argued that this collective social aspect of christianity in which 'the dominant sentiment in human relationships was not obedience to authority, but contract, reverence, loyalty, faith' (Troeltsch, 1969) was peculiarly adapted to a society based on kinship.

This being the case, it is no surprise that certain features of the medieval church were easily transposed to the post-Reformation church. The new communion service, although it 'differed from the mass in many ways . . . retained the traditional sense of collectiveness in the communal singing of psalms, in the liturgy's portrayal of the service as a communal feast, and in the sharing of the consecrated bread and wine (especially when taken from a common cup which perhaps compensated for the reformers' abolition of the paxboard)' (Grant, 1984).

In one sense the reformed church went even further in its emphasis on communal power, for elements within it proposed to 'eliminate the distinction between clergy and laity altogether and vest authority in the community or congregation, of whom the minister was merely the chosen delegate' (Donaldson, 1985). In these democratic circumstances the 'community' would have become one of the highest authorities in the land, albeit an authority founded on a theocratic vision. In the end, of course, the state triumphed over the church, the battle ground being firstly Episcopalianism and then the patronage issue. The feudal classes – the local landowners – were the beneficiaries of this:

. . . they accepted the centralised state . . . Rebellion retreated romantically into the conventicle where it could fairly easily be contained. In the meantime the church itself found new assumptions; it would either support the state or it would, in separating itself from the state, disavow political power altogether. (Makey, 1983)

In so doing, however, it helped to transform, and in the end undermine, the concept of local community.

To conclude the foregoing discussion of religious attitudes, a brief word should be added about sources for the local and family historian. Pre-Reformation material is mainly in Latin and can be studied in depth only by those who know the language. Translations of many records have been published, however, and one can certainly study the works of religious leaders and the surviving records of church courts. On the whole, parochial sources illustrating the communal functions of the church have not survived. Indeed, one must wait until the seventeenth century to find substantial local church records, such as those of the kirk sessions and the higher courts, presbytery and synod. Some extracts from these have been published; the originals are held in the Scottish Record Office and microfilm copies are sometimes available locally. Records of the general assembly of the Church of Scotland were destroyed by fire in 1834, but selections made by various hands prior to that date have been published as the *Acts and Proceedings of the General Assemblies* (Maitland and Bannatyne Club, 1839–45). The records of those churches which seceded from the Church of Scotland and have subsequently been reunited form part of the main church archive in the Scottish Record Office. Evangelical groups outside the Church of Scotland will not have deposited records with the Scottish Record Office, though Episcopalians, Quakers and Methodists have. Newspaper sources may be all that are available for the former. Roman Catholic records are kept in a separate archive centre, at Columbia House, 16 Drummond Place, Edinburgh EH3 6PL. Local history libraries are possible sources of a variety of ephemeral material including, if one is lucky, old copies of parish magazines.

Freemasonry

The past 250 years have seen a weakening of religious feeling and the substitution for it of a variety of secular influences. One development with a foot in both camps is freemasonry, of which it has been said that 'it is in times when religious values are in decline that human anxieties, deprived of God, yearn for esoteric nourishment' (Mellor, 1964); and just as the smallest Scottish town will usually have its nineteenth-century church, so it will also feature the lodge buildings of freemasons and similar orders. Scotland has boasted a disproportionate number of lodges – 25 per cent of the British total. To the family historian the movement is particularly interesting, for the esotericism of freemasonry is based upon a mystic brotherhood 'creating for itself a family when the legitimate family finds its sap drying up', again in the words of Mellor (1964).

It is no surprise therefore that freemasonry developed as the kin-based society declined in the eighteenth century, taking its inspiration, like the moderates in the Church of Scotland, from deism, which attempted to reconcile rational and scientific principles with religious belief. Deistic views were parodied by the eighteenth-century evangelical divine, John Witherspoon, as follows:

> I believe that the universe is a huge machine, wound up from everlasting and that I myself am a little glorious piece of clockwork . . . I believe that there is no ill in the universe . . . that those things vulgarly called *sins* are only *errors* in judgement, and foils to set off the beauty of Nature . . . that . . . even the devils themselves (if there be any) shall finally be happy, so that Judas Iscariot is by this time a glorified saint. (Quoted in Drummond and Bulloch, 1973)

The eighteenth-century origins of freemasonry are sometimes obscured by the 'craze for antedating which plagues masonic history', as Mellor calls it. One particular form of freemasonry *was* much older, but it bore little resemblance to the philosophical system developed in that century. In medieval times, freemasons were qualified stone workers who used passwords allowing them to be recognized and employed; in other words, they belonged to trade incorporations or guilds. The published minute books of early Scottish lodges confirm that 'the society at this time, whatever it may have become later, was strictly of an operative character' (Wallace-James, n.d.), concerned with apprenticeships and masonic trademarks. In the seventeenth century, honorary masons (usually versed in architecture) were admitted, and with the erosion of the traditional trade monopolies the latter gradually supplanted the operatives altogether, setting freemasonry on its new road, with what Mellor calls its 'speculative conception' – a unique blend of optimism and mysticism later to be copied by other groups. This was potent enough to infect the friendly societies discussed in Chapter Five with similar principles of brotherhood and secrecy. The family historian can make an interesting study of the subsequent development of this symbolic (male) 'family' to see what points of common ground it has with real families and with the kin-based societies of earlier times. Minute books may well be closed to outsiders, although some early ones have been published, as have the histories of several of the lodges.

Literary culture

One of the most effective ways of getting inside the minds of ancestors is to read the same literature which they read. There is a triple advantage in this. First, one can identify the influences which formed their thinking; as suggested at the start of this chapter, most of our ideas are second-hand. Secondly, a good deal of literature is itself a mirror held up to contemporary society, interpreting (for it and for us) its thoughts and ideas; the best literature, of course, goes further, and creates new sensitivities and perceptions so potent that people come to believe that they have arisen from their own consciousness. Thirdly, literature, especially of the more popular kind such as newspapers and magazines, reinforces and emphasizes existing values and prejudices.

Reading in pre-Reformation times more often than not meant religious reading, along with a little philosophy, classical literature and law. Before the advent of printing, which was mainly a post-Reformation development, all books had to be written by hand; churchmen were the only ones with the necessary skill and time to do this. Popular culture was therefore entirely oral. Libraries too were restricted to religious institutions – monasteries, universities and cathedrals (as at Aberdeen, Brechin, Elgin and Glasgow). At the time of the Reformation John Spottiswoode spoke of 'bibliothecks destroied, the volumes of the Fathers, Councells and other books of humane learning, with the Registers of the Church, cast into the streets, afterwards gathered in heapes and consumed with fire' (quoted in Kelly, 1966). As a result only 92 manuscripts and a somewhat larger number of printed works survive from medieval Scottish libraries. They are listed in Durkan and Ross (1961).

After the Reformation, the products of the printing press 'ranged the whole gamut from children's ABCs to learned works of law and theology' (Kelly, 1966). A bibliography of these early printed books is J.G. Aldis's *List of Books Printed in Scotland before 1700*, published by the National Library of Scotland (1970). The first catalogue of the Advocates Library (which later became the National Library of Scotland) was produced in 1692 and listed 3000 titles; the second, produced in 1742, listed 25,000. Theological works maintained their prestigious position: a parish library established in Campbeltown in the late eighteenth century is described as 'consisting of religious tracts and sacred writings . . . Books of controversy (which are read with such avidity by the common people in Scotland) are carefully excluded from the collection, as the fruit which they produce is bitter' (from a Statistical Account, quoted in Kelly, 1966). In contrast to this view stands that of James Kirkwood (c.1650–c.1708) who envisaged a free public library in each parish, arguing that it was God's will that we should 'search out and know all his wonderful works'. Seventy-seven such libraries were established in the highlands and islands between 1704 and 1708, but most had disappeared by the end of the century.

Less ambitious in concept was the endowed library at Innerpeffray in Perthshire, whose list of users included a barber, bookseller, army captain, cooper, dyer, dyer's apprentice, factor, farmer, flaxdresser, gardener, glover, mason, merchant, miller, minister, quarrier, schoolmaster, servant, shoemaker, student, smith, surgeon, surgeon's apprentice, tailor, watchmaker, weaver and wright. It is lists such as this which give credence to the widely-held view that the eighteenth century was an age of high literacy (in reading, not writing) among the Scots of all classes, a literacy which is partially attributable to the successful introduction of parish schools in 1696.

It was shortly after this date that secular libraries began to appear, two distinct types becoming prevalent in the eighteenth century. The first was the subscription library of which the earliest was established at Leadhills by lead miners in 1741, followed by that at Wanlochhead, also for miners, in 1756. Antimony miners at Westerkirk, Dumfriesshire as well as weavers and other working men from Langloan, Lanarkshire adopted the idea also, and one can study their catalogues to assess the view that 'the Scottish working-class radicals set out to develop a wide-ranging counter-culture in opposition to the one being imposed by their "masters" by means of Presbyterian sermons, the didactic novel, lectures on political economy and newspapers' (Young, 1979).

The same organizational principle applied to 'gentlemen's' subscription libraries such as those founded in Dumfries (c.1745), Kelso (1751) and Ayr (1762), but the emphasis of the reading matter was upon 'belles lettres, history, biography, travel, science and such fiction as was regarded as of literary merit: in short, what was commonly called "polite literature"' (Kelly, 1966).

Circulating libraries (also known as 'entertaining libraries') on the other hand were run by booksellers as commercial enterprises, the profits from subscriptions accruing to them alone (Edinburgh, Glasgow and Aberdeen provide eighteenth-century examples). Also, in contrast to subscription libraries, they concentrated on the light reading – novels and romances – of which Robert Wodrow complained in 1728: 'all the villainous profane and obscene books and playes printed at London [were] lent out, for an easy price, to young boyes, servant weemin of the better sort, and gentlemen, and vice and obscenity dreadfully propagated' (Wodrow, 1842–3). Wodrow would have been equally dismissive of the street literature of the day, particularly in the form of the 'chapbook', a little stitched tract sold by itinerant 'chapmen'. The subjects of chapbooks could be travel, biography or religion, but most popular of all were gruesome tales such as that of 'Sawney Bean', the purported cannibal in Dumfriesshire. Their successors are the nineteenth-century 'penny dreadful' magazines and, in our own day, the tabloid newspapers. Unsuccessful attempts have been made to dabble in the exegesis of chapbook texts, which miss the point that such tales were composed or reworked with only two criteria in mind – readability and titillation – and we should no more expect to find the 'truth' in them than we would in a modern tabloid newspaper. A more profitable approach would be to study the difference in what excited psychological curiosity then, in the nineteenth century, and now. A few chapbooks may be found in local history libraries, but the best collection is in the National Library of Scotland. A general bibliography of chapbook literature is John Cheap's *The Chapman's Library: the Scottish Chap Literature of the Last Century Classified*, published by Porteous Brothers/J. Ross & Co. in 1877 (3 volumes).

The nineteenth century saw itself as the age of self-improvement, exemplified by mechanics' institutes and similar bodies. There were 80 institutions of this kind in Scotland by the middle of the century, mostly in the central belt. The original objective of the institutes was technical education: the very first, the Edinburgh School of Arts, aimed to instruct working men 'in such branches of physical science as are of practical advantage in their several trades'. Mechanics' institutes were founded by both workers and employers and became agents for cultural as well as technical education, as the catalogues of their libraries show. They did tend however to avoid controversial political and religious issues, for the working men most attracted to the movement were skilled craftsmen who had most to benefit from the *status quo* of the prevailing values of the time. As well as libraries, the institutes and their successors ran museums, classes and lecture programmes, posters and syllabuses for which are often to be found in scrapbooks in local history library collections.

The explosion of popular literature in the nineteenth century (of newspapers and magazines as well as books) is documented in detail in Richard D. Altick's *The English Common Reader*, published by the University of Chicago Press, 1957. One illustration of this growth in popular reading matter is the fact that the third catalogue of the Advocates' Library, dated 1849, lists 148,000 printed works. A good number of these books should be borrowable through your local library by virtue of the inter-library loan system linking all United Kingdom libraries. Many of the magazines and newspapers can be consulted in the National Library of Scotland (but see also page 22–3). Through the century, men and women became exposed to an increasingly wide range of cultural experiences from home and abroad, and this fact, coupled with the dramatic advances in scientific discovery, threw traditional culture into turmoil. The local community no longer looked in on itself, and it became increasingly difficult to talk even of a Scottish culture as distinct from a British culture.

Growing literacy is reflected in the rise of the public library. The Select Committee on Public Libraries reported in 1849 and led to the Public Libraries (Ireland and Scotland) Act 1853 and the Public Libraries (Scotland) Act 1854, empowering local councils to raise a penny rate for the establishment of libraries. The consolidating Public Libraries (Scotland) Act 1867 came at a time when only one library authority had been set up in response to the previous legislation; the new act permitted library authorities to be formed by all the different types of burgh authority by that time operating in Scotland, and also by parishes. The first of these parish libraries was at Tarves in Aberdeenshire (they should not be confused with the church parish libraries such as that at Campbeltown noted above). Despite even this new act, there were still only 12 Scottish library authorities in 1886, mostly in industrial towns of the central belt, and it took the benefactions of the Scots expatriate, Andrew Carnegie to effect any radical alteration. In the words of Kelly (1973), Carnegie 'sedulously avoided any kind of poor relief, preferring to invest his money in universities, libraries, museums, parks and other institutions which would yield a long-term benefit in improving the condition of the people.' In

1887 only 8 per cent of Scotland's population had access to public libraries. By 1914, thanks to Carnegie, the figure was 50 per cent.

The catalogues of all the types of libraries mentioned in this section often survive, the most likely location being present-day local history libraries. Inventories of private book collections often appear in testaments; the libraries of great houses, like their collections of paintings, were frequently listed and kept among family papers. Catalogues can be used to recreate the social and intellectual climate of any period, and in some ways the 'poorer' the literature, the more it will tell of the day-to-day prejudices and preoccupations of the author and his or her contemporaries. One reservation about catalogues should be mentioned – that they do not always show what people were reading, but rather what other people thought they *ought* to be reading; this may, however, be instructive in itself. For example, one should take with a pinch of salt Samuel Smiles's romantic description of the Westerkirk library: '. . . we are told that it is a common thing for the Eskdale shepherd to take a book under his plaid to the hillside – a volume of Shakespeare, Prescott or Macaulay – and read it there, under the blue sky, with his sheep and the green hills before him' (Smiles, 1861–2).

Simpler than using library catalogues is to take advantage of a local history library's local author sections. Most library authorities collect the works of writers connected with their locality. Such authors, of course, were not read exclusively in their own neighbourhood, but they often commented on local issues; writers of fiction frequently drew inspiration from local landscape and character. Most library collections of this kind will give a good cross-section of Scottish writing over the last three centuries.

Chapter Seven

FAMILY, CHURCH AND STATE

The state might seem to be at the furthest remove from the interests of family historians, but in truth this is far from being the case. For the state has throughout history impinged upon the family group. Conversely, it has also offered opportunities for, and even laid obligations on, groups to participate in its processes. This last chapter investigates some of the areas of contact between family and state within three broad categories: social welfare, local politics and the law.

An initial problem is to define what is meant by a 'state'. One can enumerate its activities – maintaining internal order, operating public services, resolving political conflicts, conciliating between conflicting demands, controlling territory, defending it against external aggression, and ensuring stability while adapting to new conditions – but in many respects these objectives are much the same as in small 'primitive' communities usually considered to be without a state. These objectives also overlap with those of *society*, with its basic function of survival or self-maintenance. The state's function within this wider strategy is to bind together the widest groupings of individuals and communities, imbuing them with common purposes and values, just as a family does on a smaller scale within its kin group, through ethical systems, ceremonies, symbols and behaviour which 'both explain and justify power' (Curtis, 1968). All social institutions – families and states alike – are power systems for ordering and directing their members into certain channels or categories. Power has been defined as the 'degree to which an individual or group can get its own way in a social relationship' (Haralambos, 1965). The state is but one configuration of this, differentiated mainly by the geographic scale of its operation and its overt exercise of force within and without its boundaries. Its traditional weakness in Scotland makes the latter a particularly interesting theatre in which to study its ambiguous relationship with the systems of church, family and society.

Social welfare

In the last couple of decades, the regalia and records of the great nineteenth-century friendly societies such as the Ancient Order of Foresters have been finding their way into the collections of local museums and record offices, as a declining membership leads finally to a decision to wind up branches. This trend bears witness to a profound alteration in the relationship between community and state which has taken place in the last fifty years in the area of social welfare.

This is not to say that the state took no interest in the matter before. Indeed, the first legislation dates from 1424 when it was enacted that no person between 14 and 70 should be allowed to beg; others were issued with badges permitting them to do so. Pronouncements of this kind from the state were not implemented by the state itself, but directed towards local authorities, such as they were, who obeyed parts, ignored others and directly contravened others, as Mitchison (1974) notes. The important Poor Law Act of 1574 introduced a distinction that was to dog poor law practice up to the Second World War, between the able-bodied unemployed ('strong and idle beggars') and the destitute (the 'crippled, sick, impotent and weak folk'). Newly-appointed justices of the peace were to produce lists of the poor and the parishioners assessed for their upkeep. Another principle destined to be long-lived was that providing for the transference of a pauper to his or her parish of birth. The pauper walked, but was issued with certificates allowing him or her to pass from parish to parish during the journey and to get temporary relief. The family genealogist, however, who looks forward to consulting lists of the poor and certificates issued by justices will be sorely disappointed. This first essay at state relief existed in name only, and justice of the peace records are almost non-existent before the eighteenth century.

In the meantime, responsibility for poor relief passed, in rural areas, to kirk sessions and heritors, who became joint administrators. The abandonment of the government system, and partial reversion to the practices of medieval times, reflects the weakness of the state and its reliance on the church's institutional and ethical structures to cater for many areas of human need. In this case there was an attempt at collaboration, sources of funds for relief including a parish assessment or land tax, income from bequests or mortifications, as well as church door collections. The last-named was by far the most popular method, for it involved no legal obligation – an indication of the suspicion in which the state was still held. The only sanction available to the 'crafty clergy' was the practice of 'handing round the ladle: this exerted moral suasion as the contents of the ladle on its long handle were visible to all' (Cage, 1981). Kirk session records of the seventeenth to nineteenth centuries contain tables of recipients of relief, especially those known as the 'occasional poor' as opposed to the 'regular poor' – yet another distinction which continued in poor law practice up to the Second World War, though latterly terms such as 'cyclical unemployment' and 'structural employment' were used. Heritors' records, kept in the Scottish Record Office, deal mainly with the administration of relief.

Burgh provision was somewhat more complicated. In Glasgow, for instance, the town council, the church, the incorporated trades and the merchants' house (their guild) all contributed; and it was mainly in burghs that poorhouses were erected. Poorhouses, called by a variety of names, including 'hospital' and 'charity workhouse' provided for the very old and the very young, as well as the sick, but only to a small extent for the unemployed. The distinction between unemployment and poverty was maintained, and the unemployed in most cases felt that 'to be on the parish' was shameful, preferring the dignity of insurance through friendly society membership.

Such ideas persisted even with the onset of industrialization, though they became increasingly undermined by the prevalence of structural (i.e. longterm) unemployment which is a feature of an industrial economy. Attempts were made, notably by Thomas Chalmers, to adapt the parochial system of relief for urban areas and at the same time maintain what was seen as its most valuable feature: voluntary contribution. This was prized for the encouragement it gave to the habit of economy, the kindness of relatives, the sympathy of the poor for one another and the sympathy of the wealthy for the poor. So strong indeed was this feeling that there was an attempt in 1824 to introduce a Poor in Scotland Relief Bill intended to abolish legal assessment to 'revive a spirit of independence among the poor'. The theory espoused by its supporters, popular in the nineteenth century, was that of the *laissez faire* state, which provided merely a legal framework for the free play of market forces. Charity provided a safety-net. Cage (1981) notes that 'the existence of charities and the form they assume depend to a large extent upon the development of the market economy'. What the supporters of *laissez faire* did not comprehend, however, was that the establishment of a legal framework to permit any kind of individual freedom paradoxically involved an extension of state power, and this paradox lies at the heart of the relationship between the state and the welfare of its citizens over the last century and a half.

The problems faced by the traditional system of support from family, church and community were investigated in depth during the first half of the nineteenth century, in the Scottish Report (1818), for example, prepared for the Select Committee on the English Poor Law by the Church of Scotland. Seven hundred and seventeen returns were received from parish ministers; the originals are lost, but abstracts are preserved in the *Third Report from the Select Committee on the Poor Law with an Appendix Containing Returns from the General Assembly of the Church of Scotland*. In 1838 the General Assembly was again asked by the government to study poor relief for the years 1835–7; their report was published in 1839. 1844 saw the first report of an entirely secular body – the *Report from Her Majesty's Commissioners for Inquiry into the Administration and Practical Operation of the Poor Law in Scotland* – symptomatic of a shift of influence from church to state, further reflected in the establishment the following year of parochial boards. These were based on traditional parish areas, but the church had only nominal representation, the heritors being the dominant group.

The most radical innovation of 1845 was the superimposition of a national body, the Scottish Board of Supervision (later to be changed to the Local Government Board) to oversee the work of the parochial boards. It marked the first *direct* involvement of the state in the administration of welfare services. It also marked the introduction of the state's typical machinery: the bureaucracy. The development of this has been considered in the form of five main stages. First there is the existence of a social problem, exacerbated in our case by such phenomena as the cholera epidemic of 1831–2 which 'being a waterborne disease, attacked all, notably the middle classes with their better water supplies and struck fear into the hearts of the governors, local and national' (Fraser, 1973). The second stage is the appointment of an inspectorate to enforce compliance with the new legislation, when the voluntary principle is found wanting; the appointment of the Board of Supervision represents this stage, as does the contemporary introduction of the factory inspectorate. Thirdly, the persistent and powerful voices of professional and technical experts provide a further momentum towards intervention and superintendence; the professional expert also tends to be a scientist, whether in natural or social sciences, and his or her witness gradually pushes to one side the moral and religious approach to social problems; as the state's power advances, so does that of the church recede. A fourth stage marks a disillusionment with grand gestures in favour of a slow process of change and regulation. Finally, support and research services bring the expert into a position where his or her judgement appears to be more valuable than that of the politicians, so that discretionary executive powers are devolved upon the former.

This process can be traced over the last 150 years throughout the whole gamut of what we now regard as the state's social services: national health, education, employment, housing, town planning, national insurance and welfare benefits. This is a far cry from how the doyen of nineteenth-century liberalism, Samuel Smiles, saw its role, as 'negative and restrictive rather than positive and active'. The huge growth in the number of employees in local and central government and associated scientific and technical services, and their rise in status from the clerks of the beginning of the century to the decision-makers of today, can be traced in the stories of many recent ancestors and their families.

By the end of the nineteenth century, Smiles's argument would anyway have appeared somewhat ingenuous. The *Times* of August 1902 (quoted in Fraser, 1973) makes the point forcibly:

> The individualist town councillor will walk along the municipal pavement, lit by municipal gas and cleansed by municipal brooms with municipal water, and seeing by the municipal clock in the municipal market that he is too early to meet his children coming from the municipal school, hard by the county lunatic asylum and municipal hospital . . .

The theme of 'municipal socialism' will be taken up again later in this chapter.

When the *Times* article appeared, municipalism was already under threat from a new stage in the bureaucratic process, namely a tendency towards central government control. It is true that the local power-base of parochial boards was retained by their successors, the parish councils, established after 1894 with a wide electoral franchise, but these bodies had only been in existence for a dozen or so years when a series of statutes introduced by the Liberal government of 1905–15 laid the foundations of the welfare state. The main measures taken were the 1905 Unemployed Workmen Act, authorizing payments to local distress committees who provided public works schemes during the depression of that decade, the Old Age Pension Act of 1908 which gave pensions to all over the age of 70 and introduced the principle that payment of benefits need not bear any direct relationship to the contributions paid, and the National Insurance Act of 1911 which prescribed compulsory insurance for all workers earning less than £160 per year. The insurance cover included sickness benefit, disability benefit, maternity benefit and doctors' fees, as well as unemployment benefit to workers in seven occupations regarded as being particularly vulnerable to boom and slump. An interesting feature of the act was that it was administered not by the government but by insurance companies, friendly societies and trade unions, which were collectively known as 'approved societies'. Suspicion of government and a pride and independence were traditional attitudes which were very slow to change; only the mass unemployment of the 1930s and the collective endeavours of the Second World War brought an appreciable shift in feelings. There is a great opportunity for the family historian to investigate these attitudes through living relatives –the stigma of being on the parish, the reluctance to accept any relief seen as charitable and an unwillingness for one's family to be the responsibility of anyone outside the kin group.

The crisis of the inter-war years contributed to the demise of the parish councils in 1929. Their responsibilities were transferred to county councils and the town councils of the larger towns. 'The historic Scottish parish was now a religious and registration area: nothing more', notes Harvie (1981). In the 'land fit for heroes' of post-World War One optimism, the unemployed had been granted statutory entitlement to outdoor relief (an extension of a scheme of out-of-work donations for demobilized soldiers). Perhaps these soldiers, unlike their fathers, felt that the state owed them something for their sufferings; at any rate, applications for relief far outweighed available funds and, as Harvie again notes: 'depression-struck parishes found themselves imposing crippling burdens on local industries simply to meet relief payments, a factor which tended to accelerate industrial closures.' Attempted solutions continued to be bedevilled by old distinctions between unemployment and poverty, or, put another way, between 'insurance' and 'charity'. The distinction was, for example, enshrined in the 1927 system of *standard insurance benefit* related to a paid contribution; and *transitional benefit* drawn as of right and unrelated to contributions paid. Transitional benefit was little more than a revamped poor relief system, with the single advantage that it lacked the opprobrium attached to the latter.

One very interesting development of the period, established in the Unemployed Workers' Dependants Act 1921 and the Unemployment Act of 1934, was the acceptance for the first time of the principle of taking dependents into account when assessing need. The 1934 act in particular, with its machinery for means testing, was a belated acknowledgement by the state of the importance of the family as an institution, albeit one made in a desperate attempt to cut the amount of benefit paid to individuals in a bankrupt and depressed economy. Paradoxically, however, the act can equally be seen as a recognition of the devaluation of the family in modern industrial society. For it made the family a *responsibility* of the state, suggesting that it was no longer in a position to look after its own – a concept which would have been inconceivable two centuries earlier. The weakness of the family in industrial society has been attributed to various factors: the separation of home and workplaces, the creation of new jobs for women and the decline of the Christian ethic which 'consecrated the family through . . . imagery of God as Father, albeit an awe-inspiring Father whose sometimes harsh treatment of his children was to be accepted without question' (Farmer, 1970). Though the same author notes that 'families can and do develop their own rituals such as birthday gatherings, picnic outings to particular places which may become a form of pilgrimage with quasi-religious integrative effects for the family', these tend to lack the moral strength of previous convictions and dissipate the cohesive strength within the family group. The trauma of the 1930s therefore raises many profound questions about the relationship between individuals, church, family and state – all questions which the family historian can pursue through oral interviews.

The Unemployment Act of 1934 set up a national Unemployment Assistance Board which paid benefits to all workers no longer entitled to six-month insurance cover, guaranteed through a compulsory insurance scheme. It therefore effectively removed all able-bodied adults from the shelter of the poor law, which once again, as so often before, was intended as the refuge of the unemployable. Recently established bodies known as public assistance committees, administered by local authorities, performed this 'all-embracing, last resort general assistance service' (Frazer, 1973).

An even more radical view of the state vis-à-vis its citizens was put forward in the Beveridge Report of the war years. It is marked for its spirit of 'universalism', in tune with the exigencies of the war operation, and for its re-interpretation of freedom as 'freedom *from*' rather than 'freedom *to*': specifically freedom from the five ills of want, disease, ignorance, squalor and idleness. A series of post-war acts implemented the Beveridge philosophy: the Family Allowance Act 1945, the National Insurance Act 1946 (providing for unemployment benefit, sickness benefit and old age pensions), the National Health Service (Scotland) Act 1947 and the National Assistance Act 1948. The last-named abolished the final remnants of the poor law and the associated poorhouses, drastically curtailing the role of local government in social welfare provision. These acts also heralded a period of 30 years of consensus on the relative responsibilities of family and state – a consensus which has only recently been challenged.

Studying the written sources of the last hundred years of social welfare depends upon getting access to the local government records of the period. Where these survive (as they mostly do), they have been inherited by the present local government authorities – the regional and district councils. Broadly speaking, the regions inherited the records of the old county councils (including the various bodies such as parochial boards, parish councils and district councils whose powers were transferred to or delegated from the county councils). The district councils of today, not to be confused with the older district councils of pre-1974, inherited the records of the town councils.

It is more difficult to be precise about the current location of the records. Some are held by public libraries, some are looked after by university libraries, some are deposited in specially-established local record offices, a few are in the Scottish Record Office and a few more languish in inaccessible cellars. Those local authorities whose archives fall into the last category should be constantly pressured by family and local historians to put their house in order and to take serious responsibility for the unique material in their trust. If you want to use the records in your own area, your best course of action is to ask at your local library who should be able to tell you where they are situated.

Failing this, contact the West Register House of the Scottish Record Office where a comprehensive locations file is maintained.

The records themselves are full of interest. Parochial board and parish council minute books contain much more detailed analysis of individual cases than do the earlier kirk session minutes. As a bonus, poorhouse records sometimes survive; their day-books give a detailed picture of day-to-day life in these institutions. Details of meals can be obtained: for example, a proposed New Year dinner in the East Lothian Combination Poor's House for 1866 comprised '1½ pints rice soup, 6 oz fine bread, 1 meat pie and 4 oz plum pudding and for supper 6 oz fine bread, 8 oz currant loaf, 4 oz cheese, 1 orange and 1 pint tea.'

The development of social welfare over the centuries sets a pattern that can be followed in other areas. Schooling, for example, moved from being the responsibility of the church to that of one of the local school boards (after 1872); responsibility then shifted to the county-wide education authorities and then to county councils in 1929. A change of perspective is noted by Littlejohn (1963), talking of the disappearance of the county parish:

> Rights, which an individual once possessed by virtue of his membership of this unit, he now possesses by virtue of his membership of either the County or the State. It is now the duty of the County to educate him, for instance, and the duty of the State to aliment him should he lose his job . . . He is no longer so dependent on other members of the parish economically nor for recreation. His rights and obligations as regards employment are no longer arranged between his employer and himself. Even the social horizons of the children have been enormously widened by their being sent to schools in towns after the age of thirteen.

Once again an erosion of family responsibility is in evidence here. The traditional parish church school had as its aim to 'give all people enough literacy to read the Bible and to inculcate a set of rules about acceptable social behaviour' (Smout, 1986), and an entry in Tranent kirk session quoted by Cage (1981) 'after hearing 17 poor scholars read, decided that Peggy Hinly should be struck from the list [of pupils] as she could read fairly well' – shows the limits of its aspirations. But in its role as moral tutor to the young, the church was finely attuned to the traditional function of the family in introducing children to the social habits and standards of society. Local government schools, on the other hand, have progressively abandoned the moral stance in favour of a philosophy of mental development, in conflict to some extent with family values. As Farmer (1970) says: 'In less complex societies the old gained status because they were considered wise; age in our society brings little status, for wisdom has been dethroned by technological know-how, which is largely the prerogative of the young.' Changing patterns of education can be studied in the minute books of the different authorities noted above, which are now in the care of regional councils. School log books from 1872, some still held in the schools, give a detailed day-to-day picture of school life, and of the attitudes of teachers.

Local politics

Scottish local politics began with the parish, which grew out of the kirk session. It dealt with local taxation, with the condition of roads, maintenance of the peace and the upkeep of church, manse and school. 'Its hero' declares Makey (1983) 'was the heritor'.

The heritor was a different animal from his baronial ancestor locked into a network of kinship relationships, as investigated in Chapter Four. Brown (1986) suggests that the Reformation 'forced lay people to question their family loyalties', and that the world of the blood feud was then 'turned upside down as the corporate society of kinsmen, friends, dependents and ancestors was replaced with the awful isolation of the individual sinner standing before the judgement of God. In this new world men inherited nothing from their parents, not even their feuds . . .'

The vacuum was filled by the state, which found ready allies in landowners prepared to exploit the commercial potential of estates, where their ancestors had seen only units of jurisdiction and fodder for dependents. Prerequisites of successful commerce are stability and a powerful, widely-based law; the landowners or heritors undertook to support these, sitting as justices of the peace, commissioners of supply (for local tax collection and road maintenance) and parish elders. Their hegemony was absolute. As landowners they alone had parliamentary franchise: 'the landed interest alone should be represented in Parliament, for they only have an interest in the country' wrote Lord Braxfield in the 1790s. As employers, they effectively controlled the life of their tenants. 'The landlord', noted Saunders (1950) 'felt himself responsible for the land rather than the locality, and the performance of this increasingly private and technical duty meant interference with and control of a more dependent rural population who had to be fitted into a more imperious scheme of things.'

With industrialization the unified power-base of the landowners was to some degree broken, and by mid-Victorian times analysts have claimed to see a four-pronged power-block: capitalist bourgeoisie, landowners (who themselves were increasingly investing capital, especially after the introduction of new safeguards for capital provided by limited liability legislation), industrialists and the urban gentry, consisting of professionals and intellectuals. Because these different groups did not share absolutely the same interests, we find the emergence of local political parties during this period.

In the twentieth century a further shift has taken place in the control of local government, with a prominent role being taken by what S. and O. Checkland (1984) call the 'shopocracy' of small business men and retailers. The great capitalists, particularly those associated with the free church, had seen it as their civic duty to take a leading role in local government in the nineteenth century. They were the leading inspiration for the 'municipal socialism' which originated in Glasgow, their motivation 'a combination of civic pride and exasperation at the inefficiency of private enterprise' (Smout, 1986). Glasgow was the first town to appoint a Medical Officer of Health, in 1863, and in 1866 an Improvement Trust was founded with the remit to demolish slums, though, it has been noted, with less enthusiasm to build something in their place. Nevertheless, Glasgow served as a model, not only for the other great cities of Britain, but for the numerous tiny town councils (a population of as little as 700 could support a town council in Scotland).

One might have expected the great entrepreneurs to have responded to the challenges of twentieth-century local government as they did to those of the nineteenth, but on the whole this was not the case. Although there have been extensive additions to local government powers at certain times, such as those noted earlier in the chapter – and one could add others, such as the Housing and Town Planning Act 1919 (Addison's Act) which imposed a *duty* on local authorities to make good the housing deficiency through council house building – a combination of the need for the technical expertise of officials in an increasingly complex world with the greater degree of central government direction (in giving grants for instance) has made local government unattractive to the powerful and ambitious.

The municipal socialism of the late nineteenth century permit-ted the illusion of sturdy independence and originality, flatter-ing to the self-image of the entrepreneur. The more serious municipalization of the 1920s would have been less to their taste.

What of the rest of the population, who were not part of the small élite who actively participated in local government? Before the eighteenth century, we know little about their political views and aspirations; perhaps the majority had none, so remote were they from the practice or potential practice of power. The first popular movement was led by artisans and middle class liberals from the small towns, instrumental in setting up the Scottish Friends of the People in 1792. A radical edge was provided by hand-loom weavers who 'wished to reorder society in terms of the equality and fraternity which worked in the intimacy of their own circle' (Saunders, 1950).

Civil unrest was a feature of the early decades of the nineteenth century, including the famous and abortive Scottish insurrection of 1820 described in detail in P. Berresford Ellis and Mac A' Ghobhainn's, *The Scottish Insurrection of 1820*, published by Gollancz (1970). Extensions of parliamentary franchise were granted in 1832, 1868 and 1884, by which time virtually all adult males were enfranchised. A succession of measures also provided electorates for the mushrooming plethora of local authorities, each with their different character. School boards, for example, attracted rival sectarian candidates from the different churches.

The popular national movement of the mid-century was Chartism, which in the words of Smout (1986) 'emphasized the need for working-class self-improvement through charities and temperance societies as much as the need for franchise reform.' Moreover, Chartism was an attenuated movement deprived of the enfranchised middle classes, who distanced themselves from their erstwhile working-class allies, buying property and associating themselves with the dominant interests of a state which 'had a responsibility to protect its owners against the "jealous" ' (S. and O. Checkland, 1984). The interests of the middle class were served by the Liberal Party, composed of upper-class Whigs, middle-class radicals (evangelical and pro-temperance) and the so-called 'Lib-Labs' affected by socialist ideas of state involvement in the welfare of its citizens.

The break-up of this coalition in the late nineteenth century opened the door to the rise of the Labour Party, also favoured by a change in attitude amongst working-class men:

> By the turn of the century . . . contemporaries claimed to discern the passing of the sturdy artisan of the Victorian era as working men turned from debating societies, geological rambling clubs and self-education to football and music halls . . . (Hutchison, 1974)

A new-found self-confidence in their own solidarity and the value of their own traditions, born of a hundred years of industrial experience, was a root cause of the abandonment of deferential habits and of the self-improving morality borrowed from the middle classes.

Contributory factors can also be sought in the economic organization of cities: Briggs (1968) has analysed political development according to the range of occupations available, the size of industrial undertakings, the extent of economic mobility and vulnerability to fluctuation. Scotland's one-sided and sluggish economy explains much about its polarization of class and politics.

Political allegiances, however, have not been particularly strong in local politics. The municipal socialism of nineteenth-century Glasgow, for example, was effected without allegiance to any party ticket, and it was not until 1933 that the Labour Party took control of Glasgow Town Council. Elsewhere, the 'independents' ran most town and county councils up to reorganization in 1974 and are only now being progressively ousted in the rural areas.

What Smout (1986) calls socialism 'based on moral fervour rather than socialist analysis' was a distinctively Scottish product, drawing much of its strength from Calvinist thought (Scotland witnessed the phenomenon of socialist Sunday schools). Its belief that the 'future was in [one's] own hands and immediately improvable' inspired leaders such as John Wheatley, Tom Johnston and John Maclean. Nationalism until recently was an intellectual stimulus rather than a mass popular movement and a distinctive brand of conservatism developed in the highlands, where the domination of great sporting estates had and still has a stranglehold on the local economy.

There are many themes in local politics which the family historian might like to explore. All political activity can be seen in terms of conflict: 'organized dispute about power and its use' is one definition of this. Conflict can be constructive, and political institutions can be seen as both a means of mediating among different interest groups and of relating these groups to the community as a whole. One could look at the 'social myths' necessary in the forging of common purposes: successful myths are those which allow different groups to put different glosses on them whilst still believing that their views are identical. Another option is to look at the sociology of politics – at, for example, the political parties and their functions in the local community. Harvie (1981) speaks of the local party structure of the Labour Party 'with its newspapers, choirs, theatre groups and cycling clubs'. Mass membership of political parties was common up to the end of the 1940s, since which time it has progressively decreased. Harvie suggests that 'in the 1950s there were probably not more than 500 regular Labour activists in the whole of Scotland.'

Minute books of local political parties may well be difficult to get hold of. Many will have been destroyed or lost, and where they survive the parties concerned may not be too keen on seeing them used by others. Newspapers and oral historical records can help to fill this gap.

The Law

In trying to reach a definition of a state, one element that must be rated of importance is the making and execution of laws. This is not to say that without a state there are no laws, but in such 'primitive' societies there is no legislature (laws being established by custom) and no formal authority of enforcement. Features of primitive law survive in later legal systems, and are particularly interesting in the family historical context in that they most commonly relate to family law. This is because primitive law has its roots in the social organization of the family and the clan, which have survived as enclaves within later social structures. W.G. Sumner (1959) typifies the primitive method as 'folkways' – the group way of doing things and of solving problems, reinforced and 'legalized' by social approbation. Even today, no legal system can survive without a degree of consensus as to methods of resolving disputes, of preventive channeling to prevent disputes arising and of allocating authority; in short what Cotterell (1984) calls 'cohesion based on shared values and outlook among average members of the same society.'

Another feature of primitive law is its encouragement of private justice, as in the blood feuds discussed in Chapter Four. One can also see a similar concept at work in early Scottish court practices such as the summoning of 'compurgatores' – friends and kinsmen of the accused and plaintiff, who swore for him and with him; not, as today, as witnesses of an event, but as witnesses to his character. Equally odd to our eyes is the trial by ordeal (hot iron or water) and the duel, in which the accused was forced to fight his accuser. Innes (1872) notes caustically that 'it seems not to have revolted our forefathers to see the weak man obliged to fight the strong man who wished to strip him of his inheritance' but the practice immediately seems more logical if one takes into account the strong belief at that time in perpetual divine intervention.

Primitive law is supplanted by archaic law among settled agriculturalists. Courts and court officials arise, but not professional lawyers. Parties appear in court in person and the law is 'simple, observed and applied rather than interpreted' notes Robertson (1977). There are also signs of literacy in archaic law, for example in the writing of charters; in primitive law nothing is written. Scotland between the years 1100 and 1400 passed through this phase, and the written law books of this period make fascinating reading for the family historian, as they contain so many unexpected illustrations of the very different position then held by the kin group in legal theory. These old law books have been published and can be easily borrowed through your local library. Details are given in the notes to this chapter.

One essential new element in archaic law is the presence of the state, standing detached from kin and community and subjecting them to unprecedented strains. The crucial issue (understandably enough in an agricultural society) is land and its inheritance. Land is not only finite, it is also economically non-viable if it is divided into units of a limited size. Two solutions are possible: the land can be held collectively by a group and transmitted as a unit to its descendants (the solution of a clan-based society); or succession can be restricted to certain individuals only, thus creating friction with disinherited members of the family.

Succession in Scotland's clan society was flexible, choice being made from among brothers, uncles or others within the dominant ruling élite. This flexibility came about partly from the lack of documentation, which in turn reflected a loose concept of what 'ownership' implied. We saw in Chapter Four that highland chiefs could in fact be deposed by their clan. The charter changed all this and introduced into northern Scotland what was already prevalent elsewhere – succession by primogeniture (the eldest son inheriting all). So ingrained did primogeniture become that nowadays we regard it as natural. Yet when one reflects on the matter, there is nothing more inherently natural about eldest sons inheriting than any other member of the family. The consequences of this choice have been profound for the structure and organization both of the family and the landed economy. Potential disaffection of younger sons was a particular problem which led to aristocratic families developing networks of landed interests for their cadet branches. The complicated marriage settlements also show the manoeuverings necessary to equalize transfers of land among the great families. As for the daughters, any potential disaffection on their part had presumably been erased from their psychological consciousness by millenia of patriarchal domination, though it must be said that the legal position of women in Scotland was superior to that in England. Every family historian however must take into account that right up to the present time, 'masculine roles are more highly regarded than feminine ones' and that 'even the least prepossessing of men acquire some aura simply by virtue of their participation in the mysterious male world separate from family life' (Farmer, 1970).

Thomas Craig, the seventeenth-century Scots jurist, defended primogeniture on the grounds that it is 'conducive to the public interest by preventing the subdivision of feus, and so preserving from destruction the position of our great families who alone, as props and pillars of the state, sustain the burden of national defence in the absence of a mercenary army' (Craig, 1934). One can sum up the institution of primogeniture by saying that the cohesion of the kin group was sacrificed in the interests of its power, as embodied in the head of the group. That it was a successful power system is shown both by the size of Scottish aristocratic estates (up to 250,000 acres) and by the extension of the concept into other areas – business and the professions for example, where the eldest son was expected to take on the mantle of the father. In recognizing the importance of these power structures one can also understand those modern writers who talk of the family as a violent institution, exalting some members at the expense of others. To some degree such psychological issues can be studied by the family historian (certainly with living relatives) and related to the economic circumstances and legal framework in which the family exists.

An interesting contrast to primogeniture is provided by the rules of succession to personal possessions. For one thing, it was the church not the state which supplied the judicial machinery until 150 years ago. The personal character of goods was significant, too, infused with the spirit of their possessor. (In early societies they were often buried with the deceased.) From this concept arose, very early, a tripartite division of a deceased's goods, one-third being disposable at will, one-third going to a widow (*ius relicta*) and one third to offspring (*legitim*). One thus had no freedom not to leave moveable property to one's children; it is rules such as this which have led to family law being described as an island of *Gemeinschaft* (community) values within a legal system which has long since ceased to put community interests before individual interests. It is an interesting example of the state supporting the family as an institution whereas in so many areas it has progressively eroded family rights. Interestingly, heritable property *could* be willed to anyone (primogeniture only applied automatically in the case of intestate succession). To disinherit one's children, one needed to buy land.

The third phase in the development of law is mature law, which is fully professsionalized. Legal innovation comes from lawyers and not from court officials, while the state usurps the powers of pursuit and punishment of offenders. Prior to the seventeenth century, as Brown (1977) notes:

> . . . responsibility for pursuing a criminal, whether it resulted in a case before the courts or a private settlement, was still put on the kingroup. It was then expected not that the criminal should be punished by the state, but that he should make reparations to those he had wronged.

From the seventeenth century, by contrast, we find the 'increasingly repressive and interventionist state [which] undoubtedly indicated a new level of awareness of public authority, but it was the unpleasant face of authority which was now presented' (Wormald, 1985). It has been argued that whilst the kingroup sought reparation, the state sought retribution. The difference can be explained along the lines that the retributive brutality of the state was needed to provide an incentive to the individual and kin to forego their long-established right to deal with the offender themselves.

The dominant power of the state has also put it into a position to define the criminality or otherwise of its citizens, where before a man was defined by the kin group to which he belonged. In the words of one writer:

. . . the establishment and enforcement of laws are very much bound up with the distribution of power in a society, so that some groups may be more likely to commit 'crime' because their behaviour is more likely to be defined as 'criminal' by those in power. (*Introductory Sociology*, 1981)

'The modern idea of law as a precision instrument of wide-scale social and economic planning would hardly have been entertained when the state was less powerful', observes Cotterell (1984). One might add that its involvement in family matters would not have been countenanced either. The position now reached is summed up, again by Cotterell, if one substitutes 'family' for 'community', in the following passage:

With the triumph of individualism, autonomous organisations based on solidarity, such as communities, become largely invisible to the law (lacking personality) and so insignificant for many purposes as between the individual and the state.

The Married Women's Property (Scotland) Act 1877 gave women the right to hold property and to trade independently of their husbands, and two recent milestones along this road are the Succession (Scotland) Act 1964 which effectively abolished primogeniture (all property now being treated as personal goods, in which all offspring share) and the Divorce (Scotland) Act 1976. This act made divorce automatic in circumstances of irretrievable breakdown, defined in one way (amongst others) as two years' separation with the defender's consent. The interests of the partners of a marriage thus come to prevail over the institution itself, and over the children of the marriage as well according to some critics.

It is certain that future family historians will find the parentage of today's generation more complex than that of the past. Nevertheless, these new fluid groupings still appear to adhere strongly to the concept of a family as a small intimate defence against the depersonalization of society. For the egalitarian state, in isolating and liberating the individual, also puts him or her at a weakness when confronted by the state; and it is perhaps this perception that has contributed to the present level of interest in family history. For the individual alone, and more often than not bereft of the institutions of religion as well as of the family, looks at one extreme to create a religion out of the family itself, as does the Mormon church; and at the other to confront state power. 'Stable marriages and family life . . . make for cohesion in society, and for satisfaction with the *status quo*', suggests Farmer (1970), 'which is one reason why political extremists have attacked them'. But for the majority, historical study of one's family can provide more thoughtful conclusions about the changing roles of individual, family, church and state in society.

To end on a lighter note, the modern state has also taken exception to the untidiness and eccentricity of Scottish marriage law (irregular marriage has been prohibited since 1940), despite the fun and fees it has brought lawyers over the centuries. Perhaps one third of all alliances made in the eighteenth century were irregular (much fewer later on) and none of these are recorded in the parish registers of course, to the despair of genealogists. In compensation, one can enjoy reading the stories of the runaways at Gretna Green and other towns in the south, whose irregular marriages were celebrated by lay officiants, predecessors of the state's own laymen who conduct the subdued rituals of the registry office wedding (another innovation of 1940). The increasingly liberal interpretation of marriage law in the nineteenth century was celebrated in a poem by Lord Neave, of which a verse runs:

You'd better keep clear of love letters
Or write them with caution and care;
For, faith, they may fasten your fetters,
If wearing a conjugal air.

The possibility of contracting marriage by post was indeed seriously discussed in legal textbooks – it was agreed that such a contract was binding, provided of course that neither of the letters had an English postmark. What is perhaps most surprising is that the custom of irregular marriage was allowed to persist so long, without going the way of the penny wedding, which was also looked on askance by the authorities. The whole local community participated in such celebrations, with feasting, dancing and some sexual licence. As we have seen, the national institutions of church and state have always been suspicious of the 'little tradition' and its spontaneity.

NOTES AND
FURTHER READING

These notes should be used in conjunction with the list of references on pages 206–13; details of key works given there are not repeated in this section. Any researcher wishing to go into the subject in depth should also acquaint himself or herself with the standard bibliographical works which can supply a wealth of information only touched on here. Foremost among these are the two general bibliographical guides to Scottish writing:

MITCHELL, ARTHUR and CASH, CALEB GEORGE, *A Contribution to the Bibliography of Scottish Topography*, 2 volumes, Constable, 1917.

HANCOCK, PHILIP DAVID, *A Bibliography of Works Relating to Scotland 1916–50*, 2 volumes, Edinburgh University Press, 1959–60.

Both these works have listings under places and under subjects. Thus, for example, there are headings for 'Folklore and Tradition' and 'Freemasonry', both of which are relevant to sections in these notes. Copies of these and other bibliographies mentioned below will be on the shelves of larger reference libraries (you are unlikely to be able to borrow them for home reading, however). The bibliographical section of your local library authority may also be able to show them to you.

After 1950, bibliographical coverage is patchy until 1976–7 when the first of the annual volumes of the *Bibliography of Scotland* was published by the National Library of Scotland. Like its predecessors, it is arranged in two sections, under place and subject, though the subject headings used are much more specific. Two sample headings relevant to this work are 'Scotland, *Genealogy*' and 'Scots in . . . (followed by names of different countries)'. For the years between 1950 and 1976, one can make use of the *Reader's Guide to Scotland: A Bibliography*, published by the National Book League (1968).

A second series of bibliographies lists the published versions of historical source material. These transcripts are invaluable to amateur researchers as they allow him or her to study records at home. The bibliographies are as follows:

TERRY, CHARLES SANDFORD, *A Catalogue of the Publications of Scottish Historical and Kindred Clubs and Societies 1780–1908*, Maclehose, 1909.

MATHESON, CYRIL, *A Catalogue of the Publications of Scottish Historical and Kindred Clubs and Societies 1908–27*, Milne and Hutchinson, 1928.

Handlist of Scottish and Welsh Record Publications, British Records Association, 1954.

To a great extent all these have been superseded by a new publication:

STEVENSON, DAVID and WENDY, *Scottish Texts and Calendars: An Analytical Guide to Serial Publications*, Royal Historical Society/Scottish History Society, 1987.

Some publishing societies (for example the Scottish History Society and the Stair Society) include a list of all their publications at the back of their published volumes. Others (such as the Scottish Record Society) produce a small catalogue which you can obtain from them or from your library authority. Addresses, in this as in all other cases, can be obtained from your library; I have not given them here, because in many cases they change as office-holders change.

One specialized bibliography that is valuable for tracing the different legal works of the past is:

MAXWELL, LESLIE F. and HAROLD W., *Scottish Law to 1956*, Volume V of *A Legal Bibliography of the British Commonwealth of Nations*, 2nd edition, Sweet and Maxwell, 1957.

As well as bibliographical tools, the beginner in family history should look at various guides to sources and institutions. The magazine *Scottish Local History*, published by the Scottish Local History Forum, is essential, as is the *Scottish Genealogist*, journal of the Scottish Genealogy Society. Both these magazines give news and addresses of local history and family history societies throughout Scotland. Important academic journals include the *Scottish History Review*, *Scottish Economic and Social History* and *Scottish Studies*. Norma E.S. Armstrong's *Local Collections in Scotland*, published by the Scottish Library Association (1977) gives details of the holdings of local history libraries and record offices, though the explosion in microform copying of records since its publication means that much updating now needs to be done. This need is met in part by *Scottish Library and Information Resources*, published by the Scottish Library Association and updated every two or three years. Because this work has a wider remit, however, local collections are not described in detail. Most of the major institutions publish leaflets about their collections (in the case of the Scottish Record Office, a range of leaflets) which are normally available free of charge. The Scottish Local History Forum is publishing (1988) a new guide to local collections.

Chapter One. The Humble and the Mighty: Sources of Biography (pp. 7–36)

Getting started in family history
The study of the character and personality of individuals has received much attention in recent years. A survey of the different ideas, including the 'commonsense' layman's analysis, is:

HAMPSON, SARAH E., *The Construction of Personality*, Routledge and Kegan Paul, 1982.

American textbooks on personality and personality theory are numerous. Two samples are:

ENGLER, BARBARA O., *Personality theories: an Introduction*, 2nd edition, Houghton-Mifflin, 1985.

MISCHEL, WALTER, *Introduction to Personality*, 4th edition, Holt, R. & W., 1986.

Recent surveys of successes and failures in psychobiography are:

COLTRERA, JOSEPH T., *Lives, Events and Other Players: Studies in Psychobiography*, J. Aronson, 1980.

RUNYAN, WILLIAM MCKINLEY, *Life Histories and Psychobiography: Explorations in Theory and Method*, Oxford University Press (New York), 1983.

Methodology and advice for oral recording are given in:

DORSON, RICHARD M., *Folklore and Folklife: An Introduction*, University of Chicago Press, 1972.

HUMPHRIES, STEPHEN, *Handbook of Oral History*, Inter-Action Imprint, 1984.

THOMPSON, PAUL, *The Voice of the Past: Oral History*, Oxford University Press, 1978.

Advice and contacts can also be supplied by the Scottish Oral History Group, who publish a magazine, *By Word of Mouth*. Your local history library should be able to give the name and address of the current secretary.

Two samples of questionnaire sheets are reproduced below. In using these, one would certainly not stick rigidly to the outline given – their main value is in planting a variety of stimuli in the interviewer's mind. Note that questions are always single, never multiple, and that one never asks leading questions – the sort of questions prefixed with 'of course' or 'you must have'.

(a) *Family life questionnaire*
Who were the people who lived in your house?
Which relatives visited the house?
How was the time spent when they visited?
How often did they visit?
Who, apart from relatives, were invited into your home?
Where did your relatives live?
How often did you visit them?
Did your family keep in touch with relatives living further away?
How were births/weddings/funerals/birthdays/Christmas/New Year celebrated?
Did family reunions take place on other occasions?
How were evenings at home spent?
Did all members of the family eat together?
How were babies brought up?
Who had influence in the home? Your mother/father/grandparents/others?
Was there discipline in the home?
When did you start to have boyfriends/girlfriends?
Did you take them home?
Did your parents approve?
Did you need them to approve?
When you married, did your family help financially/with advice/in other ways?

How often did you visit after leaving home?
What relationships do you have/did you have with mother/father/siblings/
grandparents?
With which other relatives did you maintain contact?
Is/was your relationship with them different from that with non-relatives?

(b) *Local environment questionnaire*
Can you describe the house you lived in?
What was the street like where it was situated?
What sort of people lived in the houses?
Describe the furniture in the bedrooms/kitchen etc?
How were the rooms decorated?
What were the facilities for heating/lighting/water/sewage?
What were the regular household chores?
Who performed them?
What did you eat for meals?
How was the food prepared?
What clothes did you wear?
What toys did you have?
Where did you play?
Where did your friends live?
Where were the nearest shops/places of entertainment?
Can you remember the different shops?
What sort of transport did you use?
Did you have any luxuries?
Did you regard yourself as poor/average/well off?

Photographic sources
The most recent guide to the interpretation of family and local
photographs is:

OLIVER, GEORGE, *Using Old Photographs*, Batsford, 1989.

Official records
Two clear and straightforward introductions to the records in the General
Register Office are:

BEDE, TIM, *MacRoots: How to Trace your Scottish Ancestors*, Macdonald
(Edinburgh), 1982.
JAMES, ALWYN, *Scottish Roots*, Macdonald (Edinburgh), 1981.

A wider range of records is considered in:

HAMILTON-EDWARDS, GERALD, *In Search of Scottish Ancestry*, 2nd edition,
Phillimore, 1983.
WHYTE, DONALD, *Introducing Scottish Genealogical Research*, 4th edition,
Scottish Genealogy Society, 1982.

The General Register Office itself publishes a very useful *Ancestry Leaflet*,
outlining the different records; it is available free of charge. An inventory
of surviving parish registers is:

REGISTER GENERAL FOR SCOTLAND, *Detailed List of the Old Parochial Registers of Scotland*, HMSO, 1872.

These and other sources are described in:
STEEL, D.J., *Sources for Scottish Genealogy*, Society of Genealogists, 1970.

Printed biographical sources
Useful general biographical dictionaries not mentioned in the text are as follows:

ANDERSON, WILLIAM, *The Popular Scottish Biography*, Fullarton, n.d.

ANDERSON, WILLIAM, *The Scottish Nation; or the Surnames, Families, Literature, Honours and Biographical History of the People of Scotland*, 3 volumes, Fullarton, 1863.

CHAMBERS, ROBERT, *Lives of Illustrious and Distinguished Scotland . . . forming a Complete Scottish Biographical Dictionary*, 8 volumes, Blackie, 1832.

CHAMBERS, ROBERT, *A Biographical Dictionary of Eminent Scotsmen*, Blackie, 4 volumes, 1835 (with a new edition revised by Thomas Thomson in 3 volumes, Blackie, 1870).

FELLOWES-GORDON, IAN, *Famous Scottish Lives*, Odhams Books Ltd., 1967.

HOWIE, JOHN, *Biographia Scoticana*, 3rd edition, Johnson and Paton, 1796. (The fifth edition of this work was revised and enlarged 'by a clergyman of the Church of Scotland', and published in two volumes, 1828–9, the title of volume two being *The Scots Worthies*. Another edition under the latter title was published in 1870.)

IRVING, JOSEPH, *The Book of Scotsmen*, Alexander Gardner, 1881.

STARK, J., *Biographia Scotica or Scottish Biographical Dictionary containing a Short Account of the Lives and Writings of the Most Eminent Persons . . .* J. Stark, 1805.

Scottish Biographies 1938, E.J. Thurston, 1938 (this work was envisaged as the first of a regular series, but nothing further was published; a similar recent initiative is *Who's Who in Scotland*, Carrick Publishing, 1986, of which a second edition is still awaited).

There have also been some valuable regional biographical dictionaries, including:

BANNERMAN, W., *The Aberdeen Worthies, or Sketches of Characters Resident in Aberdeen During the End of the Last and the Beginning of the Present Century . . .* Smith and Maclean, 1840.

GRAY, W. FORBES, *East Lothian Biographies*, East Lothian Antiquarian and Field Naturalists' Society, 1941.

JEANS, J.S., *Western Worthies*, Star Office, 1872.

KAY, JOHN, *A Series of Original Portraits and Caricature Etchings, with Biographical Sketches and Illustrative Anecdotes*, 2 volumes, Black, 1877. (Kay's famous caricatures of Edinburgh citizens 1785–1829.)

Most of the above works should be available in large city reference libraries, and in record offices. The runs of directories mentioned in the text are often only to be found in the relevant localities. In using them it must be remembered that they were commercial productions, paid for by advertising – selective entries only were made, predominantly of householders and tradesmen.

The following publications contain lists of university graduates:

ANDERSON, PETER JOHN and JOHNSTONE, JAMES FOWLER KELLAS, *Fasti Academiae Mariscallanae Aberdonensis, 1593–1860*, 3 volumes, New Spalding Club, 1889–98.

ANDERSON, PETER JOHN, *Officers and Graduates of University and King's College, Aberdeen 1495–1860*, New Spalding Club, 1893.

ANDERSON, PETER JOHN, *Roll of Alumni in Arts of the University and King's College of Aberdeen, 1596–1860*, Aberdeen University, 1900.

DONALD, L. and MACDONALD, W.S., *Roll of the Graduates of the University of Aberdeen 1956–1970 with supplement 1860–1955*, Aberdeen University Press, 1982.

JOHNSTON, WILLIAM, *Roll of Graduates of the University of Aberdeen 1860–1900*, Aberdeen University Press, 1906 (with a supplement *Roll of Graduates 1901–1925* by THEODORE WATT, Aberdeen University Press, 1935).

ADDISON, WILLIAM INNES, *The Matriculation Albums of the University of Glasgow from 1728 to 1858*, Maclehose, 1913.

ADDISON, WILLIAM INNES, *A Roll of the Graduates of the University of Glasgow from 1727 to 1897*, Maclehose, 1898.

ADDISON, WILLIAM INNES, *The Snell Exhibitions from the University of Glasgow to Balliol College, Oxford*, Maclehose, 1901.

ANDERSON, JAMES MAITLAND, *Early Records of the University of St Andrews: the Graduate Roll 1413–1579 and the Matriculation Roll 1473–1579*, Scottish History Society, 1926.

ANDERSON, JAMES MAITLAND, *The Matriculation Roll of the University of St. Andrews, 1747–1897*, Blackwood, 1905.

The following school registers have been published:

Aberdeen Grammar School: Roll of Pupils 1795–1919, Rosemount Press, 1923.

Cargilfield Register 1873–1927, The School, 1928.

Fettes College Edinburgh: Register, 1870 to 1932, Fettes College, 1933.

The Glenalmond Register 1847–1954, Old Glenalmond Club, 1955.

The Loretto Register 1825–1948, Constable, 1949.

Merchiston Castle School Registers, 1832 to 1962, Merchiston Castle School, 1962.

St Leonard's School, St Andrews: Register Volume 1 (1877–95), 1895 and *Volume 2 (1895–1900)*, 1901.

The Watsonian Club: List of Members 1924, McKenzie and Storrie, 1924.

The Watsonian Club: List of Members of the Club and of its Branches Throughout the World, Watsonian Club, 1936.

The major biographical sources for different professions are mentioned in the text, but the following can also be usefully consulted:

(a) *Churchmen*
The following volumes of the *Fasti Ecclesiae Scoticanae* cover the ministers of the twentieth century: volume VIII, Oliver and Boyd, 1950; volume VIIII, St Andrews Press, 1961; volume X, St Andrews Press, 1982. A biographical list of Catholic churchmen 1653–1985 appears in:

DONAGH, JAMES, *The Catholic Hierarchy of Scotland*, John S. Burns, 1986.

Secessions are further covered in:

SCOTT, DAVID, *Annals and Statistics of the Original Secession Church till its Disruption and Union with the Free Church of Scotland in 1852*, Elliot/Bryce/ Milne, n.d.

SMALL, ROBERT, *History of the Congregations of the United Presbyterian Church from 1733 to 1900*, 2 volumes, David Small, 1904.

MACGREGOR, WILLIAM MALCOLM and BLAKE, BUCHANAN, *A Historical Sketch of the United Free Church College, Glasgow: with a Complete Alumnus Roll from 1856 to 1929*, Trinity College Union, 1930.

The Church College in Aberdeen: Free Church College 1843–1900, United Free Church 1900–1929, Complete roll of alumni 1843–1929, Aberdeen University Press, 1930.

Famous churchmen are the subject of;

FERGUSSON, ADAM WIGHTMAN, *Sons of the Manse*, J.P. Mathew, 1923.

(b) *Lawyers*

A History of the Society of Writers to H.M. Signet, with Lists of Members . . . from 1594 to 1890, The Society, 1890.

Register of the Society of Writers to Her Majesty's Signet, The Society, 1983.

HENDERSON, JOHN A., *History of the Society of Advocates in Aberdeen*, New Spalding Club, 1912 (includes a list of members 1549–1911 with short biographical notes).

(c) *Politicians*

FOSTER, JOSEPH, *Members of Parliament, Scotland*, Hazell, Watson and Viney, 1882.

KNOX, WILLIAM, *Scottish Labour Leaders 1918–1939*, Mainstream, 1984.

(d) *Artists*

APTED, M.R. and HANNABUS, SUSAN, *Painters in Scotland, 1301–1700: A Biographical Dictionary*, Scottish Record Society, 1978.

WOOD, CHRISTOPHER, *The Dictionary of Victorian Painters*, 2nd edition, Antique Collectors Club, 1978.

JOHNSON, J. & GREUTZNER, A. *The Dictionary of British Artists 1880–1940*, Antique Collectors Club, 1976.

(e) *Businessmen*

SLAVEN, ANTHONY and CHECKLAND, SYDNEY G., *Dictionary of Scottish Business Biography, Volume I: The Staple Industries*, Aberdeen University Press, 1986.

Other professionals, such as bankers, excise men and schoolteachers, have been the subject of biographical articles in the *Scottish Genealogist*. The *Biography Index*, from 1946, is a quarterly journal with cumulations based on 1600 periodicals, and can be used to trace any biographical articles in them during this period. The *Waterloo Directory of Victorian Periodicals 1824–1900*, Phase I, University of Waterloo: Wilfred Laurier University Press, [n.d.] (*c.*1977) lists newspapers and periodicals published in England, Ireland, Scotland and Wales. Subsequent sections will comprise indexes to the contents.

Primary sources of biography

The Rattray of Craighall Muniments are held in the Scottish Record Office GD385. Items cited are from bundle 67. That John Rattray was factor of the estate is derived from the Blairgowrie District Statute Labour Trustees Minutes 1821–74 Reference 2/17/1 (Perth and Kinross District Archive).

The following diaries, letters and memoirs have been published by the Scottish History Society:

CUNNINGHAM, THOMAS, *Journal of Thomas Cunningham 1640–1654*, Scottish History Society, 1928.

CUNNINGHAM, WILLIAM, OF CRAIGENDS, *Diary and Account Book, 1673–1680*, Scottish History Society, 1887.

CLERK, JOHN, OF PENICUIK, *Memoirs 1676–1755*, Scottish History Society, 1892.

COCKBURN, JOHN, OF ORMISTOUN, *Letters to His Gardener 1727–1743*, Scottish History Society, 1904.

ERSKINE, JOHN, OF CARNOCK, *Diary 1683–1687*, Scottish History Society, 1893.

HAY, ANDREW, OF CRAIGNETHAN, *Diary 1659–1660*, Scottish History Society, 1901.

JOHNSTON, ARCHIBALD, OF WARISTON, *Diary, Volume I, 1639*, 1896, *Volume II 1650–1654*, 1919, *Volume III, 1655–1660*, 1940.

JOHNSTON, ARCHIBALD OF WARISTON, *Memento Quamdiu Vivas and Diary from 1632–1639*, Scottish History Society, 1909.

MILL, JOHN, *Diary 1740–1803*, Scottish History Society, 1889 (the diarist was a minister in Shetland).

NIMMO, JAMES, *Narrative of a . . . Covenanter 1740–1803*, Scottish History Society, 1889.

RAMSAY, JOHN, OF OCHTERTYRE, *Letters 1799–1812*, Scottish History Society, 1966.

Other publishing societies have produced, among others:

BAILLIE, ROBERT, *Letters and journals of Robert Baillie*, 3 volumes, Bannatyne Club, 1841–2.

GORDON, JAMES, *Diary 1692–1710*, Third Spalding Club, 1949.

JAFFRAY, ALEXANDER, *Diary of Alexander Jaffray, Provost of Aberdeen*, Spalding Club, 1856.

MELVILL, JAMES, *Autobiography and Diary of Mr James Melvill*, Wodrow Society, 1842.

Shorter diaries and collections of letters have appeared in some of the miscellany volumes of the publishing societies. Two volumes of extracts from *Scottish Diaries and Memoirs* were edited by J.G. Fyfe, Mackay, 1927 and 1942.

The following work is a bibliography of published diaries:

MATTHEWS, W., *British Diaries: An Annotated Bibliography of British Diaries Written Between 1442 and 1942*, Cambridge University Press, 1980.

Reconstructing daily life

The testament of Colonel Allan MacPherson of Blairgowrie is ref SRO CC20/7/8. The precognition of Margaret Martin is ref SRO AD/14/21/ 14. Her sentence is recorded in the Minute Book of the North Circuit Justiciary Court SRO JC 11/63. The Select Committee interview with James McEwen, Perth, is taken from the *Minutes of Evidence Taken Before the Select Committee on Hand Loom Weavers 8 July 1834.*

An indispensable series of bibliographies covers parliamentary papers of the last three centuries:

FORD, P. and G., *Hansard's Catalogue and Breviate of Parliamentary Papers 1696–1834*, Irish University Press, 1968.

FORD, P. and G., *Select List of Parliamentary Papers, 1837–99*, Blackwell, 1953.

FORD, P. and G., *Select List of Parliamentary Papers, 1955–1964*, Irish University Press, 1970.

MARSHALLSAY, DIANA and SMITH, J.H., *Ford List of British Parliamentary Papers 1965–1974*, KTO Press, 1979.

The Fords have also compiled three breviates of twentieth century papers (with summaries of the contents):

FORD, P. and G., *A Breviate of Parliamentary Papers 1900–1916*, Blackwell, 1957.

FORD, P. and G., *A Breviate of Parliamentary Papers 1917–1939*, Blackwell, 1951.

FORD, P. and G., *A Breviate of Parliamentary Papers 1940–1954*, Blackwell, 1961.

Also recommended is their introductory guide to the complexities of sessional papers:

FORD, P. and G., *A Guide to Parliamentary Papers*, Irish University Press, 1972.

The testament referred to on page 31 is that of John Soutar, who died on the 16 April 1819. Published commissariot indexes up to 1800 are listed in *Sectional List No. 24: The National Archives*, HMSO (updated intermittently) and in *Scottish Texts and Calendars* (see page 180). Reconstructing local communities through these and other similar indexes does involve some patient searching to extract relevant records.

Chapter Two: Working Lives (pp. 37–53)

Life on the land

A chronological list of books relating to Scottish agriculture published down to 1850 is given in:

SYMON, J.A., *Scottish Farming: Past and Present*, Oliver and Boyd, 1959, pp 440–52.

A personal account of farming changes over the last century is contained in the trilogy:

CAMERON, DAVID KERR, *The Ballad and the Plough*, Gollancz, 1978.
CAMERON, DAVID KERR, *Willie Gavin: Crofter Man*, Gollancz, 1980.
CAMERON, DAVID KERR, *The Cornkister Days*, Gollancz, 1984.

The *Agricultural History Review* and the *Scottish Journal of Agriculture* are both magazines containing useful articles for researchers.

Trades and professions
The following are published volumes of supplications for benefices:

Calendar of Scottish Supplications to Rome 1418–1422, Scottish History Society, 1934.
Calendar of Scottish Supplications to Rome 1423–1428, Scottish History Society, 1956.
Calendar of Scottish Supplications to Rome 1428–1432, Scottish History Society, 1970.
Calendar of Scottish Supplications to Rome 1433–1447, Glasgow University, 1983.

Two published volumes of the reverse traffic in correspondence are:

Calendar of Papal Letters to Scotland of Clement VII of Avignon 1378–1394, Scottish History Society, 1976.
Calendar of Papal Letters to Scotland of Benedict XIII of Avignon, 1394–1419, Scottish History Society, 1976.

Personal accounts of schoolteaching include:

MILLER, HUGH, *My Schools and Schoolmasters*, Nimmo, 1907.
BOWIE, JANETTA, *Penny Buff: A Clydeside School in the 'Thirties*, Constable, 1975.
BOWIE, JANETTA, *Penny Boss: A Clydeside School in the 'Fifties*, Constable, 1976.
BOWIE, JANETTA, *Penny Change: Clydeside Schools in the 'Seventies*, Constable, 1977.

A soldier's life
Public Register Office inventories relevant to military studies are:

GREAT BRITAIN. *Public Record Office, List LIII: Alphabetical Guide to War Office and other Military Records Preserved in the Public Record Office*, HMSO, 1931.
GREAT BRITAIN. *Public Record Office, List LVIII: List of Admiralty Records*, HMSO, 1904.
GREAT BRITAIN. *Public Record Office, List XXVIII: List of War Office Records*, HMSO, 1908.

The addresses of institutions mentioned in the text are as follows:

Imperial War Museum, Lambeth Road, London, SE1 6HZ.
National Army Museum, Royal Hospital Road, London SW3 4HT.
National Maritime Museum, Greenwich, London, SE10 9NF.

Army service records for officers and other ranks up to 1900 and officers' records for 1900–54 are held in the Public Record Office at Kew. Other ranks' records for 1900–13 are being transferred there, but those from 1913 onwards are held by the Army Records Centre, Ministry of Defence, CS(R)2b, Bourne Avenue, Hayes, Middlesex.

For the genealogist, there is a comprehensive list of British officers in the Manuscript Army List for 1737, from which the first *Army List* was produced in 1740 (and annually since 1754). In 1840 H.G. Hart compiled and published the first edition of *Hart's Army List*, which supplements the official record until its demise in 1916. *Steel's Navy List* appeared annually between 1782 and 1817; the official *Navy List* has appeared annually since 1814. The *Air Force List* has appeared since 1918. Numerous rolls of honour for the dead of the wars of this century have also been published (including regimental, professional and school lists). They can be traced by using the bibliographies described on page 179.

Two biographical dictionaries of naval officers are:

CHARNOCK, JOHN, *Biographia Navalis*, 6 volumes, R. Faulder, 1794–8 (memoirs of naval officers 1660–1797).

O'BYRNE, WILLIAM RICHARD, *A Naval Biographical Dictionary*, Murray, 1849, (covering all officers of rank of lieutenant or higher living in 1845).

The Scottish (pre-1707) Navy is the subject of:

GRANT, J., *The Old Scots Navy, 1689–1710*, Navy Records Society, 1914.

The most graphic account of Scottish warfare is:

PATTEN, WILLIAM, *The Expedition into Scotland of . . . Prince Edward, Duke of Somerset . . . in 1547* (reprinted in *An English Garner*, volume 3, Constable, 1845).

Published army records of the Civil War period include:

Papers Relating to the Army of the Solemn League and Covenant 1643–1647, 2 volumes, Scottish History Society, 1917.

Scotland and the Commonwealth: Letters and Papers Relating to the Military Government of Scotland, August 1651–December 1653, Scottish History Society, 1895.

Scotland and the Protectorate: Letters and Papers Relating to the Military Government of Scotland from January 1654 to June 1659, Scottish History Society, 1899.

Sources of information on the Jacobite armies include:

The Prisoners of the '45, 3 volumes, Scottish History Society, 1928–9.

A List of Persons Concerned in the Rebellion (1745), Scottish History Society, 1890.

Jacobite material in the MacBean collection in Aberdeen University Library has been inventoried in:

A Catalogue of Books, Pamphlets, Broadsides, Portraits etc in the Stuart and Jacobite Collections Gathered Together by W.M. Macbean, Aberdeen University Press, 1949.

General research and bibliographical guides to military history include:

BALL, RONALD G., *Scottish Military and Militia Records Before 1707* (paper read at the World Conference on Records held at Salt Lake City, 1969).

BRUCE, A.P.C., *An Annotated Bibliography of the British Army 1660–1914*, Garland Press, 1975.

HAMILTON-EDWARDS, GERALD, *In Search of Army Ancestry*, Phillimore, 1977.

HIGHAM, ROBERT, *A Guide to the Sources of British Military History*, Routledge, 1972.

WHITE, ARTHUR S., *Bibliography of Regimental Histories of the British Army*, Edwards, 1965.

Regimental museums are listed in the annual *Museums and Galleries in Great Britain and Ireland*; some, such as the Black Watch Museum at Balhousie Castle, Hay Street, Perth, also contain regimental archives. Numerous regimental histories have been published, including a series in recent years under the imprint of Leo Cooper. One can also consult the *Journal of the Society for Army Historical Research*.

Labour and industry
Autobiographies of working men and women give an immediate feeling of experiences similar to those gained in oral history interviews. Smout (1986) suggests the following as among the best:

MCSHANE, HARRY, *No Mean Fighter*, Pluto Press, 1978 (engineering).

KIRKWOOD, DAVID, *My Life of Revolt*, Harrap, 1935 (mining).

MOFFAT, ABE, *My Life with the Miners*, Lawrence and Wishart, 1965 (mining).

SMILLIE, ROBERT, *My Life for Labour*, Mills and Boon, 1924 (mining).

BELL, THOMAS, *Pioneering Days*, Lawrence and Wishart, 1941 (foundry working).

MACGILL, PATRICK, *Children of the Dead End*, H. Jenkins, 1914 (various reprints; a semi-fictional account of navvying in Scotland, and the best of several novels by this author).

For the relationships between employed and employer, old legal textbooks are a fascinating source of information. One example is:

FRASER, PATRICK, *Treatise on Master and Servant, Employer and Workman and Master and Apprentice, according to the Law of Scotland*, 2nd edition, Hamilton 1872.

Parliamentary papers are another invaluable source of information. Not mentioned in the text are:

The Report of Commissioners Appointed to Inquire into the Truck System, 1871.
The Report of the Royal Commission on the Working of the Master and Servant Act 1867 . . . 1st Report, 1874; *2nd Report* 1875.
The Report of the Royal Commission on Trade Unions, 1867–8.
The Report of the Select Committee on Master and Servant, 1866.
Reports of the Royal Commission on Children's Employment (6 reports 1863–7).

The story of the Factory Inspectorate is celebrated in:

WUSTEMANN, P., *Her Majesty's Inspector of Factories, 1833–1983: Essays to Commemorate 150 Years of Health and Safety Inspection*, HMSO, 1983.

Many articles of interest to the researcher will be found in the *Scottish Labour History Society Journal*. The first systematic British wage census was taken in 1886 and the second in 1906. The more recent period is surveyed in:

CAMPBELL, A.D., 'Changes in Scottish Income 1924–1949', *Economic Journal*, Volume 65, 1955, pp. 225–40.

Chapter Three: Living, Dying, Moving House: the Study of Demography (pp. 54–81)

Demographic records
Of the supplementary registers kept in the General Register Office, the most important is the Register of Neglected Entries (known births, marriages and deaths between 1801 and 1854 not included in the old parish registers).

A considerable number of special registers have also been indexed in published volumes of the Scottish Record Society, as follows:

Register of Burials in the Chapel Royal or Abbey of Holyroodhouse, 1706–1900, Scottish Record Society, 1900.

Register of Interments in the Greyfriars Burying Ground, Edinburgh, 1656–1700, Scottish Record Society, 1902.

Register of Marriages for the Parish of Edinburgh, 1595–1700, Scottish Record Society, 1905.

Register of Baptisms, Chapels at Bairnie and Tillydesk, 1763–1801, Scottish Record Society, 1908.

Index to the Register of Burials in the Churchyard of Restalrig, 1728–1834, Scottish Record Society, 1908.

Register of Marriages for the Parish of Edinburgh, 1701–1750, Scottish Record Society, 1908.

Parish Register of Durness, 1764–1814, Scottish Record Society, 1908.

Register of Baptisms, Proclamations, Marriages and Mortcloth Dues, contained in the Kirk Session Records of the Parish of Torphichen, Scottish Record Society, 1911.

Index to the Register of Marriages and Baptisms in the Parish of Kilbarchan, 1649–1772, Scottish Record Society, 1912.

Parish Registers of Dunfermline, 1561–1700, Scottish Record Society, 1911–37.

Melrose Parish Registers of Baptisms, Marriages, Proclamations of Marriages, Session Minutes (1723–1741) and Mortuary Roll, 1642–1820, Scottish Record Society, 1913.

Parish of Holyroodhouse or Canongate, Register of Marriages, 1564–1800, Scottish Record Society, 1915.

Parish Registers of Canisby (Caithness), 1652–1666, Scottish Record Society, 1914.

Registers of Births, Marriages and Deaths of the Episcopal Congregation at St Andrews, 1722–1787, Scottish Record Society, 1916.

Parish Lists of Wigtownshire and Minniegaff, 1684, Scottish Record Society, 1916.

Register of Marriages of the City of Edinburgh, 1751–1800, Scottish Record Society, 1922.

Register of Marriages of the Parish of Unst, Shetland, 1797–1863, Scottish Record Society, 1947.

Marriages at Gretna Hall, 1829–1855, Scottish Record Society, 1949.

Registers of the Episcopal Congregations in Leith, 1733–1775, Scottish Record Society, 1949.

Edinburgh Poll Tax Returns for 1694, Scottish Record Society, 1951.

Calendar of Irregular Marriages in the South Leith Kirk Session Records, 1697–1818, Scottish Record Society, 1968.

Annan Parish Censuses, 1801–21, Scottish Record Society, 1975.

Censuses of Portpatrick, 1832–1852, Scottish Record Society, 1981.

West Lothian Hearth Tax Lists, 1691 (with abstracts from other counties), Scottish Record Society, 1981.

Useful articles from the *Scottish Genealogist* include:

BAIRD, J., 'Scottish Marriages', *Scottish Genealogist*, (Volume 26), 1979, pp 121–9.

MARWICK, WILLIAM HUTTON, 'Scottish Friends' Records', *Scottish Genealogist*, Volume 7, 1960, pp 1–10.

'Register of Irregular Border Marriages', *Scottish Genealogist*, 1981, pp 167–70.

Flinn (1977) apart, the major source for general Scottish demography is:

KYD, J.G., *Scottish Population Statistics*, Scottish History Society, 1952.

Local demographic studies can be profitably combined with the use of a home computer. An introductory guide to using parish registers with computers is:

EDGINGTON, SUE, *Micro-History: Local History and Computing Projects*, Hodder and Stoughton, 1985.

A quarterly periodical, *Computers in Genealogy*, is published by the Society of Genealogists.

Studying the family
A useful tip given in Bede (1982) is to look for the first column on post-1854 birth, marriage and death certificates. An entry here refers to an amendment to the original entry, be it a patrimony suit, bigamy charge or accident enquiry. The relevant papers are stored separately.
Legal treatises that throw light on attitudes to marriage include:

FRASER, PATRICK, *A Treatise on the Law of Scotland, as Applicable to the Personal and Domestic Relations*, 2 volumes, Benning, 1846.

HAY, WILLIAM, *William Hay's Lectures on Marriage*, Stair Society, 1967.

HUME, DAVID, *Baron David Hume's Lectures 1786–1822*, Volume I, Stair Society, 1939.

Migration
BIL, ALBERT, *The Shieling, 1600–1840: The Case of the Central Scottish Highlands*, John Donald, 1987 (a detailed study of transhumance).

DEVINE, T.M., 'Highland Migration to Lowland Scotland 1760–1860', *Scottish History Review*, Volume 62, 2, October 1983, pp 137–49.

Immigration

WALKER, W., 'Irish Immigrants in Scotland', *Historical Journal*, Volume XV, 1972, pp 649–67.

HANDLEY, JAMES E., *The Irish in Scotland, 1798–1845*, Cork University Press, 1943.

HANDLEY, JAMES E., *The Irish in Modern Scotland*, Oxford University Press, 1974.

The newspaper *The Glasgow Observer* reflected the interests of the Irish Catholics in Scotland.

Emigration

There is a huge literature on the Scots overseas and their emigration. A partial bibliography is:

WHYTE, DONALD, 'Scottish Emigration: a Select Bibliography', *Scottish Genealogist*, Volume XXI, 1974, pp 65–86.

The appendix to Gordon Donaldson's *The Scots Overseas*, published by Hale (1966) contains a list of some of the manuscript sources. Other general introductions to the subject are:

BURTON, JOHN HILL, *The Scot Abroad*, Blackwood, 1900.

CAGE, R.A., *The Scots Abroad*, Croom Helm 1984.

WHYTE, DONALD, *Scottish Emigration to North America* (Scottish Genealogy Society leaflet).

Dictionaries of emigrants are becoming numerous; among the most useful are:

BECKETT, J.D., *Dictionary of Scottish Emigrants into England and Wales*, Anglo-Scottish Family History Society, 1984.

DOBSON, DAVID, *Directory of Scottish Settlers in North America 1625–1825*, Volume I, Genealogical Publishing Company, 1984.

FILBY, P. WILLIAM, *Passenger and Immigration Lists Bibliography 1538–1900*, Gale Research Co., 1981 (described as a laborious work built upon the foundation of Lancour and Wolfe [1963]).

FILBY, P. WILLIAM, *Passenger and Immigrant Lists Index*, 3 volumes, Gale Research Co., 1981.

TEPPER, MICHAEL, *New World Immigrants: A Consolidation of Ship Passenger Lists and Associated Data from Periodical Literature*, 2 volumes, Genealogical Publishing Co., 1979.

WHYTE, DONALD, *Dictionary of Emigrants to the USA*, 2nd edition, Genealogical Publishing Co., 1981.

WHYTE, DONALD, *Dictionary of Scottish Emigrants to Canada Before Confederation*, Ontario Genealogical Society, 1986.

In the numerous parliamentary papers concerned with emigration, one can note in particular:

The Report of the Select Committee on Loss of Life Aboard Emigrant Ships (1st and 2nd report), 1854.

The Report of the Select Committee on Emigration from the United Kingdom, 1826–7.

Report of the Select Committee on Emigration (Scotland), 1841.

Report of the Select Committee on Agricultural Distress, 1836.

Emigration to Relieve Distress in the Highlands, (Agent General for Emigration Report), 1841.

Report of the Commissioners of Inquiry into the Condition of the Crofters and Cottars of the Highlands and Islands of Scotland, 1884.

Letter-books and lists of emigrants compiled by the Highland and Islands Emigration Society, founded in 1852, are deposited in the Scottish Record Office. Also to be consulted there is a source guide of other records relating to the highlands. The correspondence of the Highland Society of Scotland, founded in 1787 to promote development in the highlands, is deposited with the National Library of Scotland, George IV Bridge, Edinburgh.

Chapter Four: Kin, Clan and Community (pp.82–112)

Genealogy

An article on 'Heraldic Law' by Thomas Innes of Learney appears in *Sources and Literature of Scots Law*, published by the Stair Society (1936; pp 379–95). A leaflet on the *Court of the Lord Lyon* by Charles J. Burnett is published by the Scottish Genealogy Society.

James Balfour Paul's *Ordinary of Arms*, cited in the text, is brought up to date in a second volume by David Reid and Vivien Wilson, published by the Lyon Office in 1977. It covers the years 1903–73. Other works in the field include:

GAYRE, GEORGE ROBERT and GAYRE, REINOLD, *Roll of Scottish Arms*, Part I, volume I, A–G, the Armorial (1965); volume 2, H–Z, the Armorial (1969).

STODARD, ROBERT RIDDLE, *Scottish Arms, being a collection of armorial bearings, 1370–1678*, 2 volumes, Paterson, 1881.

Among the valuable indexes compiled by the Scottish Record Society is:

GRANT, FRANCIS J., *Index to genealogies, birthbriefs and funeral escutchions recorded in the Lyons office*, Scottish Record Society, 1908.

The major sources for the genealogy of aristocratic families are:

BURKE, JOHN BERNARD, *A Genealogical and Heraldic History of the Peerage and Baronetage of the United Kingdom* (from 1826, latterly infrequent; the title has varied slightly and the latest, 105th, edition, 1970 is entitled *Burke's Peerage, Baronetage and Knightage*).

DEBRETT, JOHN, *The Peerage of the United Kingdom of Great Britain and Ireland* (from 1802; latest edition *Debrett's Peerage*, Macmillan, 1985).

G.E.C., *Complete peerage*, 2nd edition, 12 volumes, St Catherine Press, 1910–59, (reprinted Alan Sutton, 1987; this standard work covers the peerage of the United Kingdom).

PAUL, JAMES BALFOUR, *The Scots Peerage*, 9 volumes, Douglas, 1904–11.

This standard work is a greatly enlarged version of:

DOUGLAS, ROBERT, *The Peerage of Scotland . . .*, 1764 (with a second edition, enlarged by J.P. Wood in 2 volumes, 1813. Robert Douglas also began the *Baronage of Scotland*, 1798).

For the lesser orders, one can consult:

BURKE, JOHN, *Genealogical and Heraldic History of the Commoners of Great Britain and Ireland, Enjoying Territorial Possessions or High Official Rank*, Coburn, 3 volumes, 1833–5; to which a fourth volume was added in 1837 under the title *A Genealogical and Heraldic History of the Landed Gentry*. The whole was republished between 1843–9 as volumes 1, 2 and 3 of *A Genealogical and Heraldic Dictionary of the Landed Gentry of Great Britain and Ireland*, by John Burke and Sir John Bernard Burke. Familiarly known as *Burke's Landed Gentry*, the 18th edition appeared 1965–72.

BURKE, JOHN, *A Genealogical History of the Dormant, Abeyant, Forfeited and Extinct Peerages of the British Empire*, Harrison, 1831. The latest edition was published in 1883, and is updated by:

PINE, L.G., *The New Extinct Peerage 1884–1971*, Heraldry Today, 1972.

MACFARLANE, WALTER, *Genealogical collections concerning families in Scotland, 1750–51*, edited by J.T. Clarke, 2 volumes, Scottish History Society, 1900.

TAYLOR, JAMES, *The Great Historic Families of Scotland*, 2 volumes, Fraser Trust, 1887.

Walford's County Families of the UK, Spottiswoode (published annually 1863–1917).

The individual noble families featuring in the volumes by Sir William Fraser are listed in:

FERGUSON, JOAN P.S., *Scottish Family Histories held in Scottish Libraries*, National Library of Scotland, 1986.

STUART, MARGARET, *Scottish Family History: A Guide to Works of Reference on the History and Genealogy of Scottish Families*, Genealogical Publishing Co. Inc., 1979 (reprint of the 1930 edition published by Oliver and Boyd).

The latter work is prefaced by *An Essay on How to Write the History of a Family* by James Balfour Paul, in one of the clearest and most scholarly accounts of Scottish genealogical records.

A recent appreciation of the work of Fraser is:

DONALDSON, GORDON, *Sir William Fraser: the Man and his Work*, Edina Press, 1986.

The wider ramifications of genealogy are discussed in an interesting article:

TRISELIOTIS, JOHN, 'Identity and Genealogy', *Scottish Genealogist*, Volume XXXIV No 1, March 1987, pp 272–6.

Genealogical records

The available introductory guides to Scottish genealogical research were noted on page 182. Of the more specialized or localized material, one can pick out in particular the following:

SCOTTISH RECORD OFFICE, *Family History* (SRO leaflet No 9). (This leaflet is a short introduction to all those records in the national archive of potential value to genealogists.)

Lennox Links: an Ancestor Hunter's Guide to the Genealogical Resources in the Registrar Offices, Cemeteries or Churchyards and Libraries in Dumbarton District, Dumbarton District Libraries, 1986. (This excellent publication – the printing apart – gives a first-class introduction to the sources to be found within the the the locality. Most similar library publications tend to deal exclusively with the library's own holding.)

MCKECHNIE, HECTOR, 'The Pursuit of Pedigree', *Juridical Review*, Volume 40, 1928, pp 205–34; 304–40 (reprinted as a monograph, W. Green, 1928).

MUNRO, ROBERT WILLIAM and MUNRO, JEAN, 'Highland Genealogy in Local Publications', *Scottish Genealogist*, Volume 11, No 1, May 1964, pp 1–7 (a guide to genealogical material in the *Celtic Magazine*, *Celtic Monthly*, *Transactions of the Gaelic Society of Inverness* and the *Transactions of the Inverness Scientific Society and Field Club*).

WHYTE, DONALD, 'Source Material for the Scottish Highlands and Islands'. *Genealogical Magazine*, Volume 20, No 9, March 1982, pp 289–91.

The specific problems of overseas researchers are the subject of:

CAIRNS-SMITH-BARTH, JOHN LAWRENCE, *Scottish Family History: A Research and Source Guide*, Volume 1, The Author, 1986 (subtitled: 'with particular emphasis on how to do your research from various sources available within Australia').

WHYTE, DONALD, *Scottish Ancestry Research: a Brief Guide*, Morgantown, West Virginia: Scotpress, 1985.

Though library and record office staff are as helpful as they can be to overseas enquiries, they can afford to do little in-depth searching, such is the volume of the demand. Few libraries are in the position of the Highland Regional Library Service, who have a full-time seasonal member of staff for genealogical work.

For detailed searching by proxy, one will need to use the services of a professional researcher. A list of names and addresses can be supplied by the General Register Office; two societies may also be of help:

Association of Scottish Genealogists' and Record Agents, PO Box 174, Edinburgh EH3 5QZ.

The Scots Ancestry Research Society, 3 Albany Street, Edinburgh 1.

Needless to say, anyone interested in Scottish genealogy should apply for membership of the Scottish Genealogy Society, and subscribe to its magazine, *Scottish Genealogist*. Most Scots genealogists will at some time come across ancestors who moved to or came from other parts of the United Kingdom. Such researchers will need a whole new set of literature to read, but for a start they can contact the equivalents of Scotland's General Register Office:

England: The General Register Office, St Catherine's House, 10 Kingsway Street, London WC2 deals with births 1837–66, and marriages and deaths from 1837. Somerset House deals only with wills and divorces. The General Register Office, Smedley Hydro, Southport, PR8 2HJ deals with births from 1866.

Northern Ireland: The General Register Office, Oxford House, 49–55 Chichester Street, Belfast BT1 4HL, has records dating from 1922.

Eire: The Register General's Office, 8–11 Lombard Street East, Dublin 2 contains records from 1864 and details of Protestant marriages from 1845.

The Federation of Family History Societies, Harts Cottage, Church Hanborough, Oxford OX7 2AB hopes to include Scottish locations in the next editions of three guides:

Where to Find the International Genealogical Index (and the Old Parochial Register Index).
Census Returns 1841–1881 on Microfilm.
Unpublished Personal Name Indexes in Record Offices and Libraries.

Sources and a complete bibliography of churchyard studies are given in:

WILLSHER, BETTY, *Understanding Scottish Graveyards*, Chambers, 1985.

The family in history
Much of the demographic and anthropological study of the family in recent years has been carried out by a group of scholars at Cambridge University; many of their works have been published by Cambridge University Press, including:

LASLETT, P., *Household and Family in Past Time*, Cambridge University Press, 1974.
GOODY, JACK, *The Development of the Family and Marriage in Europe*, Cambridge University Press, 1983.

For a continental perspective, drawing on English and French studies, one can consult:

FLANDRIN, JEAN-LOUIS, *Families in Former Times: Kinship, Household and Sexuality*, Cambridge University Press, 1979.

Although the above books do not draw on Scottish evidence, they provide many stimulating ideas for possible Scottish studies. A recent Scottish paper is:

SELLAR, W.D.H., 'Marriage, divorce and concubinage in Gaelic Scotland', *Transactions of the Gaelic Society of Inverness*, Volume LI, 1978–80, pp 464–93.

Clans
The standard works for clan studies are those cited in the text – Skene (1890) and Cunningham (1932), to which one can add:

ADAM, F., *The Clans, Septs and Regiments of the Scottish Highlands*, 8th edition, Johnston and Bacon, 1970.

The following work is an archaeological study of the Picts:

HENDERSON, ISABEL, *The Picts*, Thames and Hudson, 1967.

Popular studies of clans are numerous, but few contribute any new research material. For this one should turn to the publications of the Inverness Field Club as well as journals such as *Northern Studies* and the *Transations of the Gaelic Society of Inverness*.

Individual clan histories, especially of the 'official' type sponsored by the clan societies, often lose themselves in a detailed and uncritical exposition of the deeds of clan chiefs. They are listed under clan names in Joan P.S. Ferguson's *Scottish Family Histories Held in Scottish Libraries*, published by the National Library of Scotland (1986).

Anthropology and family history

Anthropology has not had a strong base in Scottish research. The *Proceedings of the Scottish Anthropological and Folklore Society* is now defunct, but very few of its articles pursued themes within Scotland itself anyway. The *Journal of Interdisciplinary Studies* investigates the fruitful results of serendipity among academic disciplines.

Community

Studies of community have become a dominant pursuit of oral historians, and many local publications will also provide an insight into this area. The findings of several oral studies of fishing communities are brought together and analysed in Paul Thompson's *Living the Fishing* (Routledge, 1983), a fascinating study of the diversity yet similarity of fishing towns, including several in Scotland. The evolution of another kind of community is plotted in James Hunter's *The Making of the Crofting Community* (John Donald, 1976).

The most extensive monastic rental which we have is the *Rental Book of the Cistercian Abbey of Cupar Angus, with the Breviary of the Register*, published in 2 volumes by the Grampian Club (1879–80). Rentals of other monasteries (particularly for the years immediately after the Reformation) are included in the registers and cartularies published by various nineteenth-century historical societies (the Bannatyne Club in particular). They can be checked through the sources mentioned on page 179–80 Diocesan rentals include:

Rentale Dunkeldense 1506–1517, Scottish History Society, 1915.
Rental Sancti Andree 1538–1546, Scottish History Society, 1913.

Published tacks from family papers include:

Calendar of Writs of Munro of Foulis, Scottish Record Society, 1940.
Calendar of Writs Preserved at Yester House, 1166–1625, Scottish Record Society, 1930.
Inventory of Pitfirrane Writs, 1230–1794, Scottish Record Society, 1932.
Rentals and Papers from Family Charter Chests (Miscellany of Spalding Club), 4th volume, Spalding Club, 1849; 5th volume, Spalding Club, 1852.

Chapter Five: Exploring Local Society (pp. 113–136)

Ferdinand Tonnies' ideas are developed in:

TONNIES, FERDINAND, *Community and Association*, Routledge and Kegan Paul, 1953.

Self-help groups
KINLOCH, J. and BUTT, J., *History of the Scottish Co-operative Wholesale Society Limited*, Co-operative Wholesale Society, 1981.

Histories of individual co-operative societies are listed in:

SMETHURST, JOHN BLEARS, *A Bibliography of Co-operative Societies' Histories*, Co-operative Union Ltd. [1974].

Philanthropic institutions
Parliamentary reports of relevance to the temperance movement are:

The Report of the Select Committee on Intoxication, 1834.
The Report of the Royal Commission on Excisable Liquors in Scotland, 1859.
The Report of the Royal Commission on Liquor Licensing Laws, 1896.

Sociology and Family History
Published Scottish trials from the major courts include:

ARNOT, HUGH, *A Collection and Abridgement of Celebrated Criminal Trials in Scotland from A.D. 1536 to 1784 . . .* , Smellie, 1785.
The Justiciary Records of Argyll and the Isles 1664–1704, Stair Society, Volume 1, 1949; Volume 2, 1969.
PITCAIRN, ROBERT, *Criminal Trials in Scotland*, 3 volumes, Bannatyne Club, 1833 (covering the years 1488–1625).
Proceedings of the Justiciary Court from 1661 to 1678, 2 volumes, Scottish History Society, 1905.
Selected Justiciary Cases 1624–1650, Stair Society, Volume 1, 1953; Volume 2, 1972; Volume 3, 1974.

Sociology of the family
The traditional literature in this field has been based on social history rather than sociological analysis. It includes:

LOCHHEAD, M., *The Scots Household in the Eighteenth Century*, W. & R. Chambers, 1948.
PLANT, M., *The Domestic Life of Scotland in the Eighteenth Century*, Edinburgh University Press, 1952.
WARRACK, J., *Domestic Life in Scotland 1488–1688*, Methuen, 1920.

One recent study that exploits sociological material is:

BOYD, KENNETH M., *Scottish Church Attitudes to Sex, Marriage and the Family, 1850–1914*, John Donald, 1980.

More recent is:

SMOUT, T.C., 'Scottish Marriage, regular and irregular', in OUTHWAITE, R.B., *Marriage and Society: Studies in the Social History of Marriage*, Europa, 1981.

For general sociological studies, one needs to turn to studies of Britain or of western society as a whole, and these concentrate on relatively recent times:

SHORTER, EDWARD, *The Making of the Modern Family*, Collins, 1976.
GOODE, WILLIAM J., *The Family*, 2nd edition, Prentice Hall, 1982.

The value of literary soures in historical sociology is demonstrated in:

CALDER, JENNI, *The Victorian Home*, Batsford, 1977.

Facilities, organizations and newsletters of institutions concerned in family studies are listed in:

WEEKS, JEFFREY, *Family Directory*, British Library, 1986 (British Library Information Guide No 1).

The works of Adam Petrie mentioned in the text were reprinted by the Scottish Literary Club in 1877. Petrie was known as the 'Scottish Chesterfield' after the more famous Englishman who set standards of etiquette in the eighteenth century.

Social relationships

Works by Anthony Giddens include:

GIDDENS, ANTHONY, *The Class Structure of the Advanced Societies*, 2nd edition, Hutchinson, 1981.
GIDDENS, ANTHONY, *Elites and Power in British Society*, Cambridge University Press, 1974.
GIDDENS, ANTHONY, *Studies in Social and Political Theory*, Hutchinson, 1977.

Detailed Scottish work by R.Q. Gray includes:

GRAY, R.Q., 'The Labour Aristocracy in the Victorian Class Structure', in PARKIN, F., *The Social Analysis of Class Structure*, Tavistock, 1974.

Typologies of social class today are much more complicated than the traditional working class, middle class, upper class division. The most sophisticated use matrices of various indicators; others are based on occupation, as is that used in the official census, according to the following groups: I. Professionals and managers. II. Shopkeepers/Farmers/Secondary Professions (teachers, nurses). III. Foremen/Clerks/Typists/Skilled Trades. IV. Semi-skilled/Unskilled.

Social geography

Two very different but equally fascinating studies of Glasgow gangs are:

MCARTHUR, ALEXANDER and LONG, H.K., *No Mean Streets*, Longmans, 1935 (various reprints; this a fictionalized account of the gangs).
PATRICK, J., *A Glasgow Gang Observed*, Methuen, 1973.

Chapter Six: Culture and Beliefs (pp. 137–159)

Folklore

A standard introductory study guide is:

DORSON, RICHARD M., *Folklore and Folklife: An Introduction*, University of Chicago Press, 1972.

Other folklore collections not mentioned in the text include:

BANKS, M. MACLEOD, *British Calendar Customs: Scotland*, 3 volumes, Folk Lore Society, 1937.

CAMPBELL, J. GREGORSON, *Superstitions of the Scottish Highlands, Collected Entirely from Oral Sources*, Maclehose, 1900.

CAMPBELL, J. GREGORSON, *Witchcraft and Second Sight in the Highlands and Islands of Scotland: Tales and Traditions Collected Entirely from Oral Sources*, Maclehose, 1902.

DOUGLAS, GEORGE, *Scottish Fairy Tales*, Walter Scott, 1893.

FERGUSSON, DAVID, *Fergusson's Scottish Proverbs, from the Original Print of 1641 . . .*, Scottish Text Society, 1924.

FRASER, A.S., *Dae ye Min Lang Syne?*, Routledge, 1975.

HENDERSON, ANDREW, *Scottish Proverbs*, Morrison, 1881.

MACKENZIE, WILLIAM, 'Gaelic Incantations and Charms of the Hebrides', *Transactions of the Gaelic Society of Inverness*, Volume XVIII, 1892, pp 97–182.

NICOLSON, ALEXANDER, *A Collection of Gaelic Proverbs and Familiar Phrases*, MacLachlan and Stewart, 1881 (reprinted Caledonian Press, 1951).

Folklore collections begin with the famous ballad collections of Walter Scott (*Minstrelsy of the Scottish Border*, Longmans, 3 volumes, 1802–3) and Francis Childs (*The English and Scottish Popular Ballads*, 8 volumes, Little Brown and Co, 1857–9). The latter is described by Collinson (1966) as the 'bible of balladry'. A more recent collection is Gavin Greig's archive in the Library of King's College, Aberdeen, the best of which has been published as *Last Leaves of Traditional Ballads and Ballad Airs*, Buchan Club, 1925; see also *The Greig-Duncan Folk Song Collection*, 2 volumes, Aberdeen University Press. Also available is Marjory Kennedy-Fraser's *Songs of the Hebrides* (3 volumes, 1909–21), despite criticism that she imparted an 'aura of twilight and fairy lights, when either bright noon or pitch midnight would have been more appropriate'.

Other pioneers are discussed in:

MATHESON, WILLIAM, 'Some Early Collectors of Gaelic Folk Song', *Proceedings of the Scottish Anthropological Society*, Volume 5, No 2, 1955, pp 67–82.

Collinson (1966) and Thomson (1954) give very full bibliographical leads for folk music. Gaelic sources generally are inventoried in:

MACKINNON, DONALD, *A Descriptive Catalogue of Gaelic Manuscripts in the Advocates Library, Edinburgh and Elsewhere in Scotland*, William Brown, 1912.

A detailed introduction to Gaelic literature is:

THOMSON, DERICK, *An Introduction to Gaelic Poetry*, Gollancz, 1974.

Many Gaelic texts (with English translations) were published by the Scottish Gaelic Texts Society. Alexander Carmichael's *Carmina Gadelica* was first published by Oliver and Boyd (volumes 1 and 2, 1900; reprinted 1928; volume 3, 1940; volume 4, 1941; volume 5, 1954, volume 6 (Scottish Academic Press), 1971. Volumes 1 and 2 were reprinted by the Scottish Academic Press in 1984. Folklore magazines include *Tocher* (from the School of Scottish Studies) and *Chapbook*.

Religion
The major denominational histories are as follows:

ANSON, PETER, *The Catholic Church in Modern Scotland, 1560–1937*, Burns, Oates & W, 1937.

DRUMMOND, ANDREW and BULLOCH, JAMES, *The Scottish Church 1688–1843*, St Andrews Press, 1973.

DRUMMOND, ANDREW and BULLOCH, JAMES, *The Church in Victorian Scotland 1843–1874*, St Andrews Press, 1975.

DRUMMOND, ANDREW and BULLOCH, JAMES, *The Church in Late Victorian Scotland 1874–1900*, St Andrews Press, 1978.

ESCOTT, HARRY, *A History of Scottish Congregationalism*, Congregational Union of Scotland, 1960.

GOLDIE, FREDERICK, *A Short History of the Episcopal Church in Scotland*, 2nd edition, St Andrews Press, 1976.

MCROBERTS, DAVID, *Modern Scottish Catholicism*, J. Burns, 1979.

A detailed guide to Church of Scotland records is given in: *Records of the Church of Scotland Preserved in the Scottish Record Office and General Register Office, Register House, Edinburgh*, Scottish Record Society, 1967. These records are discussed in several articles, including:

DONALDSON, GORDON, 'Church Records: Parts 1 & 2', *Scottish Genealogist*, Volume 2, July 1955, pp 14–19 and October 1955, pp 11–17.

MITCHISON, ROSALIND, 'Sources of Scottish Local History II – Kirk Session Registers', *Local Historian*, Volume XI, 1974, pp 229–35.

MITCHISON, ROSALIND, 'The Historical Use of Kirk Session Registers' *Scottish Local History*, No 12, May 1987, pp 4–6.

Two useful reports are:

GREAT BRITAIN, *General Register Office, Census 1851: Religious Worship and Education, Scotland*.

CHURCH OF SCOTLAND, *Commission on the Religious Condition of the People 1890–6* (a report on church attendance).

Two important journals are the *Records of the Church History Society* and the *Innes Review* (for articles on the Catholic church). The state of the churches in the twentieth century has been examined by the sociologist, John Highet, in *The Scottish Churches: A Review of their State 400 Years After the Reformation* (Skeffington, 1960).

Freemasonry

LYON, DAVID MURRAY, *History of the Lodge of Edinburgh (Mary's Chapel) No 1*, Gresham Publishing Co., 1900.

STEVENSON, DAVID, *The Scottish Origins of Freemasonry*, John Donald, 1987. (This argues that freemasonry was born in Scotland around 1600 when 'a number of developments conspired to focus attention on the mason craft and exalt its status above all other crafts in a remarkable and unique way'.)

Secular culture

Two bibliographies of chapbook literature are:

Catalogue of the Lauriston Castle Chapbooks, National Library of Scotland, G.K. Hall, 1964.

NEUBURG, VICTOR EDWARD, *Chapbooks: A Guide to Reference Material on English, Scottish and American Chapbook Literature of the 18th and 19th Centuries*, 2nd edition, Woburn Press, 1972.

A detailed bibliography of all authors writing up to the end of the nineteenth century and including book reviews of most titles is:

ALLIBONE, S. AUSTIN, *A Critical Dictionary of English Literature and British and American Authors . . . from the Earliest Accounts to the Latter Half of the Nineteenth Century*, 3 volumes, Lippincott, 1877 (plus a supplement of two volumes by John Foster Kirk, 1891).

For information about fiction authors of a specific locality, one can use:

LECLAIRE, LUCIEN, *A General Analytical Bibliography of the Regional Novelists of the British Isles, 1800–1950*, Debussac, 1954.

Chapter Seven: Family, Church and State (pp. 160–178)

Social welfare

Parliamentary papers for the study of poor relief include:

Annual reports of the Board of Supervision for Relief of the Poor (Scotland) 1845–93.

Annual Reports of the Unemployment Assistance Board 1935–1948.

Annual Reports of the Local Government Board for Scotland 1894–1919.

Annual Reports of the Scottish Board of Health 1919–28.

Annual Reports of the Department of Health for Scotland 1929–62.

Report by the Board of Supervision on the Measures Taken by the Local Authorities of the Principal Centres of Population in Scotland for the Relief of the Able Bodied Unemployed During the Winter of 1893–4.

Reports of the Select Committee on Distress from Want of Employment. (Distress committees were set up under the Unemployed Workmen Act 1905 and produced local reports on the background of applicants to municipal and private relief schemes.)

Royal Commission on the Poor Laws and Relief of Distress. Report on Scotland, 1909.

A two-volume detailed survey of the history of Scottish social welfare (written in a dense style which some find difficult to read) is:

FERGUSON, T., *The Dawn of Scottish Social Welfare*, Nelson, 1948.
FERGUSON, T., *Scottish Social Welfare, 1864–1914*, Livingstone, 1958.

Various official reports show the development of health services:

Report of a Departmental Committee on Poor Law Medical Relief in Scotland, 1904.
Report on the Hospital and Nursing Services in Scotland, 1920.
Report of the Committee on Scottish Health Services, 1936 (The Cathcart Report).

The specific problems of the highlands were investigated in:

Report of the Highlands and Islands Medical Services Committee, 1912.

In addition there is much valuable local material in the archive centres established by several of the health boards.
A standard work on the history of medicine is:

COMRIE, J.D., *History of Scottish Medicine*, Wellcome Research Institution, 1927.

Local politics
The development of local government institutions is outlined in:

MOODY, DAVID, *Scottish Local History: An Introductory Guide*, Batsford, 1986.
PRYDE, G.S., *Central and Local Government in Scotland Since 1707*, Historical Association, 1960.
WALKER, DAVID M., *The Scottish Legal System*, 5th edition, W. Green, 1981.

Local political studies have not been numerous, but see:
BRASH, IAN, *Papers on Scottish Electoral Politics 1832–50*, Scottish History Society, 1974.
BUDGE, I. and UNWIN, D.W., *Scottish Political Behaviour*, Longmans, 1966.
HUTCHINSON, I.G.C., *A Political History of Scotland 1832–1924*, John Donald, 1985.
LOGUE, KENNETH J., *Popular Disturbances in Scotland 1780–1815*, John Donald, 1979.
MCLEAN, IAIN, *The Legend of Red Clydeside*, John Donald, [c.1983].
WILSON, ALEXANDER, *The Chartist Movement in Scotland*, Manchester University Press, 1970.
WRIGHT, L.C., *Scottish Chartism*, Oliver and Boyd, 1953.

Law
Two miscellanies which include many of the old Scots law texts are:

Ancient Laws and Customs of the Burghs of Scotland, Volume 1 AD 1124–1424, Scottish Burgh Records Society, 1868.
Ancient Laws and Customs of the Burghs of Scotland, Volume 2 AD 1424–1707, Scottish Burgh Records Society, 1910.

Other published texts are:

COOPER, THOMAS M., *The Register of Brieves*, Stair Society, 1946.
Regiam Majestatem, Stair Society, 1947.

For background reading on the history of law, the most authoritative introduction is *An Introduction to Scottish Legal History*, Stair Society, 1958. David M. Walker (cited above, under local politics) is another very useful guide. A recent textbook on family law (only incidentally covering historical aspects) is J.M. Thomson's *Family Law in Scotland* (Butterworth, 1987). Volume One of David M. Walker's *Principles of Scottish Private Law* (3rd edition, Clarendon Press, 1982) covers family law and the law of voluntary associations.

REFERENCES

Aberdeen (1872)
Extracts from the council register of the burgh of Aberdeen 1643–1747, Scottish Burgh Records Society.

Abrams, Philip (1982)
Historical sociology, Open Books.

Barclay, Robert S. (1977)
Orkney testaments and inventories 1573–1615, Scottish Record Society (New Series 6).

Barrow, G.W.S. (1978)
'Some problems in twelfth- and thirteenth-century Scottish history – a genealogical approach', in *Scottish Genealogist*, pp 97–112.

Bascom, William (1965)
'Folklore and anthropology', in Dundes, A., *The study of folklore*, Prentice Hall.

Bede, Tim (1982)
Macroots: How to trace your Scottish ancestors, Macdonald (Midlothian)

Berger, Peter Ludwig (1966)
Invitation to sociology: a humanistic perspective, Penguin.

Beveridge, Craig (n.d.)
'Childhood and society in eighteenth-century Scotland', in Dwyer, John, Mason, Roger A & Murdoch, Alexander, *New perspectives on the politics and culture of early modern Scotland*, John Donald, pp 265–90.

Bridgers, Frank E. (1962)
'Passenger arrival records in the National Archives', in *National Genealogical Society Quarterly*, Volume 50, 1962.

Briggs, Asa (1968)
Victorian cities, Pelican.

Brown, Jennifer M. (1977)
Scottish society in the fifteenth century, Edward Arnold.

Brown, Keith M. (1986)
Bloodfeud in Scotland 1573–1625, John Donald.

Cage, R.A. (1981)
The Scottish Poor Law 1745–1845, Scottish Academic Press.

Calder, Jenni (1977)
The Victorian Home, Batsford.

Campbell, J.L. (1975)
A collection of Highland rites and customs copied by Edward Lhuyd from the MSS of the Rev. James Kirkwood, Folklore Society.

Carr, E.H. (1964)	*What is history?*, Penguin.
Carter, Ian (n.d.)	'Class and culture among farm servants in the North East 1840–1914', in Maclaren, A.A. (n.d.).
Cheape, H. (1983)	'The Lothian farm servant', in *Northern Studies*, volume 20, pp 79–104.
Checkland, Olive (1980)	*Philanthropy in Victorian Scotland*, John Donald.
Checkland, S. and O. (1984)	*Industry and ethos: Scotland 1832–1914*, Edward Arnold.
Collinson, Francis (1966)	*The traditional and national music of Scotland*, Routledge and Kegan Paul.
Cotterell, Roger (1984)	*The sociology of law: an introduction*, Butterworth.
Cox, Peter (1976)	*Demography*, 5th edition, Cambridge University Press.
Craig, Thomas (1934)	*The Jus Feudale*, translated by James Avon Clyde, Hodge.
Cregeen, E.R. (1968)	'The changing role of the House of Argyll in the Scottish Highlands', in Lewis, I.M., *History and social anthropology*, Tavistock, pp 153–92.
Cunningham, Audrey (1932)	*The loyal clans*, Cambridge University Press.
Curtis, Michael (1968)	*Comparative government and politics*, Harper and Row.
Devine, T.M. (1983)	'The merchant class of the larger Scottish towns in the late seventeenth and early eighteenth centuries', in Gordon, George and Dicks, Brian (1983), pp 92–111.
Devine, T.M. (1984)	*Farm servants and labour in lowland Scotland 1770–1914*, John Donald.
Devine, T.M. and Dickson, David (1983)	*Ireland and Scotland 1600–1850*, John Donald.
Dickson, Tony (1980)	*Scottish capitalism*, Lawrence and Wishart.
Dodgshon, Robert A. (1983)	'Agriculture change and its social consequences in the Southern Uplands of Scotland, 1600–1780', in Devine, T.M. and Dickson, David (1983).
Donaldson, Gordon (1966)	*The Scots overseas*, Hale.
Donaldson, Gordon (1981)	*Surnames and ancestry in Scotland* (privately printed).

Donaldson, Gordon (1985)   *Scottish church history*, Scottish Academic Press.

Douglas, Ronald MacDonald (1935)   *The Scots book*, Maclehose.

Dowden, John (1910)   *The medieval church in Scotland*, Maclehose.

Drummond, Andrew and Bulloch, James (1973)   *The Scottish church 1688–1843*, St Andrews Press.

Durkan, J. and Ross, A. (1961)   *Early Scottish libraries*, J.S. Burns.

Edmonson, Munro S. (1971)   *Lore: an introduction to the science of folklore and literature*, Holt, Rinehart and Winston.

Farmer, Mary (1970)   *The family*, Longmans.

Fenton, Alexander (1985)   *The shape of the past 1: essays in Scottish ethnology*, John Donald.

Ferrier, George (1873)   *North Berwick: queen of watering places*, James Drummond.

Firth, C.H. (1899)   *Scotland and the Protectorate: letters and papers relating to the military government of Scotland. From January 1654 to June 1659*, Scottish History Society.

Flandrin, Jean-Louis (1979)   *Families in former times*, Cambridge University Press

Flinn, M. (1977)   *Scottish population history*, Cambridge University Press.

Fourquin, Guy (1976)   *Lordship and feudalism in the middle ages*, Allen and Unwin.

Fox, Robin (1967)   *Kinship and marriage*, Penguin.

Fox, R.C. (1983)   'Stirling 1550–1700', in Gordon, George and Dicks, Brian (1983) pp 52–70.

Fraser, Derek (1973)   *The evolution of the British welfare state*, Macmillan.

Fraser, W. Hamish (1978)   'Trades councils in the labour movement in nineteenth-century Scotland', in Macdougall, Ian (1978).

Freeman, Derek (1973)   'Kinship, attachment behaviour and the primary bond,' in Goody, Jack, *The character of kinship*, Cambridge University Press.

Gauldie, E. (n.d.)   'The middle class and working class housing', in Maclaren, A.A. (n.d.) pp 12–35.

Gordon, George and Dicks, Brian (1873)   *Scottish urban history*, Aberdeen University Press.

Gosden, P.H.J.H. (1973)   *Self help: voluntary association in the nineteenth century*, Batsford.

Graham, Henry Grey (1969) — *The social life of Scotland in the eighteenth century*, 5th edition, Adam and Charles Black.

Grant, Alexander (1984) — *Independence and nationhood: Scotland 1306–1469*, Edward Arnold.

Gray, Malcolm (1983) — 'Migration in the rural lowlands of Scotland 1750–1850', in Devine, T.M. and Dickson, David (1983)

Gray, Malcolm (1984) — 'Farm workers in north east Scotland', in Devine, T.M. (1984)

Hamilton-Edwards, G (1983) — *In search of Scottish ancestry*, 2nd edition, Phillimore.

Haralambos, Michael (1985) — *Sociology: themes and perspectives*, 2nd edition, Bell & Hyman.

Harper, Marjory (1985) — 'Emigration from north-east Scotland 1830–1900', in *Scottish Genealogist*, volume XXII(2) June pp 33–41.

Harvie, Christopher (1981) — *No gods and precious few heroes: Scotland 1914–1980*, Edward Arnold.

Houston, Rab (1983) — '"Frequent flitting": geographical mobility and social structure in mid-nineteenth-century Greenlaw', in *Scottish Studies*, volume 27, pp 31–47.

Hutchison, Iain George Campbell (1974) — *Politics and society in mid Victorian Glasgow, 1846–1886*, University of Edinburgh PhD.

Innes, Cosmo (1872) — *Lectures on Scotch legal antiquities*, Edmonston and Douglas.

Innes of Learney, Thomas (1956) — *Scots heraldry*, 2nd edition, Oliver and Boyd.

Introductory Sociology (1981) — Macmillan.

Jackson, Peter and Smith, Susan J. (1984) — *Exploring social geography*, Allen and Unwin.

Johnston, Thomas (1929) — *The history of the working class in Scotland*, 2nd edition, Forward Publishing Co.

Jones, Emrys and Eyles, John (1977) — *An introduction to social geography*, Oxford University Press.

Kelly, Thomas (1966) — *Early public libraries*, The Library Association.

Kelly, Thomas (1973) — *History of public libraries in Great Britain*, Library Association.

Kelsall, Helen and Keith (1986) — *Scottish lifestyle 300 years ago: new light on Edinburgh and Border families*, John Donald.

Lancour, Adlour Harold (1963)   *A bibliography of ship passenger lists 1538–1825; being a guide to published lists of early immigrants to North America*, 3rd edition, New York Public Library.

Larner, Christina (1981)   *Enemies of god: the witch-hunt in Scotland*, Chatto and Windus.

Lawson, W.MacF (1979)   'Oral tradition and its use in genealogy', in *Scottish Genealogist*, pp 1–5.

Letters (1726)   *Letters from a Gentleman in the North of Scotland . . .* [Edward Burt].

Lewis, I.M. (1968)   *History and social anthropology*, Tavistock.

Littlejohn, James (1963)   *Westrigg: the sociology of a Cheviot parish*, Routledge and Kegan Paul.

Macdonald, John (1893)   *Burgh register and guide to Dunbar*, D. and J. Croal.

Macdougall, Ian (1978)   *Essays in Scotland labour history*, John Donald.

Macdougall, Norman (1983)   *Church, politics and society: Scotland 1408–1929*, John Donald.

Macfarlane, Alan (1978)   *The origins of English individualism*, Blackwell.

Mackenzie, W.C. (1950)   *The highlands and isles of Scotland*, Moray Press.

Maclaren, A.A. (1974)   *Religion and social class: the disruption years in Aberdeen*, Routledge and Kegan Paul.

Maclaren, A.A. (1983)   'Class formation and class fractions: the Aberdeen bourgeoisie 1830–1850', in Gordon, George and Dicks, Brian (1983), pp 112–29.

Maclaren, A.A. (n.d.)   *Social class in Scotland, past and present*, John Donald.

Maclean, Loraine (1981)   *The middle ages in the highlands*, Inverness Field Club.

Mcneill, F. Marian (1977)   *The silver bough*, volume 1: *Scottish folk-lore and folk-belief*, William Maclellan.

Makey, Walter (1983)   'Presbyterian and Canterburian in the Scottish revolution', in Macdougall, Norman (1983), pp 151–66.

Malcolm, Charles A. (1931)   *Minutes of the justices of the peace for Lanarkshire 1707–1723*, Scottish History Society.

Marshall, Gordon (1980)   *Presbyteries and profits: Calvinism and the development of capitalism in*

Scotland 1560–1707, Clarendon Press.

Marshall, Rosalind K. (1983)   *Virgins and viragos: a history of women in Scotland from 1080 to 1980*, Collins.

Marwick, W.H. (1967)   *A short history of labour in Scotland*, Chambers.

Mellor, Alec (1964)   *Our separated brethren: the freemasons*, Harrap.

Miller, Jean Baker (1978)   *Towards a new psychology of women*, Penguin.

Mitchell, Alison (1978)   'Monumental Inscriptions', in *Scottish Genealogist*, pp 133–6.

Mitchell, Arthur (1902)   *List of travels and tours in Scotland 1296–1900*, Society of Antiquaries of Scotland.

Mitchison, Rosalind (1974)   'A parish and its poor: Yester in the second half of the seventeenth century', in *Transactions of the East Lothian Antiquarian and Field Naturalists' Society*, volume 14, pp 15–28.

Monro, Donald (1961)   *Western Isles of Scotland and genealogies of the clans, 1549*, edited by R.W. Munro, Oliver and Boyd.

Moody, David (1986)   *Scottish local history: an introductory guide*, Batsford.

Munro, R.W. (1981)   'The clan system: fact and fiction', in Maclean, Loraine (1981).

Murray, Norman (1978)   *Scottish hand-loom weavers 1790–1850: a social history*, John Donald.

Nadel, Ira Bruce (1984)   *Biography: fiction, fact and form*, Macmillan Press.

Nicolaisen, W.F.H. (1980)   'Tension and extension: thoughts on Scottish surnames and medieval popular culture', in *Journal of Popular Culture*, volume 14, No 1, Summer 1980, pp 119–30.

Orr, Alastair (1984)   'Farm servants and farm labour in the Forth valley and south east lowlands', in Devine, T.M. (1984).

Redfield, Robert (1956)   *Peasant society and culture*, Cambridge University Press.

Richards, E. (1985)   *A history of the highland clearances*, volume 2: *Emigration, protest, reasons*, Croom Helm.

Robertson, Barbara W. (1978)   'The Scottish farm servant and his union: from encapsulation to integration', in Macdougall, Ian (1978).

Robertson, James J. (1977)   'The development of the law', in Brown, Jennifer M., *Scottish society in the fifteenth century*, Edward Arnold.

Robertson, Roland (1969)   *Sociology of religion*, Penguin.

Round, J. Horace (1901)   *Studies in peerage and family history*, Constable.

Rowntree, Joseph and Sherwell, Arthur (1901)   *British Gothenburg experiments and public house trusts*, 2nd edition, Hodder and Stoughton.

Sanderson, Margaret (1986)   'Legal records – we're all in it together', in *Scottish Records Association conference report*, No 5, March 1986.

Saunders, Lawrence James (1950)   *Scottish democracy 1815–1840*, Oliver and Boyd.

Scott, John and Hughes, Michael (n.d.)   'The Scottish ruling class: problems of analysis and data', in Maclaren, A.A. (n.d.)

Simpson, Grant G. (1985)   'The familia of Roger de Quincy', *in* Stringer, K.J., *Essays on the nobility of medieval Scotland*, John Donald.

Skene, William F. (1890)   *Celtic Scotland*, 2nd edition, Douglas, 3 volumes.

Slorance, Andrew J. (1980)   'Genealogy and the mormons', in *Scottish Genealogist*, volume 27, pp 59–61.

Smiles, Samuel (1861–2)   *Lives of the Engineers: Metcalfe and Telford*, John Murray.

Smout, T.C. (1969)   *History of the Scottish people 1560–1830*, Collins.

Smout, T.C. (1986)   *A century of the Scottish people 1830–1950*, Collins.

Sprott, Gavin (1984)   'The country tradesman', in Devine, T.M. (1984).

Steel, Don and Taylor, Lawrence, (1984)   *Family history in focus*, Lutterworth.

Sumner, W.G. (1959)   *Folkways*, Dover.

Thomson, Derick S. (1954)   'The Gaelic oral tradition', in *Proceedings of the Scottish Anthropological and Folklore Society*, volume 5, No 1, pp 1–17.

Troeltsch, E. (1969)   'Medieval christianity', in Robertson, Roland (1969), pp 115–26.

Wagner, Anthony (1975)   *Pedigree and progress: essays in the genealogical interpretation of history*, Phillimore.

Wallace-James, R.E. (n.d.) — *The minute book of the Aitchison's Haven lodge 1598–1764.*

Whyte, I.D. and K.A. (1983) — 'Some aspects of the structure of rural society in seventeenth-century lowland Scotland', in Devine, T.M. and Dickson, David (1983).

Wilson, B.R. (1970) — 'Sociological methods in the study of history,' in *Transactions of the Royal Historical Society*, pp 101–18.

Wilson, B.R. (1969) — 'A typology of sects,' in Robertson, Roland (1969), pp 361–83.

Wilson, Gordon M. (1978) — 'The strike policy of the miners of the west of Scotland, 1842–74', in Macdougall, Ian (1978).

Wodrow, R. (1842–3) — *Analecta*, Maitland Club.

Wood, Ian (1978) — 'Irish immigrants and Scottish radicalism 1880–1906', in Macdougall, Ian (1978).

Wormald, Jenny (1981) — *Court, kirk and community: Scotland 1470–1625*, Edward Arnold.

Wormald, Jenny (1985) — *Lords and men in Scotland: bonds of manrent 1442–1603*, John Donald.

Young, James D. (1979) — *The rousing of the Scottish working class*, Croom Helm.

Zelinsky, Wilbur (1970) — *A prologue to population geography*, Prentice Hall.

INDEX

Achieved status 129
Addison's Act (1919) 170
Adherence 64
Advocates, biography of 22, 185; *see also*
   Lawyers
Advocates' Library 155, 158
Affines 94
Agnatic societies 94
Agriculture *see* Farming
Aliment 64
Althorp's Act (1833) 50
Ancient Order of Foresters 117, 161
Anthropology 9, 74, 104–7, 123–4
Anti-Burghers 144
Archives, National Register of 26
Aristocracy 69–70, 101, 103, 106–7, 175
Arithmetic mean 60
Armed forces 47–8, 64–5, 188–90
Armorial seals 84–5
Arms 85, 194;
   – Public Register of 85
Ascribed status 129
Ashley's Act (1847) 50
Assedation 108
Assemblies of God 148
Associate Presbytery 144
Assythment 97
Auld Licht 144–5

Ballimote, Book of 83
Banks 119–20
Baptism 56, 60, 191
Bards 84, 140
Barony courts 39, 110
Bastardy 42, 43, 62–3
Beadles' Books 91
Beggars 44–5, 65, 161
Benefices 44, 188
Beveridge Report 167
Bibliographies 179–80
Bills of mortality 57
Biography, printed sources of 20–4, 183–5;
   – techniques of 7–8, 15, 33–6
Birlaw courts 39
Birthbrieves 85
Birth rate 60–2
Births, marriages and deaths, registers
   of 17–18, 42, 55–6, 191–2
Black's *Surnames of Scotland* 87
Bloodfeud 97–8
Blue books 32
Board of Trade 77, 78
Bondagers 40
Bonds of manrent 96–7
Bonnet lairds 39

Book of Ballimote 83
Book of Lecain 83
Books 155–9
Bothies 40, 62, 69
Bothy ballads 69, 142
British Biographical Archive 20
British Newspaper Library 23
Building societies 46, 118
Bureaucracies 163–4
Burgesses 45–6, 85
Burghers 144
Burghs 45, 47, 111–2, 121, 165, 170
   – poor law provision 65, 162
   – records 57, 85, 167–8
Burial societies 117
Burials 55, 56, 91
Burke's Peerage 18, 194

Calvinism 65, 149–50, 172
Cameras 16
Campbell, John Francis 142
Capitalism 31, 36, 79–80, 120, 130, 149–50;
   see also Free Trade
Carmichael, Alexander 142–3
Carmina Gadelica 143, 202
Carnegie, Andrew 158–9
Catechismal rolls 57
Catholic church *see* Roman Catholic
   Church
Cattle raiding 104
Celts 68, 69, 70, 84
Census enumeration books 17, 58, 60, 71,
   90, 99
Censuses 58, 75, 81, 130, 134
Chalmers, Thomas 148, 162
Chamberlain Ayre's court 45
Chapbooks 157, 203
Character 12, 35; *see also* Personality
Charities 134, 162–3; *see also* Philanthropy
Charity Organization Society 121
Charms 139
Charters 84, 85, 101, 102, 174
Chartism 171
Chaumers 40
Children 44–5
   – employment of 61–2, 93
   – folklore of 141
   – murder of 29, 117
   – number in family 61–2
   – rearing of 9
Cholera 66, 90, 163
Church 70, 143–53
   – moral attitudes 76
   – relationship with family 166
   – relationship with state 44, 145, 146,

152, 162–4
Church of Jesus Christ of Latterday
 Saints 89–90
Church of Scotland 43–4, 143–53
 – examination rolls 57
 – testimonials 73
Churchmen 22, 43–4, 46, 76, 184–5, 188
Churchyards 55, 56, 91
Circulating libraries 156–7
Civil registration 58–9
Clans 83, 88–9, 94, 95, 99–104, 174
Class see Social class
Clergymen 22, 43–4, 46, 76, 184–5, 188
Clothes 15–16, 52, 69
Coal miners 49, 50, 51, 112, 117, 119, 133–4
Coats of arms 84,194
Coffee houses 122
Cognatic societies 94, 98
Cohabitation and repute 56
Cohorts 60
Colonial Land and Emigration
 Commission 77, 78
Combination laws 52
Command papers 32
Commissary courts 28, 187
Commissioners of supply 169
Community 52, 70, 107–12
 – and society 9, 113
 – church 150–2
 – in burghs 111–2
 – in law 176, 177
Companies 49, 50, 170
Company Registration Office 132
Compurgatores 173–4
Computer File Index 90
Concubinage 100
Consanguines 94
Consignation money 55
Consistorial cases 63–4
Conspiracy and Protection of Property Act
 (1878) 52
Co-operative movement 118, 119, 199
Costume 15–16, 52, 69
Cottars 38, 107
Council houses 170
County councils 48, 165, 168
Court of Session 63, 99, 115
Craftsmen 38, 45–6, 50; see also Tradesmen
Crime 98, 126, 176–7, 199
Crofters 38, 107
Culture 69, 70, 93–4, 137
Customs commissioners 77

Daoine Uaisle 102
Davoch 107
Dean of Guild 46
Death 91, 117, 139
 – causes of 64–7
 – certificates 64
 – rates of 54, 60, 64
 – registers of 17, 55, 191–2
Declarators of marriage 64
Declarators of putting to silence 64
Decree of removing 108
Deeds, register of 20, 99

Deism 154
Demography 54–55
 – techniques 59–60
Denomination 144–9
Diaries 26–7, 186
Dictionary of National Biography 20–1, 34
Diet 30–1
Directories 21–4, 183
Diseases 64, 65–6, 90, 163
Disruption 58–9, 146
Distress committees 165, 203
District councils,167
Dividing societies 116
Divorce 63–4, 100, 177
Doctors 22, 65, 121
Domestic servants 41–2, 96
Dress 15–16, 52, 69
Duncan, Henry 119

Edinburgh Association for Improving the
 Condition of the Poor 121
Edinburgh Commissary Court 28, 63
Edinburgh School of Arts 157
Education 93–4; see also Schools
Elders 131, 147
Élites 43, 70, 95, 99, 131–3
 – burghal 111
 – eighteenth century 169
 – nineteenth century 170
 – peasant societies 106–7
Emigrant ships 75, 77–8, 193
Emigration 61, 77–80, 103, 193–4
Employers and Workmen Act (1875) 52
Entertaining libraries 156–7
Enumeration data 59
Epidemics 64, 65–6, 90, 163
Episcopalian church 153
Erskine, Ebenezer 144
Estate papers 26, 49, 71, 108
Etymology of surnames 87
Evangelism 144–9
Examination rolls 57
Exchequer records 57
Executors 28
Exogamy 94
Extended families 61, 89–90, 99, 133

Factories' Inspectorate 50, 163
Factory Acts 50, 62
Factory economy see Industry
Family 96–7, 98, 114
 – extended 61, 89–90, 99, 133
 – functions of 93–4
 – law 173, 174
 – papers 26, 49, 57
 – power structure 175
 – relationship with church 166
 – relationship with state 166, 176, 177
 – size 60, 61–2
 – sociology 126–8
Family Allowance Act (1945) 167
Famine 64–5
Farm servants 39–41, 63, 73, 132–3
Farming improvement 37, 39, 41, 72, 109,
 169–70

Farmtouns 107, 108
Fasti Ecclesiae Scoticanae 22, 184
Fecundity 60
Fertility 54, 60–2
Feudalism 84, 87, 101–3
Fishing communities 112, 133–4
Flow data 59
Folklore 138–43
Folk songs 140, 201
Folk tales 140
Food 30–1
Forbes Mackenzie Act (1853) 122
Foresters, Ancient Order of 117, 161
Fosterage 94
Franchise, extension of 171
Fraser, Sir William 86
Free Church 22, 146–7, 170
Free Trade 45, 50–1, 112; see also Capitalism
Freemasonry 153–4
Frequent flitting 73
Friendly societies 115–8, 134, 154, 162, 165
Functionalism 105, 124
Funerals 117, 138

Gaelic culture 140, 142–3
Gangs 96, 134, 200
Genealogies of the Clans 83
Genealogies, Public Register of 84, 85
Genealogy 11, 17–19, 82–6, 89–92, 182, 194–7
General Register Office 17–18, 56, 182
Gipsies 74–5
Glasgow University Archives 50
Gothenburg experiments 123
Grassmen 38
Gravestones 67, 90–1
Graveyards 55, 56, 91
Great Seal, Register of 85
Ground Officer's Books 91
Gypsies 74–5

Haldane brothers 147
Hand-loom weaving 24, 25, 30, 51, 72, 145, 171
Handwriting 27, 33, 43, 46
Hearth tax 56–7
Hearts of Oak 117–18
Heraldry 84–5
Heritable property 19, 85, 176
Heritors 43, 147, 161, 162, 169
Heroic culture 101, 140
High Court of Justiciary 30, 118
High Sennachie of Celtic Scotland 84
Highland and Island Emigration Society 78, 194
Highland Society of Scotland 78, 194
Highlands
 – clans 99–104
 – clearances 79–80
 – emigration 75, 77, 78–80
 – folklore 139, 140, 141, 142
 – libraries 156
 – literature 140
 – religion 146, 147, 148
 – social organisation 94

 – surnames 19, 88–9
Hinds 39–40
Hiring fairs 73
Holiday resorts 66
Homage 97
Homes 11–12, 60, 76–7, 126–7, 182
Honour and shame societies 97
Horseman's Word, Society of 39–40
Household books 26, 27
Household composition 60, 126–7
Housing 58, 118, 127, 135, 170
 – rural 40, 41
Housing and Town Planning Act (1919) 170
Huguenots 74
Humours 12
Husbandland 107

Ice cream shops 76
Illegitimacy 42, 43, 62–3
Immigration 74–7, 143
Incorporations 52, 154
Independent Order of Oddfellows 117
Independent Order of Rechabites 117
Indictment 30
Industry
 – industrial economy 49–53
 – industrial revolution 47, 62, 72–3, 79–80
 – industrial society 98–9, 112, 113, 129, 162, 172
Infant mortality 67
Inheritance 19, 174–6
Innerpeffray Library 156
Instruments 46
Insurance 116, 118, 165; see also Friendly Societies
Insurrection, 1820 171
International Genealogical Index 90
Interviewing technique 11–15, 181–2
Irish immigration 75
Iron manufacture 42
Irregular marriages 56, 178, 191
Italian immigration 75–7
Ius relicta 176

Jehovah's Witnesses 148
Journals 22–3
Justices of the peace 50–1, 74, 131, 161, 169
Justiciary courts 30, 118

Kindly tenants 38–9, 101
Kinship 94, 96–9, 110, 123, 142, 176
 – highland clans 100
 – tribal societies 84
Kirk sessions
 – elders 147
 – parish records 55
 – poor relief 161, 162
 – schools 43
 – sexual behaviour 62, 67
 – testimonials 73
Kirkwood, James 142, 156

Labour Party 53, 121, 172, 173
Lair registers 91

Laissez-faire 162–3; *see also* Free Trade
Land ownership 19, 37, 38, 132
 – highlands 84
 – marriage patterns 61–2
 – primogeniture 175
Latterday Saints, Church of 89–90
Law 173–8
 – company 49, 50, 170
 – criminal 98
 – leases 108
 – mercantile 111
Lawyers 22, 46–7, 174, 176, 185
Leases 85, 108
Lecain, Book of 83
Legitim 176
Letter of Slains 97
Letters 26–7
Liberal government, 1905–15 165
Liberal Party 171
Libraries 155–9
Lieutenancy records 48
Life chances 130
Life tables 59
Lineal pedigree 86
Literacy 26, 43, 85, 174
Literature 155–9
Local government 158, 161, 163, 164–5, 168
 – records 20, 91, 167; *see also* Burghs
Local Government Board 163
Local history libraries 190
 – biographical records 21, 23
 – ephemera 66, 114
 – genealogical records 17, 19, 56, 90
Local politics 169–73
Lord Lyon 84–6
Lordships 101
Lotmen 39
Lyon Office 84–6

Manrent 96–7
Marriage
 – age of 54, 61, 62, 81
 – categories of 56
 – choice of partners 81, 112, 126, 128–9
 – consistorial actions 63–4
 – contracts 99
 – irregular 56, 178
 – law 177
 – peasant societies 106
 – registers of 17, 191–2; *see also* Births, marriages and deaths
 – weddings 178
Married Women's Property (Scotland) Act (1877) 177
Marx, Karl 131
Masons 53, 154
Master and servant laws 52, 190
Matriculation rolls 21, 184
Matrilinealism 94, 100
Mechanics' Institutes 157–8
Median 60
Medical profession 22, 65, 121
Merchant Shipping Act (1872) 78
Merchants 45–6, 111
Merkland 107

Methodist church 153
Micro-history 8, 70, 102, 111, 125, 143
Middle classes 131
 – families 61–2
 – homes 28, 126, 127
 – outlook 66
 – philanthropy 120–1
 – politics 171
 – professions 47
 see also Social class
Migration 67–73, 90, 192–4
Militia 48
Mines Inspectorate 50
Mining communities 112, 119, 133–4; *see also* Coal miners
Ministers 22, 43–4, 76, 184–5
Moderates 144–5
Mormon church 89–90
Mortality *see* Death
Mortifications 161
Moveable property 19, 27–9. 175–6
Municipal socialism 164, 170, 172
Muster rolls 48

Naming customs 90–1
National Army Museum 48
National Assistance Act (1948) 167
National Coal Board 49
National Health Service (Scotland) Act (1947) 167
National Insurance Act (1911) 165
National Insurance Act (1946) 167
National Library of Scotland 26, 78, 153, 157
National Register of Archives 26
Neglected Entries, Register of 191
Neighbourhoods 133–4
New Licht 144–5
Newspapers 23, 136
Norms 129
Notaries Public 46
Nursing 121–2

Oddfellows, Independent Order of 117
Old Age Pension Act (1908) 165
Old Parochial Register for Scotland 90, 197
One-parent families 99
Oral culture 139, 140, 155
Oral history 125–6, 128, 166, 181–2
Oral recording 11–15, 181–2
Oxgate 107

Parish councils 164, 165, 168
Parish libraries 155–6, 158
Parish registers of births, marriages and deaths 17, 64, 66, 89
Parliamentary papers 32; *see also* Royal Commissions; Select Committees
Parochial boards 163, 164, 168
Passenger Act (1803) 77–8
Pastoralism 68–9, 140
Patrilinealism 94
Patronage (church) 145, 146
Patronymics 18–19, 87–8
Paxboard 152

Peasant society 105–6, 140
Penny banks 120
Penny dreadfuls 157
Penny weddings 178
Personality 12, 29, 35, 180–1
Petrie, Adam 128, 200
Philanthropy 36, 115, 119, 120–3
Photographs 15–16
Picts 70, 94
Plague 64, 65–6, 90, 163
Ploughgate 107
Ploughing 39, 107
Politics 169–73
Poll tax 56–7
Polygamy 100
Poor relief 20, 44, 65, 80, 119, 161–3, 165–8
Poorhouses 162, 167, 168
Population distribution 80–1
Population geography 80–1
Post Office Savings Bank 120
Precept of Ejection 108
Precognitions 29, 30, 67
Predestination 149
Pregnancy, concealment of 29
Priests 22, 43–4, 46, 76, 184–5, 188
Primary institutions 114
Primary sources 24
Primogeniture 84, 174–5, 177
Privy council 48, 55, 65
Procurators fiscal 30
Professional classes 46–7, 73
Professions, sociology of 43, 131
Property *see* Heritable property; Land
  ownership; Moveable property
Propinquity books 85
Proverbs 141, 201
Psychobiography 12
Psychology 12–13
Public assistance committees 167
Public libraries 119. 156, 158–9
Public Record Office 48, 77, 78
Public Register of All Arms and Bearings 85
Public Register of Genealogies 85
Public houses 122–3
Pursuivants 85

Quakers 153

Rechabites, Independent Order of 117
Record offices 167, 190
Register of All Arms and Bearings 85
Register of Births, Marriages and
  Deaths 17–18, 42, 55–6, 191–2
Register of Deeds 20
Register of Genealogies 85
Register of Neglected Entries 191
Register of Sasines 19, 85, 132
Register of the Great Seal 85
Register of the Privy Council 48
Registry offices 18
Relief Presbytery 145
Religion 143–53; *see also* Church
Religious denomination 144–9
Rentals 71, 108, 198
Retours 19

Riddles 141
Rig farming 107–8
Roman Catholic Church 43–4, 151–2
  – archives 91, 153
Royal commissions 32–3
  – agriculture 41
  – emigration 194
  – employment 190
  – friendly societies 118
  – industry 50
  – mining 49
  – poor law 204
  – temperance 199
  – trade unions 190
Ruling class 99, 131; *see also* Élites
Rundale 107
Runrig 107
Rural life 37–45, 68–9, 72, 107–11

Salt panning 49
Sampling 60
Sanctions 129
Sasines, registers of 19, 85, 132
Savings banks 119–20
Schaw's Institute 123
School boards 43, 168, 171
School of Scottish Studies 14, 143
Schools 12, 16, 62, 123, 156, 168
  – log books 43, 169
  – registers 21–2, 184
  – teachers 42–3, 188
  see also Education
Scots 100
Scottish Board of Supervision 163
Scottish Farm Servants' Union 41
Scottish Friends of the People 171
Scottish Genealogy Society 78, 90
Scottish History Society 26, 180
Scottish Record Office 20
  – army records 48
  – church records 44, 153
  – company records 115, 132
  – court records 28, 30, 52, 63–4, 110, 111
  – demographic records 57
  – friendly society records 118
  – gifts and deposits 26, 115
  – local government records 46, 51, 162,
    167
  – mining records 49
  – national register of archives 26
  – property records 19, 27–8
  – school records 43
Scottish Record Society 28, 180
Scottish Society for the Propagation of
  Christian Knowledge 147, 150–1
Scottish Trades Union Council 53
Sea bathing 66
Seals 84–5
Secessions 22, 144–7, 185
Secondary institutions 113–4
Sects 147–8
Select committees 30–3
  – agriculture 41
  – emigration 194
  – master and servant 190

– poor law 163, 203
– temperance 199
Sennachies 84
Self-help 115–20
Septs 103
Sermons 150
Servants 41–2, 96
Service of heirs 19
Sessional papers 32; *see also* Royal
  Commissions; Select Committees
Sexton's books 91
Sheriff courts 28, 30, 48, 63, 110, 118
Shipbuilding 50, 53
Ships, emigrant 75, 77–8, 193
Shopkeepers 47, 76, 118, 170
Slavery 51
Smiles, Samuel 115, 164
Smithies 42
Social class 16, 52, 57, 67, 129–33, 135–6,
  200; *see also* Élites; Middle classes;
  Working class
Social geography 133–6
Social interactionism 35
Social relationships 128–33
Social stratification 38, 129–33
Social welfare 67, 116, 161–9; *see also* Poor
  relief
Socialism 171, 172
Socialization 93–4
Society 9, 113, 160
Society of the Horseman's Word 39–40
Sociology 123–6
Songs 140
State 160, 173
  – attitude to crime 98
  – relationship with church 44, 145, 146,
    152, 162, 163, 164
  – relationship with clans 95–6
  – relationship with family 94, 160, 166,
    176
  – relationship with labour 50–1
  – relationship with localities 110–11
  – relationship with local
    government 164, 169
Statistical accounts 27, 42
Status 125, 129, 130, 145; *see also* Social class
Stock data 59
Strikes 53
Subscription libraries 156–7
Subsistence economy 72, 80
Succession (Scotland) Act (1964) 177
Superstitions 112, 139, 140
Supplications to Rome 44, 188
Surnames 18–19, 86–9

Tacks 108
Tacksmen 102–3
Tartans 100
Taskers 39
Temperance movement 122–3, 199
Tenants 38, 72, 102–3, 107–8
Testaments 28, 159

Testimonials 73
Textile industry 49–50; *see also* Hand-loom
  weaving
Theocracy 152
Theology 149–50
Tocher 99
Tombstones 67, 90–1
Town councils *see* Burghs
Towns
  – character of 113–4
  – employment in 45–7
  – social geography 133–6
Trade directories 21, 22, 183
Trade incorporations 52, 154
Trade Union Act (1871) 52
Trade unions 41, 51–3, 118, 165
Trades councils 53
Tradesmen 38, 45–6, 52, 53, 118, 145
  – rural 41–2
  – wages 50
Transhumance 68–9
Trial by ordeal 174
Tribalism 83–4, 94, 101, 102, 142
Trustee savings banks 119–20

Unemployed Workers' Dependants Act
  (1921) 166
Unemployed Workmen Act (1905) 165
Unemployment 50, 51, 161, 162, 165–7
Unemployment Act (1934) 166
Unemployment Assistance Board 166
Unemployment pay 116
United Presbyterian Church 145
United Services Museum 48
University graduates 21, 184
Urban life *see* Towns

Valuation rolls 60
Vicars 43
Video recording 14
Visitation lists 57
Volunteers 48

Wadsetters 39
Wage fixing 50–1
Weber, Max 131, 148
Webster, Alexander 57
Weddings 178
West Register House 20, 30
Westerkirk library 156, 159
Wills 28
Witherspoon, John 154
Women
  – abortion 67
  – employment 49, 50, 112, 120, 121
  – home 127–8
  – legal rights 110, 175, 177
  – rape 97
Working class 28, 49–53, 156, 157–8, 171–2;
  see also Social class

Yeomanry 48